Howard E. Covington, Jr.

A Century of Retail Leadership

The University of North Carolina Press

Chapel Hill & London

The paper in this book meets the guidelines for
permanence and durability of the Committee on
Production Guidelines for Book Longevity of the
Council on Library Resources.

Printed in the United States of America
92 91 90 89 88   5 4 3 2 1

Library of Congress Cataloging-in-Publication Data

Covington, Howard E.
    Belk.

    Includes index.
    1. Belk Stores Services—History.   2. Department
stores—United States—History.   3. Retail trade—
United States—History.   I. Title.
HF5465.U6B453   1988   381'.45'000973   88-17326
ISBN 0-8078-1822-4 (alk. paper)

Contents

Preface / vii

1. New Directions / 1

2. The New York Racket / 12

3. Elegant New Garb / 34

4. The Belks' Boys / 56

5. Bargains—and More / 74

6. Thomasville Rockers and Red Camels / 91

7. Largest in the Carolinas / 112

8. A Merchant's Democracy / 123

9. New Young Leaders / 145

10. Big B / 179

11. Coming of Age / 209

12. A Waking Giant / 231

13. "God's Good Man" / 248

14. The Next Century / 288

Index / 299

Preface

I t is fair to say that William Henry Belk would not recognize the business he left his children. Thirty-six years after his death, on the occasion of the 100th anniversary of the opening of Belk's first store in Monroe, N.C., his department stores are located in suburban shopping malls where they attract customers from an entire region, not just from a single community. Inside, the stores are showplaces for style, not discount merchandise. Many of the more than 350 stores in the Belk organization are ten times the size of the average store during Henry Belk's era. Today, Belk is modern, fashionable, and the leading retailer in more than eight out of ten of the markets it serves in sixteen states.

For the most part, the changes in his stores reflect the transformation of the South from a rural to an urban economy, from a society in which merchants filled customers' needs to one in which stores fulfill their dreams. Belk saw much of this change himself. His world opened in lamplight and closed to the silver glow of television.

During the past quarter-century, the Belk organization faced a different set of challenges. It has survived and expanded in the midst of mergers and business failures that have collapsed a once-large army of individual merchant families into a relatively small corps of vast mercantile corporations. Belk stores have emerged as America's largest family- and management-owned department-store enterprise.

Belk is prepared for its second century. The next generation of leaders finds a corporate culture built on solid business principles and values that emphasizes integrity and an unwavering belief in people, a Belk hallmark from the beginning. In place is a program of strategic planning that analyzes past results, evaluates present trends, and follows the market. The stores meet a merchandising program that includes prestigious national brands and one of the nation's most accepted and valued family of private brands. Computers, data management systems, and electronic communications connect the most diverse units in buildings that are either new or recently remodeled and feature the most advanced techniques in architecture and design. Belk people have been trained for the future challenges in retailing through a comprehensive internal training and career development program that has more than a quarter-century of experience. Professional management programs, complemented by a tradition of formal personnel practices, produce Belk leaders that match the company's sophisticated retail image. And the balance sheet is as solid as it ever was with the individual companies primed for future expansion and growth.

William Henry Belk would be most heartened to find that with all the electronic advances, consolidation of services, and coordination of merchandising, modern retailing has not eliminated what he cherished most—his unique organization with its premium on the individual enterprise and initiative of the people who managed his stores. Today, a Belk Stores Services (BSS) buyer in New York may place large orders with some of the world's leading fashion houses, but those orders are only as good as the endorsement of the managers in hundreds of communities throughout the South who want that merchandise for their customers. Indeed, Belk would probably chuckle to think that what today's students of business call "Japanese management" is what he considered just plain good sense. Long before corporate America had begun to stumble under its own size and concentration of power, Belk had discovered the value of placing the responsibility for his business close to the customers.

Another tradition that has survived the social and economic changes of the thirty-six years since William Henry Belk's passing is the fundamental commitment that Belk and his partners made to their communities. They dedicated themselves to their neighbors who shopped in their stores and to the people of the factories and mills of the region that produced many of the products that filled their shelves. The Belk stores and the stores with hyphenated names like Hudson-Belk, Belk-Matthews, Belk-Leggett, and Belk-Beery were as close as good neighbors. Today, about 95 percent of Belk's private-label merchandise is made in America. In addition, the Belks and their partners continue to extend their personal and corporate stewardship to hospitals and colleges, churches and civic enterprises.

Yet, as familiar as the Belk name is to the Southeast, the story of the growth and development of the business has been a private matter, particularly as those chapters of the Belk history have been written by the second generation of leaders. Rarely have the Belks and their partners invited outsiders in to share in the story of their businesses, which remain privately held corporations. Recently, however, Ray Killian, a senior vice-president with Belk Stores Services, included plans for an update of a history of the business since William Henry Belk's days as part of the organization's preparations for its centennial celebration. Early on, Killian enlisted the help of John and Tom Belk, who endorsed the project and gave it their unqualified support. Thus Belk Stores Services commissioned this book. During my research the Belks gave me access to people and company records, inviting me into meetings and conversations reserved in most cases for decision makers only. They were open, candid, and gave freely of their time to my questions and calls as did their sister, Sarah Belk Gambrell, and brothers, Irwin and Henderson. I thank them for their help. In addition, their supervising partners, Von Autry, Jr., William Beery III, Frank Matthews II, Karl Hudson, Jr., Leroy Robinson, and Robert Gallant were helpful and open to my inquiries. BSS senior vice-presidents Joe H. Robinson, I. N. Howard, and John L. Green provided not only information but encouragement and guidance.

For information about William Henry Belk, I relied on those who knew him, worked with him, and learned by his example. Sarah Pharr Caddell of Charlotte was Henry Belk's secretary for more than twenty years and served the company for more than fifty years. She provided particular insight into Belk's relationships with his partners, his associates, his customers, and his church. R. D. McCraw described the early days of the New York buying office, and former BSS executives Sam Elliott, Guy Byerly, Jr., and David McConnell helped with an understanding of the man and the business during the post–World War II expansion and transition to management by his heirs. And any historian of this company must acknowledge an indebtedness to LeGette Blythe's biography of Henry Belk. Through the foresight of Belk's children, Blythe was invited to record their father's recollections of the building of his business in *William Henry Belk, Merchant of the South*, published in 1952 by the University of North Carolina Press.

Additional information on Belk's relationship with early partners Houston Matthews, Karl Hudson, and Erskine Gallant came from Frank Matthews II, whose uncles were Belk's chief assistants in Charlotte; from Karl Hudson, Jr., whose father and uncles founded the Hudson-Belk group in Raleigh, N.C., and from Robert Gallant, whose father, Erskine, opened stores in South Carolina and Georgia.

I found a rich history in the files of Belk Stores Services, including transcribed recollections of Sam Scott's nearly thirty years with William Henry Belk. A taped interview with Yates Laney, prepared by Becky Moser of the Belk Stores Services corporate communications staff, and interviews with M. C. Quattlebaum, Archie Hampton, and others who managed early stores helped complete the merchandise circle from wholesaler to customers. Henderson Belk made available his historical files containing correspondence, photographs, company periodicals, and newspaper articles from the early years of the business as well as his library of studies of the department store business.

I am thankful too for the history that Hazel Caton Brown compiled during her more than twenty years as editor of *Busy Bees*, the company magazine. She and others shared a sense of the company's heritage and presented it bimonthly in the magazine's column, "Story of a Store." Within the pages of Mrs. Brown's publication I found important anecdotal material about those who had experienced the first years in the Belk stores throughout the South and a contemporary account of the Belk organization as it changed from a loose confederation to a major retail force.

For information on the Leggett brothers and their relationship with William Henry Belk and his brother, John, I relied on interviews with their sons, who now manage the Leggett stores, and on *The Leggett Story: A Southern Retailing Family* by Booten Herndon.

I appreciate the advice of those who encouraged me to tell the Belk story in the context of the region and the guidance of others who led me to information about the growth of and change in America's department stores. Most helpful in my research on North Carolina was *North Carolina: The History of a Southern State* by Hugh Talmage Lefler and Albert Ray Newsome. I referred to *The Emerging South* by Thomas D. Clark and to George B. Tindall's *The Emergence of the New South* for an understanding of the era of Belk's early expansion. *Hornets' Nest: The Story of Charlotte and Mecklenburg County* by LeGette Blythe and Charles Raven Brockman provided background on Belk's principal city. The illustrations and accounts in *Charlotte: Spirit of the New South* by Mary Norton Kratt were helpful in describing Charlotte during the time when the Belk brothers were establishing the leading store in their organization. In *These Are Our Lives*, produced by members of the Federal Writers' Project of the Works Progress Administration in North Carolina, Tennessee, and Georgia, I found detail about life in the kind of towns and communities that supported Belk stores throughout the 1920s and 1930s. Jonathan Daniels's report, *Tar Heels*, also provided a look at life during these times.

Mrs. Sarah Aull of Landis, N.C., an experienced researcher and librarian, helped me find in the University of North Carolina libraries at campuses in Charlotte, Greensboro, and Chapel Hill books, monographs, and periodical literature on the history of retailing, most particularly on the development of shopping centers in America.

I relied on Thomas A. Nipper and Robert N. Wildrick, both BSS senior vice-presidents, for the story of the emergence of Belk as a major customer of the world's leading fashion houses. They and their assistants carefully explained the subtleties of fashion retailing and made available to me the people who buy the merchandise that customers find in Belk stores. I also appreciate the time and attention of Belk store managers and buyers who postponed some of their own pressing business to guide me through the markets in New York and the Belk stores' shows in Charlotte.

For editorial assistance and guidance, I turned to Liz Smith and Darrell Williams of the BSS corporate communications department. Smith carefully transcribed hours of taped interviews while Williams and Ray Killian helped me keep in sight the goal of this effort, a complete account of the development and transformation of one of the nation's unique retail businesses. I thank them for their encouragement and support as I do others, including my family, who put aside their daily concerns and duties to help me complete this project.

Finally, this book is made possible by the more than thirty-five thousand salespeople, buyers, store managers and their assistants, truck drivers, computer clerks, accountants, secretaries, and dedicated Belk employees who live the Belk tradition each day.

1. New Directions

The final soft, warm, orange hues of the setting sun burned on the horizon, silhouetting Belk's South-Park store in Charlotte, N.C., as guests for a pre-opening celebration began arriving on the evening of September 21, 1986. Doormen in tuxedos greeted the first of the Belks' 1,800 richly dressed guests as they stepped from their cars onto the red carpet beneath a canopy extending from the store's south entrance. Renovation of this flagship store of the vast Belk network of stores had cost $13 million and had taken fourteen months to complete. Now, as part of a popular charity benefit, the Belks themselves were introducing their new 290,000-square-foot store in unforgettable style.

Inside, Tom Belk moved easily through the black-tie crowd with acclaimed designer Oscar de la Renta in tow. Belk steered the deeply tanned de la Renta, who stood nearly as tall as his lanky, beaming host, from one small knot of guests to another. Businessmen, bankers, politicians and dignitaries, and friends and neighbors from Charlotte's fashionable suburbs stopped long enough to chat and graciously accept Belk's introductions. The two men gathered compliments— Belk on his new store and de la Renta on his fashions being modeled on the floor above—as they walked from cosmetics to men's, from linens to juniors', from gourmet shops to electronics. When Belk moved on, the guests returned to feast on the delicacies offered at nearby buffet tables, constantly in resupply with a broader selection of light and heavy hors d'oeuvres, desserts, and drink than Belk had boutiques in this, the company's most stylish store.

The Belks had created this store like no other. It now was the brightest star in the 350-store Belk constellation. Included in the lineup of famous brands and designer merchandise were labels from Fendi, Ralph Lauren, Calvin Klein, Burberrys, Perry Ellis, Baccarat, and soon to come, Gucci. Belk executives had searched the country for ideas, borrowing a bit here, a bit there, and had blended them together in a final design prepared by the New York design firm of Hambrecht Terrell International. There was a little of Bloomingdale's in the gourmet boutiques on Level One, a bit of Saks in the latest fashions in Level Three ladies' wear, styles as exclusive as Beverly Hills in the signature boutiques strategically placed throughout. The overall design was as contemporary as Dallas. And it was all carefully arranged in perfect detail beneath the store's high, vaulted glass skylight, an architectural centerpiece both functional and distinctive.

This opening was special for Tom Belk, president of Belk Stores Services Incorporated, the corporate connection for the Belk network of stores, and his older brother, John, chairman of BSS and chairman of the many Belk store corporations. Taken altogether—the live mannequins freeze-modeling the latest fashions, motionless even to the poking of unbelievers; the musicians, from the jazz quartet in the first-level gift department to the sophisticated piano in Regency Sportswear; the de la Renta appearance—SouthPark was a statement about the future of the Belk stores that these two brothers had been waiting to make for years. This new store clearly established that the Belk department store business their father had begun nearly ninety-eight years before was now as sophisticated and contemporary as any retail outfit in the country.

Not quite twenty-five years before this evening, in 1962, John and Tom Belk had been preparing for another grand company celebration, the company's seventy-fifth anniversary. They could not have imagined SouthPark as it would appear on a warm, late summer's evening in 1986. Most of the vendors whose fashion merchandise would be tucked away in Macy's-style boutiques were not on the market. If they were, they had not heard of Belk stores. Charlotte was a growing, thriving Southern city, but the land that was to become the home of SouthPark was still green pasture for the prize black Angus grazing within sight of the estate of Cameron Morrison, former governor of North Carolina. Yet, as

Tom Belk carefully compiled the guest lists for seventy-fifth anniversary festivities, he wanted the year-long celebration and sales extravaganza to be more than one to recognize the past.

On the schedule for the birthday celebration to begin in late 1962 were major events involving governors, mayors, senators, and dignitaries turned out for fine dinners and plenty of congratulatory speeches. Artists had designed a diamond logo colored in magenta and turquoise, special advertising had been arranged, store clerks had been given specific dress instructions, and Belk buyers had collected the usual array of souvenirs, including silver dollars set in Lucite. In the stores, customers would find plenty of special sales to make the cash registers ring. Even if founder William Henry Belk might have frowned about the expense of all the publicity, he would have liked the idea of special sales to get customers into his stores.

For Tom Belk, then a meticulous young merchant who had inherited his father's attention to detail, the weekend of October 12, 1962, was particularly important. Billed simply as an Advance Celebration, the festivities included an evening reception, then a day of luncheons, speeches, and honors. The Belks' guests were the manufacturers and suppliers who kept Belk stores stocked with goods. Some of the early acceptances came from familiar faces and names from textile concerns in the region. These were old friends. Many of these companies had been supplying Belk stores since William Henry Belk and his brother first expanded beyond their one small store in Monroe, N.C., before the turn of the century.

The Belks valued their relationship with suppliers and were sincere in their desire to say thank you to new and old alike. But the Belks had another goal as well, as they fashioned their anniversary programs for manufacturers who supplied their stores, for the bankers who financed their business, and for newspaper publishers who carried their miles of advertising columns. They wanted to say that the Belk organization was changing from a collection of mostly small stores in country towns. A second generation of Belks was planning to flex its muscle as the leading mercantile business in the South.

The Belk that was paled in contrast to the promise of things to come offered by Henry Belk's sons. Belk in the fall of 1962 remained much as it had been under its founder, whose operation was simply organized and easily understood. His success, he often said, was the result of the hard work of his "partners," as he called the men who owned shares in their stores and whose names appeared right along with his on the store signs, on the invoices, and on the sales slips and stationery. They ran the business.

Individuality was such a part of the Belk stores' corporate culture that Henry Belk would proudly claim there was no such thing as a typical Belk store. Instead there were many Belk stores, each serving a local community with a different array of goods, operating under a hodgepodge of corporate and store names. Sometimes the Belk name preceded the partner's name, such as Belk-Leggett in Danville, Va., and sometimes it followed the partner's name, such as Hudson-Belk in Raleigh, N.C. The signs simply read "Belk's" on other stores, as in Charlotte where the Belks themselves were the "partner."

Henry Belk's children, sons Tom, John, Henderson, Irwin, and Henry Jr. and daughter Sarah, had not changed the basic organization since they assumed responsibility for the business following their father's death in 1952. Many stores still stocked staples, work clothes, and sturdy shoes, for shoppers who came to Belk looking for the most for their dollar. Piece goods, the backbone of the business in Henry Belk's day, generated twenty percent or more of a year's sales. "The store's image of 'value,'" *Women's Wear Daily* reported in a rare article on the Belk stores in 1961, "is so well-established in some communities that the beginnings of a mild recession may be reflected by a moderate sales increase as customers seek to extend the buying power of their dollars by switching from other outlets to the local Belk store."

The Belk name meant more than just a place to shop.

Henry Belk was a leading benefactor of the region. Belk had helped hundreds of congregations build new churches, and he had donated money for dormitories, chapels, and other buildings for colleges and hospitals in the Carolinas, especially those run by fellow Presbyterians. And his business interests extended beyond the stores. During hard times, Belk purchases from local mills and factories had been large enough to reopen closed plants and put North Carolinians back to work. Indeed, the Belk logo, a sunburst with more points than you would bother to count, was as much a part of the region as bib overalls and brogans.

This same heritage presented a vexing problem as brothers Tom and John Belk thought about the future. Since assuming leadership of the Belk organization in 1956, they had worked to upgrade the image of the stores and improve internal organization while retaining the strength of local autonomy. They faced a multitude of handicaps, not the least of which was the Belk image outside the South as a chain of "little country stores."

Certain national, brand name manufacturers and fashion houses, whose clothing Tom Belk wanted stocked in the stores, had refused to sell to Belk buyers often enough that the Belks knew their reputation for value also translated into low-budget stores in a land of low-budget shoppers. For vendors in New York and California, the South was still on Main Street while the rest of America was shopping in the suburbs and in large regional malls; the South bought simple shifts and Sunday suits while America was buying fashion. If these vendors sold in the South at all, they preferred to put their higher-priced goods in more fashionable stores like Ivey's, Belk's competitor immediately across Charlotte's North Tryon Street, and specialty shops in cities like Columbia, S.C., Greensboro, N.C., and Raleigh, N.C.

In addition, the almost sacred autonomy of the stores and the resulting plethora of company names had diluted Belk's buying power. Some manufacturers were not even aware that Belk was one of their best customers because the Belk orders often arrived separately from various stores, were then filed under separate names, and were paid by checks drawn on banks all across the South.

The October seventy-fifth anniversary program honoring manufacturers, which carried the theme "Big Belk Country," was designed to begin changing these perceptions. The morning's program included a film on Belk Stores with a script that was liberally salted with words like "sparkling boutique" and "fashion trends" and that illustrated the broad reach of the Belk organization. At lunch, guests heard a Duke Power Company official describe the anticipated economic growth in the region. The day concluded with an evening dinner address by Luther Hodges, the former governor of North Carolina, who was then U.S. secretary of commerce. But it was the afternoon awards sessions that left the Belks' guests something to think about.

With special ceremony, including the presentation of shiny plaques by the Belks themselves, manufacturers who had sold the most to Belk stores were singled out for special favors. Craddock-Terry Shoe Corporation, which supplied Belk's private-label shoes, was the largest Belk vendor with $4 million in sales. Cannon Mills Company, whose looms turned out sheets and towels under Belk's private label of State Pride, was honored for doing more than $1 million in business with Belk for the previous year. In addition to the plaques, each guest was given a sealed model rocket containing a prediction of the amount of business the Belks believed each vendor should be doing with Belk at the next anniversary celebrating one hundred years of business. The numbers were not small, but as it turned out, they were woefully short of the mark.

"There was no question," recalls Belk executive Ray Killian, "that we wanted to say to these leading resources, 'If you expect to do business in the Southeast, then you need to build up a team relationship with the Belk and Leggett stores.'" The Belks hoped the top executives not receiving awards would return to their offices the following Monday and get their regional sales managers to explain why the competition had been honored by the Belks and their company had not. The strategy worked.

Thank-you letters poured in from across the country. Many included references to a new understanding of the Belk organization. Vanity Fair, a major line that had previously refused to put its labels in Belk stores now was ready to write orders. Another New York guest wrote, "my impression of Belk stores was obtained solely from quick glimpses on U.S. Route 301, as I drove down to Florida. Those impressions were completely wiped away by the pictures shown at the Friday morning meeting and my visit to your Charlotte store and the stores' Services Center." A St. Louis manufacturer was so impressed that he called to offer Tom Belk a special price on a line he was preparing to close out. The price was so low that the store's markup allowed the Belks to earn enough on the deal to pay for the cost of the entire Advance Celebration weekend.

Attending another of the series of anniversary celebrations was Joe Robinson, a top executive of Wachovia Bank and Trust Company. Tall, thin, the very picture of a flinty banker of the old school, Robinson had been doing business with the Belks since he arrived in Charlotte in 1938. He had known Henry Belk, who had served on the Wachovia board of directors from 1938 until his death in 1952, and when the bank had begun looking for a successor, Robinson had recommended John Belk as his father's replacement. Later, as John learned the banking business and Robinson learned more about merchandising, the two talked often about adapting the bank's program of planning to the Belk organization. "He was fascinated with the idea that we would plan five years out and actually do what we planned," Robinson said later. A year after the seventy-fifth anniversary, John and Tom Belk convinced Robinson to leave banking and come to work for them. The two wanted a plan for the future of the stores, and they saw Robinson as the man who could produce it for them.

In October 1964, Robinson became a banker's merchant—a

retail executive who could talk the language of the financial world—instead of a merchant's banker. On the organization chart, Robinson replaced Gibson Smith, who had retired a few months earlier after managing the Belks' vast collection of corporate and personal real estate for more than twenty years. Of course, John Belk had more than real estate closings and property management in mind for Robinson. Robinson quietly moved into a vacant office on the first floor of the Belk Stores Services building at 308 E. Fifth Street in Charlotte and set to work.

Robinson thought he knew the Belks' business. After all, he had been their banker for more than twenty-five years. But all the Belk companies were privately held corporations, and the Belks and their partners shared little financial information with outsiders, even a close confidant like Robinson. They revealed only that information absolutely necessary to secure a loan or obtain a line of credit. When Robinson moved inside the company and began to look around, he was not impressed.

He quickly learned that before he could plan for the future, he had to organize the present. There were few systems in place to collect timely vital sales and financial information from more than four hundred separate store corporations. The organization of individual companies for each store had served Henry Belk well in many ways. Stock ownership had provided local managers with incentive to grow and prosper, and at one time there had been certain tax advantages to the arrangement. But the unique arrangement had created a corporate nest of interlocking stock ownership and directorates that amazed outsiders and was difficult to comprehend.

Robinson found that the company still used the founder's measure of success. Performance standards were based on where the company had been, not on where it was going. Store managers and partners kept score by whether they had beaten last year's sales. In addition, Tom Belk's plan to upgrade merchandise and transform the company from emphasizing value to promoting fashion was not universally shared. Some partners, well senior to the young Belks, objected to changing a Belk store from its traditional role of providing customers with what they needed to providing what they wanted. Despite merchandising trends elsewhere in the country, John Belk could not budge some partners who saw no need to consider shopping centers in the suburbs when their downtown stores were doing just fine.

In short, the image of the stores that the seventy-fifth anniversary celebration had intended to convey did not fit reality, at least not universally across the nineteen mid-Atlantic and Southern states where the Belks operated stores. Indeed, the very building that housed Belk Stores Services was not even square. Checking on the odd shape of ceiling tiles in his office, Robinson learned that when Henry Belk, Jr., had stepped off the corners for the building in 1948, he had staked out a foundation six feet wider in the rear than the front. No one had bothered to correct the error.

Because of the lack of information inside the Belk organization, it took Robinson a year to gather everything he needed to produce the plan John and Tom Belk had requested. Late one afternoon in early 1966, Robinson presented his findings to John Belk: Belk stores had plenty of money in the bank but was losing its share of the market. "With all our money," Robinson later recalled, "we still were far behind the market, far behind the opportunities."

Robinson then backed up his analysis with cold, unforgiving statistics. Most Belk stores were downtown when every trend showed retailing moving to the suburbs. Most stores were trading in cash while customers were looking for ways to use credit. Belk store managers were filling their shelves and counters with clothes for rural folk and low- to middle-income customers with limited buying power while the population was moving to the cities and shopping for fashion. Finally, Belk stores were anchored in tradition while the Carolinas and much of the rest of the South were becoming part of mainstream consumer America. "In many markets, we are not keeping up," Robinson told the Belks.

Robinson's analysis was one of the first in-depth assessments of the future of the business ever conducted within the organization. If his report was correct, then the Belks and their partners were faced with the job of totally redirecting not just one company, but hundreds—a mammoth, almost overwhelming task for a company organized in conventional fashion. The autonomy Henry Belk had granted his partners, once considered a strength that encouraged local leadership and kept Belk stores close to their customers, now appeared to be a major liability. And while most corporations could simply redirect their business, the change at Belk would have to come with the cooperation of minority stockholders who were perfectly satisfied with the condition of their business. Within a few months, however, the Belks had organized a long range planning committee with the endorsement of the most influential of the senior partners, Arthur Tyler of Rocky Mount. Things would never be the same.

On April 16, 1969, William B. Beery III of Wilmington, N.C., clipped a ribbon and opened a new Belk store in Oglethorpe Mall outside of Savannah, Ga. The store was shiny, new, and large, the largest that the Belks had ever opened outside of Charlotte, containing more than 80,000 square feet of carefully laid out shopping space. Another 20,000 square feet on a second level could be used for offices and expansion. Moreover, the store was in a large regional mall, another first. The Belks' own shopping mall, SouthPark in Charlotte, was still under construction and the opening still several months away.

Belk was one of two major stores in the new regional center at Savannah. Sears was the other and its presence fulfilled a promise John Belk had made to himself in Savannah years before. Fresh out of the Army in 1947 and working as a young troubleshooter for his father, John Belk had helped open the Savannah store. The store had not fared well in that location, one vacated by Sears, which had moved closer to the suburbs, and Belk had resolved that when Sears next moved in Savannah the Belks would be right there with them.

The Savannah mall building was simple enough, a tall, wide, windowless, brick box, with the entrance highlighted by three high arches side by side. Architects had struggled with the design, trying to come up with something that looked stylish, but at the same time was inexpensive. After presenting nothing that satisfied the Belks, Joe Robinson and Bill Beery had sketched the arches onto a restaurant napkin during a meeting with developers in Atlanta. They thought the entrance columns added elegance without ostentation. They also cost less than anything else on the drawing table.

This store's name also was different. Hanging from the exterior wall was the company's new graphic identifier, the Belk name spelled in a new specially designed alphabet highlighted with a large, curlicued capital *B*. And it was there alone, without the hyphenated addition of Beery's name, although he was the operating partner. Adopted as a new logo, the distinctive "Big B" had been going up on Belk storefronts across the South for about a year, replacing the designer's nightmare of type styles in store signage and other identification that varied even within the same store.

While Savannah's attention focused on the new mall store, which began making money from the first day it opened, workers were closing up Belk's former location downtown. This would not be the Belks' last store closing or gala opening. During the next fifteen years, as the company headed into its centennial year, the Belks and their partners would embark on the most ambitious building and remodeling program in the company's history. In the first ten years alone, their plans called for the yearly opening of 500,000 square feet of new retail sales space and the remodeling of yet another half million square feet. They were not stores Henry Belk would have opened, but the South of the 1970s was a very different world from Monroe on May 29, 1888.

William Henry Belk swelled with pride as he opened the doors of the New York Racket for his first day of business on the corner of Main and Morgan streets in Monroe, N.C. It was late May 1888. He could not remember when he had not wanted to be a merchant, and twelve years of work in B. D. Heath's store a few blocks down the street were merely a prelude to this day.

The name "Racket" was a common handle for the dry-goods trade among merchants in small Southern towns. And they usually lived up to the promise, making noise about their latest shipments of goods from Northern markets sold at what would come to be known as discount prices. Henry Belk announced, in large letters painted on the side of the two-story building, that his was the "Cheapest Store on Earth." He added New York to the name for panache.

His leased store was modest, only twenty-two by seventy feet, but the building was of substantial brick and it even carried a title. The name "Marsh & Lee" was painted in a recess just below the filigree at the roof line. When the afternoon sun baked the dirt street, Belk could pull a canvas awning out from the fixtures mounted just below the second story windows and shade the brick sidewalk and storefront with its two large entrances flanked by display windows. On busy days, the awning also protected the overflow of goods that spilled out of the store and were stacked on crates for display along the front near the curb.

Inside the store, Henry had carefully laid out stacks of bargains on rough boards and packing crates that passed for store fixtures. He offered a stock of cloth in dull, conservative patterns and drab colors—a family of six required about four bolts a year to keep everyone clothed—and notions, men's work clothes, ladies' shoes and wooden-pegged brogans that could cripple a man until shaped by a season in the fields. Henry Belk had the basic staples ready for the farmers and their families of Union County, N.C.

If Henry Belk was proud, he also was nervous. At a time of economic uncertainty in the South, he had left a good job at Heath's store, one that paid fifty dollars a quarter, and had opened his own place on borrowed money. He had matched a $500 loan from Col. John McCain's widow with $750 from his savings and had picked up goods on consignment from Capt. John Austin, whose own fortune as a merchant had turned sour. But Henry Belk was confident. He knew the business, and he knew his customers—the strong, sturdy Carolina farmers whose livelihood came from raising small crops of corn and cotton.

Union County and the town of Monroe also knew Henry Belk. This tall, lean, handsome man of twenty-six had been a familiar figure in Heath's store. He had worked there since he was fourteen, arriving early in the day and leaving late, for his starting pay of five dollars a month (merchants followed no established hours, remaining open for business as long as there were customers). Heath had liked his apprentice and increased the young man's responsibilities as time passed and he became more experienced. When Heath traveled in search of bargains to New York, Philadelphia, Baltimore, and other Northern markets, Belk managed the store in his place. This gave him a chance to pick up tips of the trade from drummers who called on the store as part of their regular tour of the region selling everything from pills to plowshares. Heath rewarded Belk's enterprise and ambition, following one raise with another. Heath said Belk was a born merchant, and was eager to hang on to this able young man.

With each payday Belk had added to his savings, but he had also carried part of his earnings home to his mother, a strong woman who had rebuilt her life after the Civil War left her widowed and virtually homeless. Belk's father, Abel Nelson Washington Belk, had been drowned in a creek near the Belk homestead by marauding Union soldiers just weeks before Gen. Joseph Johnston surrendered to Sherman's conquering force at Durham Station, N.C. Sarah Walkup Belk had managed to save the family farm in the Waxhaws just across the South Carolina line near Rock Hill, but it was heavily mortgaged as she worked it with hired help after the war. In 1866 she remarried, bringing John R. Simpson, the man she had hired to manage the farm, into the family. In 1873, when Henry Belk was eleven years old, the Simpsons moved to Monroe.

Henry Belk already knew he wanted to be a merchant when he moved to Monroe. As a lad on the farm in the Waxhaws, he had hurried to finish his chores in time to go with the family to see the circus in nearby Rock Hill, S.C. He had enjoyed the circus, but Belk had gone home even more fascinated with the stores he had seen on the country town's main street.

Sarah Belk, a woman of great religious faith, instilled in her children the stout Presbyterian tenets of faith and hard work. She was an educated woman and had graduated from the Carolina Female Academy in Ansonville, N.C., in 1853. The school included Latin and music in the curriculum and was designed to accommodate the daughters of plantation owners along the Pee Dee River. She had passed her education along to her children and the children of Negroes hired to work the farm, using the Bible and its stories to help them learn their lessons. Such training did not go unnoticed in the community, where hard work and religion, and plenty of both, were part of life. So was improving one's situation.

Belk had continued his studies while he worked in Heath's store. The county commissioners recognized his talent and offered him a scholarship at the University of North Carolina. Belk went to Heath with his choices: business or a college education. Heath argued against college and raised Belk's pay to fifty dollars a quarter, a third more than he had been making. The increase made the decision all the harder because Belk's mother was prepared to sell land to raise money for college expenses—the scholarship was for tuition only. Finally, Belk made his decision to remain in the business. His brother John, two years younger and full of promise, would be the college student in the family.

Confidence in a merchant was something to cherish in rural communities like Monroe in the late 1880s. The South was recovering from the war and Reconstruction, but the periodic upheavals in the economy usually meant harder times for the farmers, who were locked in a one-crop system. While Henry Belk was planning his future with the New York Racket, farmers meeting in Raleigh were organizing a political challenge to a system that produced low prices for their crops and ever-increasing prices for their basic needs. The farmers' political strength was rising to its peak, and the legislature that convened in 1888 included the highest proportion of farmers elected since the Civil War. Two years before Belk opened his store, Leonidas L. Polk of Raleigh had begun publication of the *Progressive Farmer* and had given thousands of farmers and people of the land a voice in the state's political affairs.

Chief among the farmers' complaints was the credit system upon which they depended for their livelihood. Farmers had money in their pockets one time a year, when they sold their crops at harvest. To survive, to keep food on their tables and seed in their fields, farmers depended on credit from country merchants. Thus, the merchant was a banker as well as a retailer, at a time when there was only one bank for every 58,000 citizens and bankers held little sympathy for the small farmer. Many merchants took advantage of their captive customers and increased the credit prices of their goods by 20 to 50 percent above cash prices, and then they charged interest on the outstanding balance. When farmers arrived to settle affairs at harvest time, they sometimes found themselves paying the equivalent of 40 to 100 percent more than the cost of an item if they had paid cash.

Belk had seen this system work, both as a merchant and earlier when his own mother had struggled to get the family farm working again. It left customers with overpriced goods and with their dignity ground into the Carolina clay. Merchants, meanwhile, were caught in the middle, risking their own future to keep farmers in goods. Neither condition suited Henry Belk.

Belk had heard about another way of doing business, in Philadelphia. In 1878, a successful merchant named John Wanamaker had opened what he called a "New Kind of Store," which incorporated something called the one-price system. Instead of negotiating a price with each customer, the merchant marked the price plainly and customers paid the posted price. Wanamaker was not the first merchant to adopt the one-price system—Lord and Taylor in New York used it as early as 1835—but he was the first to adopt it on such a large scale. Drummers and traveling salesmen, who carried trade news from town to town, as well as advice on stock and credit, and a few tall tales, also told Belk that Wanamaker's plan was founded on four principles. In addition to selling goods at a fixed price with no haggling, Wanamaker made cash sales and did not offer long credit. He had a generous money-back guarantee and was totally committed to fully satisfying his customers.

Wanamaker's success with one-price shopping worked in Philadelphia, where customers had steady incomes from factory paychecks and office jobs; a man's income was not dependent on the weather and changes in the price of cotton. Factories were beginning to open in the Carolina Piedmont. Many new textile mills had started operating in the 1880s; James W. Cannon's first cotton mill was running in Kannapolis. There was a furniture factory in High Point. But North Carolina was a farm economy, and there was no guarantee that a cash-sales policy could be transplanted to Monroe, where credit terms and haggling over a merchant's asking price were accepted parts of the business. Belk's friends told him he was foolish to try something different. He persisted, nonetheless. On May 29, when he opened the doors of the New York Racket, he announced his new policy up front.

Belk told his customers that if he did not have to carry their debts, his goods would be cheaper than those they might find at his competitors. In addition, Belk could take advantage of his own discounts from vendors who normally gave him 5 percent off if he paid bills promptly. The policy meant turning over a lot of stock during the year, but Henry

William Henry Belk, founder of Belk stores, as a successful Charlotte merchant.

Dr. John Belk, brother of William Henry Belk and early partner in the company, died in 1928.

Posed in the stiff, pretentious style of the late 1800s, the staff of the Monroe store set up shop on the sidewalk for the photographer. The group includes (from left) Frank Thomas, Walter Crowell, Alice Norwood, Carrie Rudge Coble, Henry Brown, Dr. Redfern, Ed Austin, Will Rudge (seated), Henry Walkup (a Belk cousin), and William A. "Billy" Benton. Alice Norwood continued with the store for years. Benton opened his own Belk store in Hamlet, N.C., in the 1930s.

Belk was prepared to take the chance. He carried through with his lower prices, sold for cash, and promised full value and full service. If a customer was unhappy with goods, he knew Henry Belk would make good on the sale, without any questions. This strategy made sense economically as long as Belk could find stock for his store and keep turning his investment over and over. It also fit comfortably with Belk's own Scotch-Irish independence. If a man paid cash for his goods, Belk said, he would be happier than if he had a debt hanging over his head.

Six months after Henry Belk opened the New York Racket, as 1888 came to a close, he tallied his accounts. His books showed he had sales of just more than $17,000, an average of $100 a day since he opened his doors. He had repaid the

ENTHUSIASM!

The Boy Orator of the Platte with his Silver Proclamation is Carrying the Country by Storm. Such Enthusiasm has never been known.

Belk Bros.,

Are also, with the Biggest Stock of Goods and the Lowest Prices, drawing the Thousands every day into their Mammoth Establishment.

CARGO AFTER CARGO of Boots, Shoes, Clothing, Dry Goods, Hats, Tinware etc., now arriving daily.

Prices cut in two in the middle and set on fire at both ends.

☞ Cheapest Store on Earth.

BELK BROS.,

19 & 21 EAST TRADE STREET,
White Front.   Charlotte, N. C.

William Henry Belk wrote the copy for his newspaper ads in the Charlotte newspapers. This one, pegged to the political campaign of William Jennings Bryan, was typical of the topical nature of his promotions.

William Henry Belk opened his first store in Monroe on May 29, 1888. He called it the New York Racket and advertised that his was the "Cheapest Store On Earth."

The Belk brothers broke with the tradition of merchants who carried large accounts for their customers. They sold for cash, a proposition that Belk said allowed him to give his customers lower prices. This receipt, dated July 12, 1893, included a boy's suit at $4.50 for Johnnie Stewart.

$500 loan to Mrs. McCain, had long since paid Capt. Austin for his goods, and had restocked the store. In addition, he had a profit of $3,300. Belk's strategy had not only worked, but worked well. The New York Racket was a success.

The promise that more could be achieved sent Henry Belk shopping the markets in Philadelphia, Baltimore, and New York, looking for bargains, closeouts, bankruptcies, and deals from merchants on the narrow streets of Manhattan. The eager young man from the South won friends easily in the market. Belk established relationships with merchants who would be selling to him and his stores thirty and forty years later. His years with Heath, and his years of listening to salesmen who provided an education beyond what he found in the small store, had taught Belk how to buy. He not only looked for deals, he knew the prices of raw materials and what was involved in making a pair of shoes or a shirt. As a result, he bought well. When the goods were shipped home, Belk sold them straight from the heavy wooden packing crates. With each sale he turned a small profit and was

Traveling to markets in Baltimore, Philadelphia, and New York was a family affair. During one trip, probably about 1910, Belk led his buyers on a tour of Washington in an "automobile coach." Seated beside Belk on the front seat is Presbyterian evangelist Reverend William Black. Houston Matthews from the Gastonia store is beside Black. Belk's brother, John, is seated in the rear with Nealie, one of his seven daughters.

back on the road again. His slogan: "Cheap Goods Sell Themselves." When the decade closed, Belk's sales had more than doubled.

As the business grew, Belk hired more clerks for the store. The additional help made a difference, but Henry Belk needed more than hired hands. He needed someone who could tend the store in his absence, someone in whom he had absolute and unqualified confidence that customers would receive the same service he offered when he was in the store. In 1891, he paid a visit to his brother, John, who for five years had been building a country doctor's practice about thirty miles east of Monroe in the Anson County town of Morven, N.C. John had married two years earlier and started his family. Times were tough in John's country practice, but as his income permitted he paid on loans his brother

Charlotte bargain hunters turned out for the Belk brothers' special sales. On the occasion of the store's 16th anniversary in 1911, Belk recorded the event with a photograph. Store clerks and others climbed out on the ledge of the store's large bay windows on the second floor while a crowd gathered at the door. The image is blurred, but the man standing by himself at the far left of the crowd appears to be William Henry Belk.

Inside, Belk's store was crowded on Saturdays. This photograph of the interior of Belk's Charlotte store shows the rigging (near the top of the walls at the ceiling) for the Lamson system that directed wire baskets carrying cash and receipts to and from the store's cashiers.

The Trade Street trolley rolled right by the front door of the Belk store just off the square in downtown Charlotte. William Henry Belk could leave his home on Hawthorne Lane, board the trolley at the top of the hill near Presbyterian Hospital, and be at his store in minutes.

When the Belks remodeled their store in 1927 they replaced the troublesome rigging of the Lamson system with miles of brass tubes. A vacuum system carried large capsules filled with cash and receipts to cashiers who prepared the correct change and stuffed them back into a return for quick delivery to the sales floor.

The staff of the Greensboro store worked under the direction of D. R.
"Dick" Harry (the man with the hat and mustache), who had been trained
by William Henry Belk in the Charlotte store before Belk opened the store
in Greensboro in 1899. This photograph was taken in 1907.

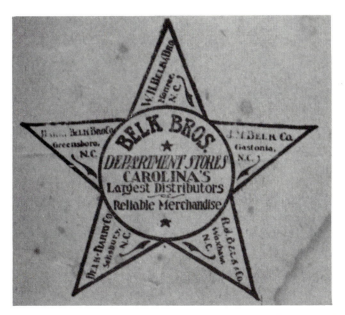

With the addition of each new store, William Henry Belk just added
another point to his logo, which eventually evolved into the familiar
sunburst that served the company for more than sixty years. (See also
illustrations on pages 26 and 27.)

had made to him for his education. On a particularly difficult night, when John had been called out late in bad weather to tend to some neighbor's maladies, Henry Belk made his pitch. Leave medicine, he told his brother, and come into business with me. They talked it over through the night. By daybreak, John had decided that his future was in retailing, not medicine. John Montgomery Belk took a one-half interest in the business and soon returned to Monroe with his young wife and daughter. As soon as a painter could be found, the New York Racket Store sign was changed to W. H. Belk & Bro.

Two years later, cotton prices dropped to four cents per

In 1920 the Charlotte Observer *featured the Charlotte Belk store in a full-page display of photographs of company employees. Prominent in the foreground is Sarah Houston, who managed the ladies' wear and millinery departments with little or no interference or questions from Belk for more than thirty years.*

The Belk family gathered on the steps of the Belk mansion in 1926 with their cousin Mary VanWie. The children standing behind their parents are (from left) Henry, Sarah, and John. Tom Belk is in his mother's lap. Brothers Irwin and Henderson and cousin VanWie's child are in the foreground.

The Belk brothers had a commanding position in the Charlotte market in 1927 when they expanded their building, which they advertised at 119,180 square feet as the largest department store in the Carolinas.

Belk store ads competed for attention with other major retailers in Charlotte, including Ivey's and Efird's department stores.

pound and economic panic began closing banks and businesses all across the country. Farmers and businessmen in North Carolina suffered, but Belk's system of cash sales and quick turnover of inventory resulted in cash on hand with which to buy more goods. This put the Belk brothers in a stronger position than most. Where other merchants waited for the economy to improve, strapped to the farmers' losses as surely as if they were spending their days behind a mule themselves, the Belks found opportunities.

Belk hawked his goods from the sidewalk and in the *Monroe Journal* with advertisements that promised much. One ad, in the July 26, 1895, edition, said the New York Racket "has more real bargains to offer than any store in North Carolina. On many lines prices cut in the middle and set on fire at both ends." Belk advertised he had silk umbrellas at fifty cents each and 5,000 men's and ladies' handkerchiefs at below cost. "Come in and inspect our stock whether you wish to buy or not. No trouble to show you. W. H. Belk and Bro."

Henry Belk had not opened the New York Racket with plans for expansion. At first, he was simply a merchant who wanted his own store. But he and his brother had an eye for investment opportunities, and they saw a chance to do something different after a visit from Alex Kluttz, who had married a Belk cousin from South Carolina. The brothers had recently purchased the stock of a bankrupt business in Monroe when Kluttz walked into their store in 1893. Like many, Kluttz had fallen on hard times and his business had gone bankrupt. But he had paid his debts and was looking for an opportunity to start anew. The Belk brothers liked that. As the brothers talked, they made Kluttz a proposition: Take the goods they had recently purchased, rent a store building in Chester, S.C., and open a store. Kluttz would own a share of the business, the Belks would own the rest.

That year, in the depths of a severe economic depression, the Kluttz Department Store opened. A year later the two brothers repeated the process in Union, S.C., where Reece P. Harry opened a store. The two liked the determination and honesty of Harry, one of seven children of a widowed mother, and they helped him get together between $4,000 and $5,000 in dry goods to start the business. Harry's store opened as another New York Racket Store, but it also was known as Harry and Belk Company. As such, this location

became the first store to carry the Belk name beyond Monroe.

The Belks began looking for other opportunities as economic conditions remained severe in the South in 1894. Despite the expansion, Belk stores' sales declined for the first time since the New York Racket had opened six years earlier. Moreover, Henry and brother John had lost more than $1,000 in the bankruptcy of a Monroe cotton mill they had invested in. People envious of the Belk brothers' prosperity and growth expressed satisfaction that their bubble had burst. When word of this envy reached Henry he was angry. He did not need the petty politics of Monroe. Henry's travels to the nation's largest cities had extended his horizons far beyond the dusty streets of Monroe. He enjoyed the New York theaters when he was in Manhattan and occasionally stopped off in Washington, D.C., for a visit to the Capitol, where, he once wrote his half-brother Will Simpson, he had seen many senators and representatives and was unimpressed with either lot. When he had had enough of the Monroe gossip, he began looking for another part of a growing nation to do business.

He had heard of the booming economy in the West and set off on a scouting trip to Houston, Texas. He found the Texas economy alive and well, and Houston riding a wave of expansion. Belk shopped the stores of the city and discovered that goods from his contacts in the East would bring two and three times the purchase price when sold in Houston. He felt confident he could compete with any merchant he had seen on the streets of Houston, and he returned home full of optimism and enthusiasm, ready to sell out everything and head west.

Henry discussed the opportunity with his mother and brother and was eager to leave behind the petty differences over the cotton mill failure and move to the Gulf Coast.

Sarah Belk Simpson was against the plan. She had endured much and struggled hard to get her sons started in life. She told them if they moved to Texas it would be the same as telling her goodbye forever. She argued that they knew the South and knew the people of the region, and their future was as certain as the strength of these roots of family and tradition. They should stay at home.

Henry Belk listened and took his mother's advice. But he was not going to stay in Monroe. That was settled. He began looking for a new opportunity closer to home, in Charlotte, the growing city just twenty-five miles up the newly laid railway line. Years later, Henry Belk told a friend that, if it had not been for the incident over the cotton mill, he might have remained in Monroe forever.

Henry Belk was no stranger to Charlotte when he stepped off the train from Monroe in the summer of 1895 to scout a location for the Belk brothers' next store. Daily, more than thirty trains pulled out of two rail stations in this growing city, and for years Henry Belk had switched cars in Charlotte on his way to the markets in the Northeast. After the destructive isolation and bitterness of Reconstruction, America's trains, which boasted of traveling 439 miles in just more than ten hours, were tying the nation together. The tracks through the center of Charlotte linked Henry Belk's growing new business to the world. Washington was only a little more than twelve hours up the line.

Charlotte was North Carolina's second largest city. With a population of about 15,000, she was fast approaching Wilmington as number one. Local boosters and businessmen were beginning to open textile mills along the main line of the Southern Railway at such a fast clip that the road from Danville to Gastonia would earn the title of "Gold Avenue." Piedmont Carolina communities soon would rally to the cry of a "mill a mile." Seventy-three mills already were in operation or under construction in the Charlotte area. In June 1895, James W. Cannon announced additions to his mills. His plans included adding 5,000 spindles and 125 looms to his growing complex in Kannapolis, just twenty miles north of Charlotte. About eighty miles up the line in Greensboro, Moses and Ceasar Cone had opened their Proximity Mill and were turning out prints, flannels, and denims, fabrics that Belk knew he could buy at a good price for his customers in the stores in Monroe and Chester and Union, S.C.

Charlotte joined in the boom times that relieved the severe depression of 1893 as a center for trade and finance. The only sound of machinery in the center of town was the cotton compress, where the city's official cotton weigher and inspector prepared for shipping the bales hauled in by area farmers. The people of Charlotte were proud of their banks, insurance companies, electric streetcars, and busy retail trade. Charlotte had private schools for men and women, blacks and whites—nearby Davidson College was preparing for a fall enrollment of 160—a daily newspaper, and crank telephones. Electric power had replaced kerosene lamps in the grand homes along North Tryon Street. E. L. Latta was selling lots just south of downtown in a residential development called Dilworth. "Buy a house with the rent money," Latta told Charlotte.

As Belk walked up South Tryon Street to the square at the intersection of Trade and Tryon streets, he passed handsome buildings of brick and granite that were several stories taller than his modest store in Monroe. Buggies and wagons clattered along the broad street, past the handsome Central Hotel on the southeast corner at the square. The hotel was home to the city's telephone exchange and provided lodgings and meals for most of the traveling men who filled their order books in Charlotte.

The *Charlotte Daily Observer* carried advertisements from merchants who would be tough competitors for Belk. His new ideas in Monroe were not new here. Belk would not even be able to bring his Racket Store name to town. It was already taken by Williams and Hood Company. "Call at the Racket," the store's daily newspaper ads announced, "and see the great pile of goods gathered in, bought cheap for dollars and see how very cheap we are selling goods." And some of his other sales strategies were in place. Long, Tate and Company advertised as a "one-price clothier." And more new stores were already in the works. Herman Baruch, whose previous business had fallen on hard times, was announcing to the city that he was in the markets looking for new fall stock and "will in a very short time have my shelves laden with the most correct fabrics for the coming FALL and WINTER SEASON." He also asked those who owed him money to pay up. He needed the cash for his season's purchases.

Henry Belk knew there was only one spot for his store, right in the thick of Charlotte's merchants at the Square, one of North Carolina's busiest commercial corners. Belk located an empty building, near the Oestreicher brothers' Charlotte Dry Goods Emporium at 11 East Trade. It was three stories tall and owned by E. L. Baxter Davidson, whose family had donated land and lent support to open Davidson College about fifty years earlier. The college had graduated four of Belk's uncles and one had served on the college's board of trustees. Davidson needed no better recommendation, and Belk acquired a lease immediately and began filling his new selling floor with goods. He had nearly twice the floor space he had in Monroe, but he was now in a city, not a country town, and he would need a wider range of merchandise to compete. His reputation had preceded him. The business he and his brother were doing in Monroe was known to Charlotte merchants, who said he would not last the year.

Belk opened for business on Wednesday, September 25, 1895. The *Daily Observer*, which carried detailed reports of local interest, paid him no heed. The paper's attention was focused on politics and the silver convention in Raleigh. A patent fight between the government and Alexander Graham Bell was being heard in a federal courtroom in Richmond. It was not that the paper ignored matters of commerce. For example, the *Daily Observer* reported two days after Belk's opening that S. T. Cooper, formerly of the Bee Hive store near Belk's new establishment, had opened a store in Rockingham, N.C., and Mr. Cooper had been in town to share his news of his new venture. Belk probably noted that particular news item with interest. Here was someone going the other direction. Belk and other downtown merchants probably were pleased to read that the mayor had announced that the fire department would no longer be permitted to exercise the fire horses on the city's principal streets. The last time the fire crew had taken the team out, they had wrecked the fire wagon and broken its tongue.

Timing and Henry Belk's eye for opportunity and keen

sense of promotion produced a grand-opening extravaganza no other merchant in town could afford. Rather than announce his new store on the first day of business, Belk waited a week. Then, on the eve of the opening of the Sells Brothers Circus, an event sure to draw thousands of potential shoppers to Charlotte, Henry Belk purchased a larger-than-average, two-column advertisement in the *Daily Observer* to say:

Belk Bros.

claim to be the

"Cheapest Store on Earth."

In a word, we know no competition—mean to be second to none. Kind attention shown everybody. Call for anything and you shall have it

Folks will hear from

Belk Bros.

19–21 E. Trade St.

Backed by years of experience, untiring energy and the mighty dollar, have just returned from the markets with the largest stock of goods ever shipped to North Carolina. We simply announce to the trading public that we intend doing the business of Charlotte and the surrounding country. Watch us and see the dizzy pinnacle of success reached in this statement.

Belk's plan worked perfectly. At five o'clock on the morning of October 4, 500 people gathered at the Southern Railway station a few blocks south of his store just to watch the unloading of the circus animals. By midmorning Trade and Tryon streets were lined with people for the circus's mile-long parade up Tryon Street. That left visitors to the city plenty of time to shop before the ringmaster opened the show at 3:00 P.M. More than 6,000 people filled the circus tents and caught the one-day show before it left for Spartanburg the next day. Three rings of exotic entertainment, with educated seals, monkeys that could ride horses, clowns, and trapeze artists were just about as good a grand-opening celebration as a merchant could want.

Belk declared his opening in Charlotte a rousing success. A week after the circus left town, Belk was in the newspapers again when he told Charlotte:

New Store, New Goods, New Men

We have worked for three weeks from early morn till 12 o'clock at night in order to get our stock opened, marked and placed, and yet the goods pour in by the carload. However, the day is beginning to dawn and people are moving this way to find, as announced, that we keep the

Cheapest Store on Earth

The ready cash does the work. Then we divide the profit, and a short quick one it is. Circus day was a hummer for us. Saturday the same and Monday just as good. The largest deal of this season consummated Saturday night—buying for four large stores, you remember. Spot cash is the lever we use. Don't mean to oversell, but UNDERSELL. Keep up with us.

Belk Brothers

19 & 21 E. Trade

Henry Belk was ready to sell anybody anything. His store was a combination of services, part novelty and part dry goods, which aimed for the business of the solid, hard-working people in the community and in the country. He sold overalls to the well digger, spectacles to the man's grandmother, and suits for his Sunday meetings. Belk had a feeling for these people. He knew they wanted high-quality goods for their hard-earned dollars. He had given them that in Monroe, and he found that shoppers in Charlotte were not any different.

He constantly searched for ways to promote his trade in the city and beyond. When country folk came to Charlotte to load their wagons with supplies, he arranged with some to have Belk signs painted on the sides of their wagons in exchange for an extra bolt of cloth. The painted notice helped, to be sure, but perhaps more important was the word of mouth that spread in the small communities and mountain hollows about the values neighbors found in Belk's store, where every customer was king. Belk's strategy was simple: sell the working man necessities like sturdy work shoes at a low price, and he would return to outfit his entire family.

Belk was off to a fine start, and Christmas brought a new level of success. The stores Henry and John Belk had started were doing well; forty employees in the four locations were needed to handle the business. While others were selling for cash, while others were selling at low prices, and while others might have sturdy staples just like Belk, Henry Belk was succeeding against stiff competition. He crowed about his large crowds in his Christmas ads and by year's end had adopted a new slogan, "Goods sell themselves because they are bought right." That was but a slight variation of the slogan printed on his invoices of the New York Racket—"Goods Cheap Enough Sell Themselves."

When Henry and John Belk settled accounts for the year 1895, they knew they had made the right decision to move beyond their small business in Monroe. The store there was doing well under John's management, and the two stores in South Carolina were growing, but Charlotte moved Belk Brothers Company into a league that neither had believed possible. In 1894, with three stores in small towns, the brothers had sold just more than $50,000 in goods. Sales for 1895 were six times that. With Charlotte added to the group of stores, the brothers had sold more than $326,000 in goods.

Soon other Charlotte merchants were copying Belk. The Bee Hive, Mr. Cooper's old store just a half-block away at the corner of College Street, adopted the slogan, "The Cheapest Store in North Carolina." Another competitor, J. G. Hood and Company, under the name of the "Old Racket," used price to counter Belk. Using the same typeface and advertising style, Hood said, "We buy our goods cheap and sell them cheap. The field of credit disaster, the slaughter pens of the sheriff and the auction rooms are our prolific play-grounds."

Belk just upped the ante. He opened a "bargain shoe counter" and offered to outfit men, ladies, misses, and children at prices below his own low prices. He made his own deals, negotiating with manufacturers and mills in the area to get bargains on the best piece goods. The shoes came from Craddock-Terry Shoe Corporation in Lynchburg, Va., which started business the same year Belk opened his first store in Monroe. The company would be a supplier for nearly one hundred years. Belk also shopped Cannon's mills in Kannapolis and got into the manufacturing business himself, investing in mills and other enterprises that kept him close to the demands of the market.

Belk, like other merchants, offered mail-order service, picking up on the popularity of this new kind of trading. Lower postage rates and expansion of postal service had helped bring city life a little closer to the Carolina farmers. Belk's main business was in the city, however. The mail business was just a sideline.

Belk always offered one-cent items, from fishhooks to playing marbles, that helped draw young customers into the store. And he often worked as his own "puller-in" and stood at the front doors chatting with passersby and inviting them into his store.

By 1897, Belk had established a loose cooperative buying network that tied together the purchasing power of the Belk stores in Charlotte and Monroe and Union and Chester, S.C., and of two other stores in which Henry and John Belk had no financial interest. They purchased goods in large lots, buying as many as 1,500 pairs of pants at one time, for example. They also had a buyer in New York who scouted the market on their behalf, particularly looking for bargains in hats.

Reece Harry's store in Union now occupied two floors and a basement of one building and a floor of a new building erected by the company. Harry stocked more than just basic goods for farmers and field hands. Dress goods were a specialty of the house, and in the spring of 1897 he had added a millinery department which Ruth Anthony of Baltimore managed. He had ten clerks, three check boys, a cashier, a wrapper, and a porter.

While the Kluttz store remained part of the buying cooperative, the Belks sold their interest in the Chester store. They shifted their investment to Charlotte and Monroe, where they were adding new lines and expanding the range of goods. But the basic premise of the business remained the same. Buy cheap, sell at a modest profit, and return to the market with the cash.

A newspaper reported on the brothers' style of trade, saying "No books are kept in this house. All goods are sold for cash. 'Short profits and quick sales' is their motto. 'No credit' is their slogan. One of the proprietors informed the writer that not a dollar's worth of goods was charged on the books. The success of this business is a monument to industry, enterprise, business sagacity, honesty and temperance."

Competition took its toll on the mercantile trade in Charlotte during the last decade of the old century. Belk bought out one store, that belonging to T. L. Alexander and Company, and, shopping the bankruptcies and auctions in Baltimore and New York, he saw what could happen to merchants who overextended themselves with credit or strayed from their customers.

But Belk knew his business and his customers and had chosen his location well, right in the center of Charlotte's commercial activity. The city's three banks were within a block of the square where the city's horse-drawn trolleys exchanged riders. In the block with the Belk brothers' store were a drug store on the corner at the square and, next door, the offices of the Life Insurance Company of Virginia, a dentist's office, a hardware store, a barbershop, a shoemaker's shop, and the Odd Fellows Hall. To the east, at the corner of Trade and College streets, was the Bee Hive. Three saloons were in the second block. Charlotte's new City Hall, a grand, ornate affair with a tall tower topped by weathervane, was just a block away, around the corner at Tryon and Fifth. The First Presbyterian Church, with its broad lawn and park, was two blocks west on the other side of the square.

Henry Belk and the rest of Charlotte and Mecklenburg County were on the square for the traditional May 20 celebration in 1898. Patriotic fervor was at its peak. America had cheerfully declared war on Spain, and citizens were eager for a fight. The *Daily Observer* headline on April 23 was solemn: "War A Grim Fact." But Henry Belk's topical advertisements, eye-catching in their association with the news, read:

OPEN FIRE, BOOM BOOM BOOM. Don't you hear the cannon roar and the bursting of shells on Havana's shore; crashing through the timbers of Morro Castle, laying low the Spanish army drawn up to battle.

Two weeks earlier, as Washington moved closer to war, Belk all but declared action himself. His ad that week read:

SHOOT LUKE, or GIVE UP YOUR GUN

This will apply to Uncle Sam at this writing. No time to cater Wall Street or the money power. Independent action is absolutely necessary. Take the situation by the horns and risk the consequences. Assume an aggressive attitude. Move things, set the country on fire. That is the way BELK BROS. carried everything before them: raised the flag on low prices and swept the country from center to circumference; knocked the credit system, high prices and big profits into a crooked hat.

While affairs offshore had united the nation, Charlotte had not forgotten the Civil War. Veterans' groups were holding reunions and Gen. Stonewall Jackson's widow, who lived in

Charlotte, was accorded reverential treatment, particularly at public events. Charlotte also concentrated on its place in the founding of America. Mecklenburg patriots are said to have declared their independence from the British crown a full year before John Hancock boldly signed the Declaration of Independence in Philadelphia. Historians still debate the validity of the event, but to dispute the existence of the document in Charlotte's proud early days of growth was nothing short of heresy. In early May 1898, all the city was preparing for a special observance of the signing of the Mecklenburg Declaration of Independence on May 20, 1775.

By eight o'clock on the morning of May 20, a Friday, units that made up the mile-long parade began forming on South Tryon Street. The day was sunny and bright as Drum Major Baxtor Todd led off with the Charlotte Drum Corps in red jackets and white trousers. Floats for the twenty-one descendants of the signers carried young ladies in brilliant white dresses. Three more young women rode the float for the Old Ship of State. The line of march also included forty-five more floats, representing each of the "re-united states now fighting under the old flag for the same country and in a cause of freedom."

The parade moved out onto a route that passed right in front of Henry Belk's store before making a turn on College Street and heading north in a circle around the city's finest homes. As Mrs. Jackson's carriage passed by, Civil War veterans fell in behind. "Now and then a wooden leg labored earnestly to do as good work as the spared number," the *Daily Observer* reported, "and empty sleeves swung in eloquent silence from many a veteran's arm." The veterans carried battle flags lovingly preserved despite the bloodstains and bullet holes from battles now a glorious memory. The Hornet's Nest Riflemen, who fought at the battle of Big Bethel in 1861, where Henry Wyatt of Edgecombe County became the first to fall for the South, marched proudly to the elms at First Presbyterian Church. There, thousands waited to hear a patriotic speech by Adlai Stevenson, the grandfather of a statesman of a later time. Mrs. Jackson sat on a tier just below the speaker's podium, a small Confederate flag in her hand.

It was a grand day, and Henry Belk had prepared for it. The May 19 newspapers carried his advertisement that read like a program for the day's festivities. He invited shoppers to be at his store early in the day to "deposit their baggage, lunches and take a drink of water to revive them after their long journey." Then, Belk said, shoppers could watch the parade from right in front of the store and still have plenty of time to hear the noontime speeches scheduled for the First Presbyterian lawn. The newspapers devoted page after page to the event, which included the unveiling of a monument to the declaration's signers. Belk and other merchants could not have asked for a better way to start the summer season.

Henry Belk entered the twentieth century established and respected in the Charlotte business community. He was not yet forty but he and his brother owned a majority interest in a network of successful stores, the most recent opening in Greensboro in 1899. In addition, the Belk brothers owned stock in a hardware store, a grocery store, a bookstore, a roller mill, and a telephone company in Monroe. Henry Belk was a director of the Piedmont Fire Insurance Company, president of the Piedmont Clothing Company, and an investor in the Cole Cotton Planter Manufacturing Company, all in Charlotte. The Belks also owned stock in three other textile mills and a New York hat-manufacturing concern. Through cousins, Walkups from his mother's family, Henry Belk had even invested in orange groves in Florida.

The brothers had expanded the Charlotte store, leasing adjoining buildings, taking Belk's front door closer to the square. A shopper turning the corner off Tryon passed the Charlotte National Bank and came next to Belk's millinery department, followed by its clothes, dry goods and shoe departments. Weddington Hardware's three-story building was next door, with four more stores before the corner of College Street.

No other North Carolina city could match the growth of Charlotte, whose population was just more than 18,000 in

1900. And that count did not include the families living in the bustling streetcar suburb of Dilworth, which, if included, would have made Charlotte the state's largest city, with a population of more than 27,750. Despite the city's growth, the Belk brothers had not seen another year like the one that followed their entrance into Charlotte. Sales volume had declined, but the stores were busy and so was Henry Belk.

Customers would find the Belk brothers all over their stores. They were the first in the building each morning, organizing the display tables and merchandise for the day, supervising the young check boys as they swept the floors and pulled the tarpaulins off the display tables. Bolts of cloth and stacks of men's denim jeans and other goods were placed on upended wooden shipping crates on the sidewalk. Throughout the day, when clerks were overrun with business, Henry Belk waded into the crowd of customers, eager to sell and thriving on the exchange with people. He always carried a small pair of scissors in his vest pocket which he used to snip the corner of a measure of cloth before he tore it across with a flourish. The brothers were in their stores until the late evening hours. Closing time depended on the traffic and the competition. No store wanted its selling floor dark when another store up the street still had bright lights burning for customers.

Such a schedule was nothing new to Henry Belk. B. D. Heath had taught him the rudiments of retail clerking, and he had worked like that since he was fourteen. Moreover, Belk had been raised in a simple home, his early years marked by severe economic hardship. Hard work had been a necessity as well as a virtue honored daily with Bible readings. He took these lessons learned from his mother to Charlotte, where they were as much a part of his business as cash sales and low prices. Indeed, Henry Belk seemed all but consumed by his efforts to retain an edge over his tough competition in Charlotte. His clever ads helped, but success was due to a keen eye for opportunity and a single-mindedness of purpose.

Except for trips to markets in Northern cities, and excursions into the Carolina countryside to buy from the growing textile concerns in the Piedmont, Belk did not stray far from the front door of his store on East Trade Street. He lived in rooms on the upper floor of the taller of the two buildings that housed his store and took his meals across the street at the Central Hotel. Many of the city's businessmen, and most of the travelers, found substantial portions of well-cooked food there. Some businessmen, including bachelors like Henry Belk and newspaper editor J. P. Caldwell, listed the hotel as their residential address. After dinner, Belk would take a chair with the others at the hotel and pass the time before returning to the store to prepare for the next day's business. He had counters to restock, accounts to settle, and another round of advertisements to write. Though a handsome and eligible bachelor, he was too busy for an evening of social events or time with the ladies. His only vice was chewing tobacco, which was as popular with men of the day as cigarettes were considered evil. Cigarettes, however, were growing in popularity, largely due to aggressive sales and marketing by James B. Duke's American Tobacco Company. North Carolina had large cigarette factories in Durham, Winston-Salem, and Reidsville, along with smaller operations that turned out plugs for chewers like Henry Belk. Gentlemen and preachers in Charlotte, many of them with tobacco stains on their lapels, condemned smokers to eternal punishment. Belk, meanwhile, carried a plug and enjoyed his quid all day long.

On occasion, John Belk left the store in Monroe to join Henry for meals at the Central. He also was a familiar figure on East Trade Street. In time, John Belk was even listed in the Charlotte City Directory though he maintained a fine home with his wife and seven daughters in Monroe. The brothers were a notable pair. Their deference to each other— they referred to one another as "Brother John" or "Brother Henry"—and to their mother was known to all. Henry Belk was the decisive one of the two, making decisions quickly and finally. John Belk, demonstrating the bedside manner of the country physician, was quieter, more deliberate. The two conferred on major questions about the business. Despite his stern appearance and occasional brusque manner, Henry ducked some of the more difficult tasks. He often called upon John to dismiss employees, for example. Some of Henry Belk's supper companions at the Central could tell when an employee was getting the axe, because Henry would leave town, and John would arrive to manage affairs for a day or two.

Every weekend, except when he was traveling outside of Charlotte, Henry climbed aboard the train for the twenty-five mile ride to Monroe. He joined his brother and his family, and they attended church with their mother. Afterward, they returned to Sarah Simpson's house, located just behind the Monroe store, for a Sunday dinner of fried chicken and vegetables always cooked the day before. She permitted no work on the Sabbath. Henry Belk enjoyed his nieces and spent time with John talking about the future or coordinating their schedules. But Sundays were mainly devoted to their mother, who treasured family ties.

Monroe was convenient to Charlotte by train. But within a couple of years after Osmond Barringer introduced the first automobiles to Charlotte in 1904, Henry Belk had one of these new machines and could control his scheduled departure even more. One of his first trips was not without its problems, however. Henry Belk picked up his new automobile and headed to Monroe for the weekend. On his return, the confounded thing gave out, right in the middle of the road. Henry was stumped. He was as inept at things mechanical as he was adept at merchandising. Not until a nearby farmer explained that the gas tank needed refilling did Henry understand what kept the machine running.

Mrs. Simpson's request to her sons that they forsake their dreams of expansion to Texas and remain in North Carolina to build their business was paying off, for her and for them. She had told Henry on his return from Texas that he should remain where he was known, where he knew his customers and their needs. The brothers certainly knew the people in Monroe and Charlotte, and they enjoyed a reputation as hard-working, honest merchants who had successfully made the transition from country storekeepers to prominent businessmen of the city. The word of their success spread and brought them more customers and more business and, most important, a steady stream of young men eager to leave the farm and follow Henry Belk's example.

Belk was partial to the ambition he found in the young men who showed up at his stores asking for work. He knew life on the farm had tempered them to long hours and tough duty, and he knew just how much they wanted to succeed. Their alternative was a return to pushing a mule across acres of Carolina clay. Belk also knew the families these young men represented. The first who came into the business were cousins, close family members. Ralph J. Belk, for example, opened a store in Waxhaw in 1897, just as cousin Fred Kluttz had opened the Belks' first expansion store in Chester. While others were not blood kin, Belk was familiar with their families through his years in the area and his work with the Presbyterian Church. Before long, the Charlotte and Monroe stores were a reservoir of talent.

In 1899, the brothers opened a store in Greensboro, which like many of the textile towns of North Carolina was enjoying newfound growth and prosperity. The process followed closely what they had already done in opening businesses with their cousins in South Carolina. They found a suitable building, on the corner of Washington and Elm Streets a few blocks north of the railroad, laid in a stock of basic dry goods, and opened for business. But this move was different and set the stage for a pattern that would continue for more than fifty years.

The Chester and Union stores had been good business opportunities that the brothers approached much as they did an investment in a new cotton mill or other business. They had confidence in the management and put up the necessary capital, expecting a return, as with any other investment. In the meantime, the power of buying for four stores instead of one helped Henry when he was negotiating in the Northern markets or traveling to regional mills for goods. But the brothers had made no plans for any more stores. In fact, the Belks sold their interest in the Union, S.C., store before the century closed and early company records do not include the York and Chester stores as part of the organization.

Greensboro was to be different. Greensboro, located about 100 miles north of Charlotte, was developing as a major textile manufacturing center. Henry had passed through the city hundreds of times on his way north. He had purchased goods from Cone Mills' large plants located north of the city. Like Charlotte, the city showed promise with good rail connections and a busy downtown retail district. In 1899, John and Henry Belk prevailed upon D. R. Harry of Charlotte, who had once worked in the Charlotte store, to leave his insurance business, take a one-third interest in a new company, and open a store in Greensboro. The brothers knew the young man could sell. They had trained him. And they knew he came from a hard-working family. His brother Sam had clerked in the Chester, S.C., store before opening his own business in Salisbury in 1894, one year before Henry Belk moved to Charlotte. In addition, the Belks had helped put his brother Reece in business in Union, S.C. Shortly after the first of the year, Dick Harry agreed to the Belks' proposition and in March 1899, Harry–Belk Brothers Company opened for business.

Business in the Greensboro store was good, and two years later the Belk brothers looked for a location for yet another store. Across the Catawba River, the textile-mill fever was rapidly changing Gaston County. Gastonia, the county seat, was humming with business. More than 4,000 Gaston County workers were employed in the nearly one hundred manufacturing plants in the county. The city had replaced the oil lamps along Main Street with electric lights, and the same bond issue had raised money for a municipal water works. The city had successfully converted from a rural farm market to a factory town with steady wages and a solid economy. Only the Gaston County liquor distilleries seemed to be in trouble, but that was just fine with the Belks. They preferred to count the number of churches in the communities where they did business.

On February 25, 1901, Will Kindley opened Kindley-Belk Company on Gastonia's Main Street in a small, two-story brick building not much larger than Henry Belk's first store in Monroe. Within a few months, however, business had increased, and Kindley added five more sales people to his original staff of three. And the staff got a raise. Some of the first records of the Belk network of stores show women now earned seven dollars a week, instead of five; the men went from eight dollars to ten. The check boy got a quarter a week.

Greensboro, Gastonia, Monroe, Charlotte. A year later, in March 1902, the Belk brothers were meeting in their office in Charlotte with Sam and Arthur Harry. Three years earlier, Arthur Harry had left Belk's Charlotte store, where Henry Belk had trained him in the business, to join his brother at his store in Salisbury, one of the state's oldest cities, about forty-five miles north of Charlotte.

This morning, Henry Belk had his sales figures at his fingertips and the ledger showed a steady increase from year to year. His four stores had nearly doubled in volume in just two years. Belk's staff of young eager clerks had sold more than $300,000 in goods that Henry had had shipped south from vendors in the North. After hearing the Harry brothers out, the Belks decided to join forces. No team of brothers was better known to the Belks. And Salisbury was convenient, a prime location just up the rails from Charlotte. Henry Belk had passed through it countless times. It was a vigorous, growing community that also was caught up in the campaign to attract new business. After all, a town that could foster the slogan, "Next to the grace of God, what Salisbury needs is a textile mill" had to be a city on the move. When the Harrys returned home, they pulled down their own sign and erected a new one, Belk-Harry Company.

With the addition of Salisbury, the Belk name was now a part of the retail life of towns and cities in the busiest sec-

tion of the Carolina Piedmont. Only seven years had passed
since Henry Belk had opened his store on East Trade Street,
greeted by the skepticism of competitors, and now Belk's
goods were available in stores throughout the Piedmont. By
the tenth anniversary of the opening of the Charlotte store,
an event that prompted no special sales or promotions, the
Belk sales had doubled and Belk was clearly a part of the
booming growth of the area.

By 1904, Charlotte had seventeen textile mills in the city
limits and three hundred within a 100-mile radius. Most of
the spindles in these mills were turned by electricity supplied
by Charlotte's Southern Power Company, which was convert-
ing the strength of the Catawba River for use by town boosters and entrepreneurs for miles around. Charlotte's slogan,
"Watch our town grow," perhaps lacked the character and
flair of others, but local businessmen were organizing to see
that people had something to watch and could watch in the
proper atmosphere. On January 1, 1905, following a vigorous
campaign against prohibition, the city closed all its saloons
and watering holes, including the elegant bar at Henry Belk's
favorite, the Central Hotel. The town went dry.

While the Belk brothers had been staking claims on main
streets throughout the Piedmont, Charlotte was preoccupied
with itself and the growth right at home. The city claimed
that half of the South's looms and spindles were within a
two-hour ride of the city. In Charlotte alone, 10,000 wage
earners pumped an annual payroll of $2 million a year into
the local economy. In 1905, a group of businessmen gathered
to pool their resources and build the Independence Building,
the state's tallest building, right on the northwest corner of
the square. Every morning, as workmen stacked the bricks
higher and higher, citizens marveled at their work. The
building was an object of intense civic pride when it topped
out at twelve floors of mercantile and office space. The street
level was home to the Charlotte National Bank, which even
provided a concealed corner for use by lady customers, who
could enter from a door on Tryon Street and avoid the "shov-
ing of the general crowd."

Henry Belk joined in to support the growth of the city. He helped underwrite the construction of the city's first tall building, and he helped organize the Piedmont Fire Insurance Company, which built the Piedmont Building on South Tryon Street. And in 1907, he became a member of the Board of School Commissioners at the request of some of the city's leaders.

Despite the boom-town growth, Charlotte citizens still had to contend with dirt streets, which produced shoe-sticking mud in rain and clouds of dust in the dry summertime. Little could be done about the mud, but the city provided horse-drawn water wagons to help control the dust that settled on the goods that Henry Belk and other merchants stacked on their sidewalk displays and on counters in the stores.

While Henry Belk had been expanding his business throughout the Carolina countryside, other merchants had been establishing themselves right down the street from his Charlotte store. The Efird brothers, who came from Anson County, virtual neighbors to the Belks, followed their oldest brother Hugh to Charlotte. Hugh began as a clerk at the Bee Hive, and in 1907, he and his kin bought the store and reopened it with their own name prominent on the storefront. By 1907, they had expanded, opening a store in Concord. J. B. Ivey, the son of a Methodist minister, was growing a substantial business at his store on West Trade Street. Ivey had clerked in a small store in Belwood, about thirteen miles north of Shelby, N.C., before coming to Charlotte in 1900 to start his own business, which had begun to cater to the city's more fashionable families.

The Efirds, the Belk brothers, and Ivey personified the opportunity that attracted young men to Trade and Tryon streets in Charlotte. Some, like the Harrys, had already received their training from the Belks and were running their own operations. Others were still in their apprenticeships or assuming growing responsibilities in the Belks' ever-expanding Charlotte store, which now occupied much of the street frontage in the middle of the first block of East Trade Street. Already in the Charlotte or Monroe stores were young men by the name of Matthews, Gallant, Hudson, and Parks, whose families the Belks had known in Union and Anson counties.

These young men considered themselves "Mr. Henry's boys," and Belk turned his attention to developing them as merchants. They took the menial jobs at first, but if Henry or John Belk liked their industry and ambition, they were promoted to more responsible positions. If deemed good merchants by the Belks, they then began accompanying Belk and his buyers on their semiannual trips to market, meeting the merchants and dealers Belk had cultivated as his resources over the years. As the number of stores in the group increased, Belk began gathering buyers from the various stores together in Charlotte before leaving. Belk met with them the night before to talk about their stores and goods needed for the season. The group then departed together by train the next day. On occasion Belk even led his protégés on tours of the cities, special places like Washington and Philadelphia, that they passed through on their way to market.

Belk had strict rules about travel that remained in place for years. No one was allowed to travel on Sunday, and women were never permitted to travel alone. Henry Belk also carried his own snacks onto the train. The sandwiches he tucked into his bag helped cut expenses. Belk also was not fond of food cooked on the road. Despite the wealth of culinary delights available to him in a city like New York, he often ordered scrambled eggs and sliced tomatoes for breakfast, lunch, and dinner. He figured even a bad cook could not mess up that simple fare.

Belk's recruiting system fed itself. Many of those who arrived at the store looking for a start in the business came from large families. B. Frank Matthews, for example, was just a teenager when he started with Belk in 1899 cleaning wool hats. In a few years, his brother W. M. ("Mac") Matthews joined the company as a cashier. After a time, Mac Matthews took a year off to study at Massey's Business College in Richmond, an education financed by Belk. He returned and became Belk's office manager while brother Frank

helped manage the store. One day, in 1907, as Frank Matthews was headed home to the Providence community for
the weekend, Belk asked him to bring his brother Houston
back with him. Three years later, Henry Belk named Houston the new manager at the Belk brothers' store in Gastonia.

The number of Belk employees increased as business increased. In 1910, sales were approaching $1 million a year,
and the Belks had perhaps their boldest effort yet laid out on
the drawing boards of architects Oliver D. Wheeler and Eugene J. Stern. Two years earlier (and twenty years after Belk
had leased about 2,000 square feet of space in a building on a
dusty Monroe Street), the Belk brothers had commissioned
plans for a new five-story building for their Charlotte store.
They would keep the men's store in the building Henry Belk
had leased in 1895, plus one adjacent building. The new
structure would rise beside these buildings and be the finest
department store in town.

On October 4, 1910, Belk announced to the readers of the
Charlotte Observer that Belk Brothers store would be closed
October 5 and would reopen at 8:00 P.M. on Thursday, October 6, with an "informal reception" for the city's newest business address. The *Observer*'s reporter was overwhelmed with
what he found as he joined the crowds that turned out to see
Henry and John Belk's new store. "It might be regarded," the
writer said in the morning paper, "in a sense as a debut
party, in which Belk Bros. store was introduced anew to the
people of Charlotte and surrounding towns in its elegant
new garb."

Despite a light rain carried over the city by warm southerly
winds, more than 2,500 turned out to stroll the aisles and
view the new merchandise Belk and his buyers had purchased for the special occasion. Just inside the front door, a
large staircase led to the basement, where toys and holiday
goods were laid out on tables along with Belk's bargain merchandise. Carpets, rugs, and home furnishings were on the
third floor. Ladies' wear on the second floor was under the
close watch of Sarah Houston, whose word even Henry Belk
did not dispute when it came to purchases of ladies' fash-

ions. Miss Houston commanded her position as firmly as Frank Matthews his in menswear, located next door in the original building. The main floor was the home for woolens, linens, and notions, and ladies' accessories and hosiery. Belk's desk was moved to the new mezzanine where, from about midway between the front door and the back loading dock, he could oversee the main floor.

Charlotte was ready for the new store. The city was busting with pride over its growth, and "modern" conveniences were readily available for the new homes in the suburbs. The newspapers advertised new appliances such as the "suction cleaner," a vacuum cleaner that came with sixty-five feet of cord, and the Charlotte Gas and Electric Company was presenting free lectures for cooks on the proper handling of a gas range. A Ford roadster was $680. Belk's grand-opening sale featured ladies' suits for $18.95, nickel handkerchiefs, and Sarah Houston's best selection of millinery, wraps, and coats. Not to be outdone by the new store, one of Belk's competitors, Little-Long Company announced that the forty show girls appearing in the musical "The Girls Behind The Counter" would be in their store to serve customers.

The opening-night rain continued into Friday and through the weekend. Unperturbed, Belk extended his grand-opening sale another week. When the skies finally cleared and the evening sun broke through over Charlotte, Henry Belk could look across Trade Street from his table at the Central Hotel and see reflections off the new copper and shiny prism glass that decorated the storefront. Just above a high tier of windows, the name "Belk Bros." was set firmly in terra cotta, flanked by ornate cartouches featuring a large capital *B*.

In 1910 John Wanamaker completed construction of his grand, twelve-story granite emporium that covered three acres of Philadelphia real estate. Wanamaker, Henry Belk's model for one-price selling, a money-back guarantee, and clever advertising, was not satisfied with just offering customers more shopping opportunities than they could find anywhere else. He made shopping an experience, offering goods in seventy-six different departments. His store included a free sickroom with a doctor in attendance, a tearoom that could serve 10,000 at one time, and a courtyard featuring an immense eagle he had bought from the St. Louis World's Fair. He had installed that exposition's mammoth organ in a gallery above the Grand Court.

Wanamaker was just one of the great merchant princes who had emerged by the turn of the century. Most had started with little money—much of it borrowed—and they had expanded their small dry-goods businesses into multi-million-dollar mercantile enterprises offering merchandise and services unimaginable to most Americans outside of the major cities. For example, in addition to the latest fashions for ladies, gentlemen, and their children, Macy's in New York offered fine crystal, appliances, and lessons in riding the bicycles they sold. The store even offered to pack provisions for their wealthy customers' yachting trips and made deliveries in a fleet of Mercedes-Benz trucks, the first imported motor vehicles in the country.

In Chicago, Marshall Field's dominated. Field, who died in 1906 leaving an estate of $120 million, had created a store that was the merchandising center of the Midwest. Even before Field opened his twelve-story building on State Street, his staff had changed department-store marketing by stylishly decorating display windows with special, featured items rather than crowding them with samples of everything in stock.

In Atlanta, Rich's new building had opened in 1907, making it the largest store in the South's largest city. By 1910, the company had an expanded mail-order business and was clearly a Georgia institution, its generous policy on returned merchandise already a tradition. In one annual sales event, on the anniversary of Eli Whitney's cotton gin, Rich's sold more cotton goods than any other store in the world.

Big merchants. Big cities. Field, Wanamaker, Rich, the Straus family at Macy's, Filene in Boston, J. L. Hudson in Detroit—all were selling millions and millions of dollars in goods as cities grew with the migration of people from the farm and from abroad. America was on its way to becoming a nation of consumers, buying what it wanted as well as what it needed, and these men and their stores were prepared to supply any and all. The department store, a merchandising phenomenon of the late 1800s, had become a necessity in the nation's major cities.

Charlotte was North Carolina's largest city by 1910. The official population count was 34,010, though the local boosters reported in the city directory that just more than 50,000 lived in the area they considered to be the city. Downtown, the city had five office buildings, including the tallest one in the state, seven banks, and five hotels, with another under construction. Seven hundred houses had been built the previous year, and construction would soon begin in Myers Park, the city's first residential development for the wealthy, which had been described as the finest subdivision south of Baltimore. James B. Duke, impatient with the developer's choice of small saplings for landscaping, would bring his own crews in from his New Jersey estate to plant larger trees.

Most of Charlotte's streets were unpaved, but Charlotte boasted of 294 miles of gravel and stone macadamized roads. Residents got about the city on twenty-six miles of "electric railway." Intercity travel was excellent, if you went by rail. Thirty-four passenger trains departed each day. Despite the bad roads, automobiles were common. Before America became involved in the war in Europe, the Ford Motor Company was turning out nearly 7,000 cars a year at a plant on Statesville Avenue just north of downtown. With more than three-fourths of the textile mills in the South within 100 miles of the city, Charlotte claimed to be North Carolina's leading city of commerce, the textile center of the state.

Belk Brothers Department Store thrived on Charlotte's growth, but success and a growing affluent population had not changed Henry Belk's marketing strategy. His store did not cater to the new rich in Myers Park homes. He left that to Ivey's and specialty shops along Tryon Street. Belk's store attracted a broad base of customers that included less affluent shoppers, factory hands, farmers, and workers who looked to Belk for the best prices for sturdy, reliable everyday goods. Belk did not ignore the rich, but no matter how fine his new store, or how prim the dresses in ladies' ready-to-wear, or how stylish the feathers and plumes in millinery, Belk insisted that the store prominently display an inexpensive suit or pair of shoes that the workingman could afford.

On the eve of the opening of the new store in 1910, Belk Brothers Company published full-page ads celebrating the fall millinery fashions. The newspaper obliged with a fashion story reporting that the season's hats, with wide brims and plenty of feathers, "were rather on the Eiffel Tower order rather than of the aeroplane proportions which we have been dodging all summer."

Competition was stiff in Charlotte. There were men's specialty shops like Tate-Brown close by, and Ivey's, catering to the silk-stocking trade, was just around the corner. The newspapers were growing wealthy from the city's competitive retail trade. J. B. Ivey conversed with his customers in his chatty "Ivey's Weekly Store News," a large ad that ran each Monday in the *Charlotte Observer*. These merchants crowed about the good deals they had found in the "market." In Belk's basement, Mother could find dresses for fifty-nine cents. Father could pick up a straw hat for ninety-five cents, a cap for a quarter. Just down the block, the Efird brothers offered damaged bedspreads or closeouts on runs of piece goods for prices that made Belk sharpen his pencil.

While Belk offered low prices, he also gave his customers something extra to remember him by. On occasion, he would pull the bolt just a little harder and give a woman an extra measure of cloth. He would throw in an extra spool of thread for a steady customer or at least knock a penny or two off the cost. Consideration like that kept customers coming back—and out of his competitors' stores.

Even while Henry and John Belk were building their new Charlotte store, they were continuing to expand as opportunities arose. In February 1910, six months before the Charlotte store opened, the brothers opened a store in York, S.C., just south of Charlotte. J. W. Kirkpatrick, formerly the manager of the brothers' Gastonia store, opened Kirkpatrick-Belk Company in a building bought from Jim Heath, a nephew of B. D. Heath, the Monroe merchant who had given Henry Belk his first job. Jim Heath had sold dry goods, farmers' supplies, and groceries from a location just across from the York County courthouse, a prime location from Henry Belk's point of view.

In late 1909, the brothers paid a call on their old schoolmate from Union County, Hugh McRae Williams, who owned a dry-goods business in Sanford. "Mack" Williams's son, Jim, had worked in the Belks' Waxhaw store for three years before going to work for his father in 1906 when the elder Williams opened his store. The Belks had heard the father-son team was doing well.

Emma Hart, then a young seamstress, was working in the Sanford store when the Belks came in to talk business with their old friend and she overheard the conversation of the three businessmen. Recalling the meeting years later, she said the three talked about their childhood, about local crops, about business and payrolls in the town. Henry Belk looked Williams's store over, and soon they were discussing doing business together. Then, in the midst of Henry's questions about the economy, he abruptly changed his line of inquiry.

"Never mind all that," Henry Belk said. "Mack, how many churches are there around here?" Williams told him and Belk followed with another question. "Do the people here attend church services pretty well?" Williams assured him that Sanford was as fine a Christian community as the Belks would find anywhere. "In that case," Belk said turning to his brother, "I don't think we can go wrong by coming to Sanford."

The opening of Williams-Belk Company in January 1910 extended the Belk name to eastern North Carolina, where the Belks were not well known. Aside from a few textile mills on the edge of the Piedmont region, eastern North Carolina was farm country. Cotton, tobacco, and corn were prime cash crops. But if towns like Sanford were not like Charlotte, they were like Monroe, which the Belks knew very well. The streets filled on Saturdays when farm families came to town to shop and pick up supplies. The economy followed crops. This was Henry Belk's kind of town.

The Belks expanded to York and Sanford much as they had to Greensboro, Gastonia, or Salisbury, where they simply had invested in a local owner and manager, much the same way they invested in any other enterprise. In each case it had been someone they knew well, either through business or family. Usually their new partners took a third of the stock in the new corporation, and the Belks owned the balance. Then the brothers left town and let their partners run the business as they saw fit. The partners would join the rest of the Belk buyers for the semiannual buying trips to New York and, along with the employees from the stores, climb aboard the train for the annual Thanksgiving convention trip to Charlotte. But, as in any family, each member was free to make his own fortune.

By the time the Belks' new store opened in Charlotte, this growing confederation of stores had its own logo, a star, with "Belk Bros. Co." featured in a circle at the center. Points on the star carried the names of the associated store corporations. The Belks simply added points as stores opened. By the end of 1910, the Belks either owned or had a majority interest in stores in Monroe, Gastonia, Charlotte, Greensboro, Salisbury, Sanford, Waxhaw, and Union and in York, S.C. Gross sales topped the million dollar mark. In twenty-five years, Henry Belk had grown from a dry-goods shop-keeper in a small rented store building in Monroe to the most successful merchant in the region.

Henry Belk's life remained as simple in success as it had been in hard times. He lived at the store and appeared the perfect example of the confirmed bachelor. He showed no inclination toward marriage or starting a family of his own and took little or no time for a social life. His life was his business and the Presbyterian Church. He was a charter member of the Oasis Shrine and served on the Charlotte school board, but his other civic involvement was generally behind the scenes. He helped build the new Selwyn Hotel and continued to invest in local mills and manufacturing concerns. Generally, he left the local boosterism to others and concentrated his outside activities on the church. For example, although he was one of Charlotte's largest and most successful merchants, he was not on hand when the Charlotte Chamber of Commerce was organized.

Henry Belk's business life was as simple as the neat, clean Calvinist doctrine he followed in the Presbyterian Church. He worked hard and made the most of his situation. Years later, he told an interviewer he never really planned to be what others called the merchant prince. He merely took advantage of opportunities that came his way and worked hard to succeed.

In their first twenty-five years, the Belks' expansion often amounted to little more than a merger or a purchase of an existing store. The brothers did not so much increase the competition in a community where they hung out their sign as replace local merchants whose plans had changed, or whose plans had been changed by swings in the economy. Other merchants were using the same strategy, including the Belks' chief Charlotte competitor, J. B. Efird, who by 1910 had about as many stores throughout the Piedmont as the Belks did. What made the Belks' style of expansion unique was their ability to pick the right business partners for their stores and the confidence they showed by leaving partners alone to make their own business decisions.

Henry Belk had to look no further than his own stores to exercise this advantage over the competition. Working in the Belks' stores were a number of young clerks, department managers, and eager merchants-to-be. They were a hardworking and steady lot, all churchgoers, and most of them Presbyterians. Henry Belk was partial to Presbyterians and often checked a newcomer's background with his local minister. The young men were loyal and dependable, honest, respectful, and deeply grateful for the chance to get a job in the Belks' store in Monroe or Charlotte. To be accepted into the Belk fold spoke well of them and their families back on farms in counties around Charlotte, especially Union, Mecklenburg, and Anson counties, where an informal recruiting network had emerged. At one time or another, one small post office in rural Anson County had delivered mail to John Belk when he was a country doctor and to the families of Hudsons and Leggetts, who later emerged as leaders within the Belk organization.

The Belks trained their protégés in the basics—piece goods their steady customers purchased to make a season's dress or to outfit the children for the summer. Henry Belk believed a merchant must know his goods, must have an understanding of the raw materials of the finished suits and dresses, particularly if he was going to be sufficiently armed to compete in the Northern markets. After all, what kind of merchant would a man be if he did not know how much cotton yarn the weaver used to manufacture the cloth for a shirt? Henry had started that way, and his boys did the same.

"Before you buy a man's shirt, look at the button," Belk told his new men. "They never will put a cheap button on a good shirt. And, when buying pants, look at the pockets. You will never see a cheap pocket on a good pair of pants. Look at a suit and examine the buttonholes," he would say. "If it's not clipped around don't buy it. You will never see a cheap buttonhole on a good suit of clothes."

The brothers taught courtesy and respect for any and all customers. While North Carolina had gone through racial retrenchment, thoroughly disenfranchising blacks, the Belks permitted no color lines on the sales floor. Whites and blacks bumped and jostled one another to reach the bargains Henry Belk had laid out on his tables on sale days.

The Belks permitted no idle time. If business was slow or foul weather kept shoppers at home, clerks stayed busy refreshing the stock, stringing up socks, handkerchiefs, belts, and other items on Coats No. 50 thread to hang from the ceiling, ready to be pulled quickly for a customer. Clerks straightened the tables and prepared advertising posters and show cards to hang just over shoppers' heads. When the store was crowded, the signs were traffic signals and answered customers' questions. "Please Don't Ask For Credit," one read. "It's Unpleasant To Be Refused." Another popular line was "If You Don't See It—Ask—It's All Reduced."

And Belk clerks dusted. The open doors and windows of the store sucked the street dust straight into the store. As late as 1915, the city regularly watered West Trade Street on dry summer days. Clerks groused that if the store was clean and not a speck of dust in sight, Henry Belk would send them to the basement to clean the coal.

When the store closed and the selling floors were in order, some of Henry Belk's boys retired to the rooms above the men's store, the three-story building beside the new store, where they shared simple rooms just like their boss's. Belk pay was low and the hours long, but they dreamed of the future. Belk once told a young partner-to-be, "Everybody talks about Henry Belk being so stingy and tight. But any man who will serve an apprenticeship with me for three years, just like a doctor or a lawyer, I'll give them a store if they're worth a cent."

Some did not stay and moved on, often after having words with their boss. Frequently, with long apologies, they returned to seek readmittance into the fold, and Belk usually took them back. "I believe we might as well have him back," Belk would tell those who might argue against this policy. "I am sure that what he said about us was said without really thinking. I don't believe he really meant it. He is a good fellow and I believe we had better take him back. Don't you think so?"

As these young merchants came of age, their ambition, bolstered by years of on-the-job training in Charlotte and Monroe, became the foundation for a period of expansion that even the Belks had not quite imagined. In the ensuing ten years, men named Parks, Hudson, Matthews, Leggett, and Stevens would leave their jobs in Charlotte and Monroe not only to open stores of their own but to begin to expand and establish their own groups of stores, all with the Belks' help. Also established during this time was the beginning of an organization linking these independent corporations that gave small individual stores the buying power of a much larger operation.

One of the first to branch out was J. G. Parks from Union County. Parks had begun work for John Belk in the Monroe store in 1899, pedaling a bicycle over sixteen miles of dirt roads to reach the store. Three years later, he had opened a store in Waxhaw for R. J. Belk, one of the Belks' cousins. In September 1911, Parks opened his own store, Parks-Belk Company, in Concord, an old, established community about twenty miles north of Charlotte.

Concord was a first-rate location for Belk. The town had long been a commercial center for the steady farmers of Cabarrrus County, and it was emerging as a major textile center. The town grew with each loom that Cannon Mills Company installed in plants in Concord and nearby Kannapolis. Other merchants already had spotted the opportunity. Efird had opened a store there two years earlier.

Parks found an available building on the west side of South Union Street, right downtown near the Cabarrus County courthouse. The store prospered, and Parks, looking for new ways to expand the business, added groceries to the store's daily stock of goods. In October 1916, Parks opened another store, this one in Kannapolis, the Cannon Mills company town, under the same arrangement he had in Concord. He took a third of the stock, and the Belk brothers took a third each. Parks sent Cyrus White, from his Concord store, to be the manager in Kannapolis.

The grocery business was Parks's own invention and illustrates the freedom permitted a Belk partner. The Belks owned an interest in a Monroe grocery business, but no other Belk partner combined the grocery business with the dry-goods trade. Backed by his success in Concord, Parks carried his grocery business with him to Kannapolis and it flourished. The store kept a Model T Ford and a wagon busy until midnight on Saturdays completing deliveries of the day's sales. When Parks approached the Belks about adding more delivery vehicles, however, they decided the additional investment was too expensive and closed the grocery business, returning to dry goods only.

A year after Parks had opened the Kannapolis store, he repeated the process in Albemarle, a farming community of about 3,000 people about twenty miles east of Concord. The two men he dispatched from Concord to open the store, Karl W. Broome and George Ridenhour, left shortly after to join the military as America entered World War I. Parks's brother, C. E. Parks, became the manager. By the end of the decade, Parks-Belk signs were hanging over storefronts in three more cities, Hickory and Newton, N.C., and Spartanburg, S.C., where the store was called White-Parks-Belk Company. Cyrus White, who had begun with Parks in Concord and had later moved to Kannapolis, had now graduated to become a managing partner.

The Parks' stores looked no different from the other small textile-town stores carrying the Belk name. They were all located in rented buildings and were outfitted simply, but the stores carried the Belk name and that was worth more than expensive fixtures. Usually, the partner's name appeared before Belk's in the signage over the front door and on letterheads and sales receipts. Although the Belk name lent prestige and let those familiar with a Belk store know what to expect in a new location, the Belks believed that a new store would succeed based on the reputation of the local manager. He came first.

A solid reputation was important to Henry Belk, and he passed that along to his partners. Belk admonished a young man who left for a store of his own to be mindful of his position in the community and remember his Christian up-bringing. Join a local church, he said, before getting involved in anything else. After building a reputation as a churchman, then the young man could consider other civic involvement. Actually, a new merchant had little time for anything more than building his business. And a little prayer for divine guidance was helpful on days when the cash box held just a few dollars.

While Parks was establishing stores in communities of North Carolina's central Piedmont, the Belks were expanding with the Williams family in eastern North Carolina. In 1915, the Belks went to Wilmington and bought out an existing business, the Gaylord Company. They brought in Jim Williams, who had trained with the Belks before entering business with his father in Sanford, as their partner and opened Williams-Belk Company in Wilmington in October of that year.

A month earlier, three Hudson brothers from Anson County, Karl, Will, and Grier, had opened Hudson-Belk Company in Raleigh. Karl Hudson had managed the store in Waxhaw, the one his uncle J. G. Parks had opened for one of the Belks' cousins. Hudson's mentor was John Belk, who often devoted his evenings to talking business with young Karl, who had taken the train from Waxhaw to Monroe. Hudson also sought out Henry Belk, who, though patient, was not above a good swift verbal kick in the pants when necessary.

Karl Hudson never forgot a trip he made to Charlotte in the early fall of his first year as manager in Waxhaw. He had bought too heavily, and the future looked grim. He found Henry Belk sitting on a barrel in the basement of the Charlotte store. Belk told him what he already knew, that the

Waxhaw store was broke, and, Hudson said, Belk "declared, very emphatically, that if I didn't get down to business I would be a flat failure and wouldn't amount to a jelly bean." Belk's stern warning stirred Hudson to action. He reorganized the store, and by Christmas, the business was out of debt. The day before Christmas, the store sold $750 in goods, the most it had ever done on a single day. Hudson was feeling proud of his accomplishment and was in Monroe a few days later to tell Henry Belk about his success. Before he could make his report, Belk said, "Karl, did you sell a thousand dollars yesterday?"

The Hudsons chose Raleigh because the town looked right for a store. Although not the state's largest city, Raleigh was the capital city, and well-established clothing stores lined Fayetteville Street. They would provide stiff competition for the three merchants, still young and unseasoned. Karl was the oldest at twenty-six. Brother Will was twenty-two and young Grier was only seventeen. But the three did have relatives in the city who could provide them a place to stay while they got their business started, and the city looked promising. The year 1915 was being heralded locally as the year of "returning prosperity." Raleigh had seven banks, two telegraph and telephone companies, and the service of three railroads. And new businesses were opening all the time.

The brothers found a location just off Fayetteville Street that was even smaller than Henry Belk's first store. They arranged for goods to be shipped in and set to work with a local carpenter to build display tables. While the older brothers selected merchandise for the store—silks, woolens, cottons, laces, notions, and clothing for men, women, and children—young Grier hired a wagon and with the manager of the store's shoe department circled the county nailing up opening announcements within a ten-mile radius of the downtown store. On Thursday morning, September 9, they opened their doors, announcing in the News and Observer that their store would be one where "you can buy goods knowing you are getting the very best Merchandise that can be bought for the money." The ad continued: "The Opening of Hudson-Belk Company this morning at 8:30 o'clock means that the standards of prices in Raleigh on Reliable Merchandise will go down with a crash." It was, as Karl's son said some years later, "what you would call an outlet store today."

The Belks had trained their partners to buy cheap and sell fast, turning over goods that could be purchased as mill ends, closeouts, or odd lots at low prices. The stores opened early to catch farmers on the way to market and clerks stayed late to give factory workers a chance to shop. The lights were on late at Hudson-Belk most every night except Wednesday, when the Hudsons and many of their employees headed to prayer meeting.

A Belk manager also used anything and everything to promote his business. One day in the late teens, Henry Belk was visiting his brother's store in Monroe when he asked some youngsters working at the back why they did not use the slats from the shipping crates to make some store signs. They had the wood, even the nails from the crates, at hand. All they needed was imagination and some paint, Belk told the boys. Yates Laney, who later became a Belk manager and opened stores in South Carolina, was one of the group. He and the others soon had every road leading to Monroe posted with Belk Brothers' signs. One read, "All Roads Lead to Belk Bros.," another, "Long John Work Shirts that cover your body," and another, "If We Ain't Got it We Will Get It." On seeing the last one, Belk replied, "Boys, that covers a lot of ground, and you had better be careful." But the sign remained in the tree.

By the end of the decade, other partners had followed the Parks's lead of expanding from their initial location to nearby communities. J. W. Kirkpatrick expanded from York, S.C., to Greenville, S.C., where he opened a store in 1916. In 1919, Karl Hudson's brother Will opened a store in Durham, N.C. And that same year, the Belks asked W. E. Gallant, who had started work in the Charlotte store in 1906, to find a location. Gallant looked over Virginia and North Carolina. He scouted the railroad north of Charlotte and investigated Danville as a location, but everywhere he turned he came up short. There were just no available spaces in the towns that looked promising. Business was booming and Gallant was afraid he had missed the tide. He turned south and was working his way north from Charleston, S.C., when his train stopped in Anderson, S.C. With a few hours to kill, Gallant stepped off the train and set off to look over yet another Carolina city. While walking the streets, he found a merchant ready to retire. By the time the conductor announced his departure he had a tentative deal. As soon as he returned to Charlotte, Gallant presented his proposition to Belk, who agreed to back him in the business. Gallant-Belk Company opened a short time later.

Less than ten years after the Belk brothers had opened their new store in Charlotte, the Belk name was on stores throughout much of North Carolina and South Carolina. The *Charlotte Observer* spotlighted the growth of the Belks' business in a special promotional section published that year that carried the headline: "HOW THE BELKS BUILT UP BIGGEST DEPARTMENT STORE BUSINESS IN SOUTH." It continued, "W. H. and J. M. Belk founded what is to-day known as the Belk Chain of Stores in a small building, with 2,000 feet of floor space, in Monroe, N.C., in May, 1888. To-day the Belk chain of department stores embraces twenty-six large stores in three states—North and South Carolina and Virginia. They employ 1,100 people.

"The Belk idea of selling REAL merchandise for LESS MONEY has been the principal factor in the Belk success. The policy of Belk Brothers has been promotion from the inside, and the men in charge of these stores to-day are men brought up in the Belk business."

The newspaper also featured the chain of Efird stores. The Efird brothers had started later than the Belks—their first store opened in 1907—but they had expanded more rapidly. "Since the artist made the sketch for this page," the Efird advertisement said, "three new stores have been added to the chain (for a total of 24) and by the end of the year the chain will contain forty links, according to present plans."

The Belks and Efirds shared a lot in common. They had

come from Piedmont North Carolina farm towns, the Belks from Monroe and the Efirds from nearby Anson County. They both had started small: Henry Belk in Monroe in 1888; the Efirds as clerks earning fifteen dollars a month in the Bee Hive, which they subsequently bought. Both were active in their churches and were generous contributors. Both expanded into the growing towns and cities of the Piedmont with virtually the same low-cost, discount-store strategy. And they were fierce competitors.

The following paragraph from the Efirds' promotional ad must have really nettled Henry Belk when he picked up his newspaper. "The Efirds were the originators of the One Price Cash Stores in the Carolinas, and from the very first the Efird brothers have followed the policy of buying merchandise from the country's largest manufacturers, thus eliminating the middleman's profit, and then of 'Selling it for less.' "

The Belks and the Efirds enjoyed their greatest expansion during the years immediately following the end of World War I, when the Southern economy received its biggest boost in years. Returning veterans, many of whom had left their stores to fight in Europe, were eager to get their lives together, and the companies had a good supply of new store managers. Karl Broome returned to work with J. G. Parks, who sent him to open the Hickory, N.C., store. Cy White moved to Spartanburg, S.C. Gallant moved to Anderson, S.C. During this time, the Efirds opened twelve stores in two years. The Belks opened ten.

The growing number of stores changed Henry Belk's responsibilities. He had moved from a manager of stores to a manager of people. His boys were in cities across three states, and he stayed close to their operations, checking the weekly sales reports and visiting frequently in their stores. In addition, the staff of the Charlotte store had grown and was changing. In 1919, Charlotte store manager Herbert McDonald died of pneumonia. He was not quite forty and had been a mainstay in the Charlotte store. He had been with Belk since the store first opened twenty-five years earlier and had helped Belk train many of his new managers now spread across the Carolinas. The loss was deep, but Belk knew he had a successor. He named Frank Matthews, who was managing the men's and boys' department, as store manager.

Belk remained close to the business, but in addition to the expansion something else now divided his attention from the stores. Belk was now a married man with a family. In 1915, Henry Belk was fifty-two years old and had spared little of his time away from the stores. By this time, brother John had raised seven daughters, built a fine house in Monroe, and enjoyed his success by traveling the world. Henry was still living alone above the store. John did entice his brother away for a trip to Europe in the summer of 1914, a trip that brought unexpected attention. The two were sought after by newspaper reporters when they returned home. An assassin had killed Archduke Ferdinand, heir to the Austro-Hungarian empire, while the Belks were on their return cruise, and immediately local people wanted to know all they could about conditions in Europe. Henry Belk matter-of-factly explained that the countryside was beautiful, but he did notice an absence of able-bodied men.

The year before, Henry Belk had taken a summer trip to Canada. On board his train, in a group of other young ladies from Charlotte, was Mary Irwin, the thirty-two-year-old daughter of Dr. John R. Irwin, a prominent Charlotte surgeon and active Presbyterian churchman. Henry Belk knew Mary Irwin—he was on the Charlotte school board, and she was a teacher—but Belk had never expressed any special interest in her. A widower traveling with the group had his eye on Mary and asked Henry Belk to help him out in his quest for Mary's hand. Belk warned him he might be interested in Miss Irwin himself. In later years, Belk delighted in the telling of the story of this courtship and always concluded with the wry comment: "I helped him clean out with Mary."

The two were married June 9, 1915, a fine day for a wedding. The weather was fair, cotton prices were stable, and agriculture officials were reporting a good year. Political trouble was brewing over U.S. involvement in Europe, but Charlotte was more excited about Belk's annual white sale, which was to begin on Thursday, and about the mayor's continuing negotiations to arrange a Charlotte stopover for the train carrying the Liberty Bell to the San Francisco Exposition. According to the *Charlotte Observer*, "It rang out the news of the National Declaration of Independence a little more than a year after the sturdy settlers of Mecklenburg County had met here and started the movement for independence by declaring themselves independent." On Wednesday evening at 8:30, in the parlor of the Irwin home on North Tryon Street, Dr. John R. Irwin, a direct descendant of the Mecklenburgers spoken of by the mayor, gave his daughter's hand to Henry Belk, described in the morning paper as "one of North Carolina's most prominent and successful businessmen." Mary wore a pearl pin and necklace, with diamonds set in platinum, given her by the groom. A reception for several hundred followed and the couple left the following day for a trip to New York and Canada.

Indeed, Henry Belk was successful. He was on the board of a growing Charlotte bank and several Charlotte businesses as well as the boards of trustees for Davidson College, Queens College, the Barium Springs Orphanage, and the Montreat Association. But when the couple returned from the honeymoon, they moved into the Selwyn Hotel until a home on North Tryon Street came available. Henry Belk may have owned stores across two states, but he did not have a home other than rooms over the store. His new bride was not going to live there. In fact, she confided to her son Henderson years later, she burned the sheets from Henry's rooms when he moved out.

Most of the monied families in Charlotte were attracted to Myers Park for their new homes, but in 1917, Henry and Mary Belk purchased, for $50,000, a portion of the property of the bankrupt Elizabeth College on a hill overlooking the downtown and moved into the large, white frame president's home. The college property was not only a prime piece of land but very convenient for Belk, who could leave his front door, walk a few feet to the corner, and catch the trolley that ran down Elizabeth to West Trade and his store. He might have moved from the store with his marriage, but his business was not far from his front door.

T he end of the war in Europe brought prosperity to the South. Cotton prices were the highest they had ever been, seven or eight times more than buyers had offered four years earlier. R. J. Reynolds's new smoke, Camel, was the most popular cigarette in America, and Winston-Salem swelled with workers turning out the new fad. The nation's furniture manufacturers were looking to North Carolina where, in 1921, the twelve-story Southern Furniture Exposition building opened in High Point.

Textile mills, the backbone of the North Carolina industrial economy, declared unusually high dividends and boosted wages. The money that went into workers' pockets found its way into the hands of cashiers in Belk stores across the Carolinas. Between 1918 and 1920, total sales at Belk stores more than doubled, from $5.6 million to almost $12 million a year.

Shoppers indulged in ready-to-wear clothes and paid more attention to the latest fashions, even if all could not afford the finest. One observer called it the "Lipstick Era," when women forsook the prewar interest in durability and quality and bought what looked right. Department stores continued their "white sales," begun during the war to help the war effort, but now the goods were in lively colors. The new homemakers also began shopping for new appliances and home furnishings, purchases postponed by shortages or limited means during the war. A "suburban model" of the player piano was available for $495. Kelvinator had something called a refrigerator that did not require ice.

Charlotte's first supermarket, the Piggly Wiggly, opened in 1919. And new stores were opening downtown. Folks carried their portable Victrolas to Lakewood Park outside Charlotte, where the music played in the background for bathing, boating, and fishing. Motion pictures were replacing live minstrel shows in the music houses, and Belk's had adopted the slogan, "The Home of Better Values—We Sell It For Less."

Houses were going up everywhere, particularly in the cities. If you were not building one, you had applied a fresh coat of paint to the one you had.

North Carolina, long stuck in the mud, embarked on an ambitious road-building campaign. When Charlotte's Cameron Morrison reached the governor's office in 1921, he pushed through a program to link the county seats of the state's one hundred counties with hard-surface roads. One observer reported that "good roads became the third god in the trinity of Southern progress" after industry and education. No doubt Henry Belk subscribed to Morrison's ambitious plans, but the choice facing Belk in the 1920 general election was a tough one. Morrison's Republican opponent was John J. Parker, a Monroe lawyer who had once clerked in Belk's Monroe store.

The road program of fellow Presbyterian Morrison literally paved the way for the future of the Belk network of stores. The Belk brothers had chosen the location for most of their early stores based on access to the railroad. During the first twenty-five years, they picked towns close to the Southern Railway line that cut through the Carolina Piedmont. Stores opened in Greensboro, Salisbury, Concord, Kannapolis, and Charlotte. Governor Morrison's road program would pave roads to every county seat and every state institution, from the mountains to the coast. As a result, the North Carolina road-building campaign, and similar ones undertaken in other Southern states in the 1920s, would open hundreds of opportunities to Henry Belk.

The Belks believed they had the men to open and manage the stores in the communities that good roads would make more accessible. Particular favorites were the Leggetts— brothers Fred, Will, Robert, Harold, and George. They were from Morven, the small Anson County community where John Belk had opened his brief medical practice. Belk had worked there only a few years, but it was long enough for him to meet and marry Hallie Little, whose sister was the Leggetts' mother. Shortly after the turn of the century, Hallie Belk opened her home to her sister's oldest son, Fred. His mother wanted him to have the advantage of the better schools in Monroe, and Fred all but became a member of the Belk family while he finished his schooling.

John Belk, the father of seven daughters, the last two named Johny and Henry, was happy to have the young man about. On Saturdays and afternoons after school, Fred was in the store learning everything he could about the business. On weekends, he got the benefit of the two Belk brothers, who always visited together after Sunday services. Later, after Fred left to attend N.C. State College, Will Leggett followed his older brother to Monroe and similar on-the-job training.

Henry and John Belk gave Will his early training, but Frank Stevens, John Belk's son-in-law, provided Leggett the opportunity to use what he had learned. Stevens was a hard worker and had considered a career as a professional baseball player before he returned to Monroe and went to work at John Belk's store. In 1910 he married Belk's oldest daughter, Nealie, and settled into managing the Monroe store. He loved the area, but he did not want to be under his father-in-law forever. Shortly after a new rail line provided direct connections from Winston-Salem to Charlotte, he chose Winston-Salem as the home of his new store. In December 1916, Stevens opened Belk-Stevens Company, and Will Leggett was his assistant manager.

It was an ambitious move. Belk stores had done well in small towns, but the Hudsons were fighting to stay afloat in Raleigh, where they were competing against established business. Stevens's store would have stiff competition too, but Stevens would have an advantage the Hudsons could not claim. Winston-Salem was growing bigger with each passing day. For a brief time around 1920, it would pass Charlotte as the state's largest city. The expanding city had plenty of room for new merchants on the streets near the tobacco factories downtown.

The Winston-Salem store prospered during the boom times and experienced steady growth in the city. Stevens stocked his store with basic goods and clothing for tobacco workers,

ninety-eight-cent men's overalls, fifty-cent shirts and Pepper-
ell sheets at eight cents each. Stevens put his store right in
the center of town, on the courthouse square within easy
walking distance of Reynolds's plants and tobacco warehouses. He kept a close eye on his competition in Winston-
Salem, but was looking for opportunity elsewhere in the
northern Piedmont of North Carolina.

He picked Burlington, just eighteen miles east of Greensboro on the main line to Durham. Burlington was changing
from a railway repair town to a textile mill community by
1919, when Stevens arrived to find a location for his next
Belk-Stevens Company store. Stevens's store would complete the Belk linkage across the center of the state. Since
Stevens had moved to Winston-Salem, the Hudson brothers
had opened a satellite store in Durham from their base in
Raleigh. The Greensboro store was well established. If Stevens opened a store in Burlington, then customers could
find a Belk store almost every twenty-five miles from eastern
North Carolina to the mountain foothills. Stevens knew he
could pick no better person for the job of manager of the
Burlington store than twenty-five-year-old Will Leggett. The
Belks agreed and put up their share of the working capital
for stock in the store.

Leggett opened the store in March. Within a short time,
Will had moved from his hotel room to a house and had
brought his three younger brothers (Robert, Harold, and
George), his two sisters (Hallie and Julia), and their mother
from their home in Wadesboro. The move not only kept the
family together after their father's death, but provided Will
with extra help around the store.

Anxious to please their older brother, Robert, Harold, and
George were eager workers. They distributed advertising fly-
ers, nailed signs to trees along roads leading to town, and
helped Will with all manner of chores in the store. Leggett's
store was small, about 3,000 square feet, but he wanted it to
look like the best in town. Years later, his brother Harold
recalled that he and his brothers could never satisfy Will on
that score. "You'd knock yourself out setting up a table of

merchandise. Shirts, yard goods, it doesn't matter what. Then Will would come along and he'd say, 'Oh, that's fine. That looks just right.' Then he'd step back, and look at it again, and he'd say, 'Now, don't you think if we just move this one over here, it would look a little better?' So you'd knock yourself out again, trying to please him."

Handsome, always well-dressed and well-groomed, Will Leggett presented himself as the perfect merchant. He shopped the mills in the surrounding towns and became a familiar figure with the mill owners in the area. He was a popular customer and always would find bargains to ship to his store, stacking the rolls of yard goods "just so." Immediately, he would announce a sale and draw folks into his store, which they left with his specials and other merchandise as well. The Belk style of loss-leader selling worked as well in Burlington as it did in Charlotte and Monroe.

In 1920, home from Europe with thousands of other veterans, Fred Leggett returned to Monroe and paid a call on John Belk. Without hesitation, John Belk told him to find a location for a store. Leggett roamed North Carolina and returned to Monroe excited about his choice. He would not open another North Carolina store. He wanted to set the Belk flag in Virginia and had chosen Danville, a busy railroad and textile town on the Dan River. He had better luck finding a suitable building than had Erskine Gallant, who had passed through a year before. Belk-Leggett opened in Danville in March 1920.

The expansion fueled by available and talented managers like the Leggetts soon came to a halt. The boom days of postwar prosperity were followed by a recession that sent farm and factory incomes plummeting. Merchants like the Belks were left with goods that they could not sell for what they had in them. By the end of 1921, sales were down by about 25 percent from the previous year and would remain there for the next few years. Will Leggett, like many merchants, spent worried nights wondering whether local bankers would renew their notes and give him time to recover from the setbacks. Karl Hudson wondered at times if he would ever catch up. He carefully set aside a small portion of each day's sales to pay off his loans and have some profit for dividends at year's end.

Charlotte merchants scrambled for business. Belk's store had soap sales, drew up special lists of items for sale from one penny to nineteen cents, and tailored specials for special occasions, such as the Fordson tractor demonstrations held in 1922. The Ford Motor Company, which was making automobiles in a plant just north of downtown, invited dealers from across the South to the city. Belk's, and other stores, offered special prices on men's fall suits—$14.95 to $25.00—and dropped prices on work shirts and pants. A farmer in town to see the new machines could walk out of Belk's with new work pants, work shirt, and shoes and spend less than five dollars.

Some sales just did not work. In his Monday morning "Weekly Store News," J. B. Ivey reported on one previous week's special sales. "The folks just didn't come in," Ivey said candidly.

The Belk brothers retrenched, concentrating on the stores they had. Not a single new location was opened between 1922 and 1925, the year after the nation's economy began to improve. And managers were careful about adding any new lines. New merchandise tied up more of the few dollars they had for operating expenses. The Belks did not lose any stores, but some, like the Durham store, were in trouble. In 1924, the Belks asked Will Leggett to take it over. The store was larger and a likely next step for the ambitious young merchant. And Will would not have to worry about his investment in the Burlington store. Brother Robert, who had worked with him for more than four years, could manage the store there.

In 1924, Henry Belk joined the crowds on the street in Durham waiting for the new manager to open the doors. After the usual ceremonies, customers pushed through the entrance and Belk was swept along with everyone else. Inside, he tried to stand aside and let customers get to the bargains Will Leggett had gathered for his opening day sale, but he stepped back a bit too far behind the notions counter to suit a nervous salesclerk. "Grandpa," the clerk said to Belk, "you just get out from behind this counter and I will wait on you next." Belk did not say a word and moved. Later, he told Leggett about the exchange. Leggett's reply was, "Well, Mr. Belk, I hope you bought something." Belk said he had purchased a paper of pins and asked Leggett not to embarrass the young woman by telling her about the incident. Leggett complied and kept the story to himself until the clerk's retirement dinner years later, when he presented her with a diamond stickpin.

As the economy improved, other retailers were discovering the opportunities in Southern cities and towns. National retail chain stores, with grocery companies leading the way, opened on Main Streets throughout the South, threatening the future of local merchants who had neither the capital nor the resources in the market to compete. Local merchants fanned resentment against out-of-town ownership of businesses just as they had campaigned against the mail-order houses twenty years earlier.

At one point, a North Carolina legislator described chain stores as "a giant octopus of capital . . . (which) by their methods of buying force the truck farmers and producers to sell their products at cost or less." He added, "And if the chain stores are not checked, the independent merchants who have supported institutions of city and state will be pushed aside," destroying the community and creating what he called a "deserted village." A letter writer to the *Charlotte Observer* responded in defense of Belk that "the 'Belk boys,' as they have been termed, have been community builders, support churches and build structures that are a credit to any town in which they operate, and not only do they turn their money over to our banks, but give employment to hundreds of people. I know of no other chain store that pays such taxes, helps build good roads and is a benefactor in general."

By most accounts, the Belks' and the Efirds' stores qualified as chains, and just a few years earlier the owners had proudly called their businesses such in local advertising.

These references now disappeared. When any subsequent new Belk store opened, the new manager promoted the unique local personality of the Belk business. That helped to fortify Belk against the growing resentment of local merchants, who appealed to the legislature for help.

Most attempts to stem this changing tide in the retail business would fail. By the end of the decade, more than half of the department stores in the country belonged to chains. While Belk was little more than a collection of stores, each independent of the other, the business would survive the challenge from national chains because of the system of local ownership, because of the special interest Belk's managers took in tailoring their stores for local customers, and because of new business unfolding at Henry Belk's store in Charlotte.

By 1925, Belk Brothers Company was a complete mercantile business with a successful retail business on East Trade Street and an expanding wholesale trade throughout the Carolinas. The center of the business was Henry Belk's desk on the mezzanine of the Charlotte store. Frank Matthews and other store employees had replaced his simple pine desk with a fancier rolltop model, but it was still located close enough to the edge of the balcony so he could see the sales floor below. From this vantage point Belk could look down the long aisles between the counters stacked with goods and pick out customers who might need attention. If his main floor clerks were busy, then he would leave his post and descend to make the sale himself.

Though past sixty years of age, Belk's pace had not slowed. He had turned certain day-to-day responsibilities over to others, but he still traveled frequently to New York and at least once a week was on his way to visit his stores. A vest-pocket booklet in which Belk recorded his travel expenses shows that during the first two weeks of July 1924, he was in Gastonia to see Houston Matthews and left from there to visit the store in York. He was in Concord, Kannapolis, and Salisbury on another day, Greensboro and High Point on another, and he took a two-day trip to Spartanburg, Greenville, and Asheville before returning for a meeting in Monroe with his brother. He was a demanding driver, pushing his Buick roadster to the limit. The car took the punishment, but at a cost. That same year he had to spend $247.50 on automobile repairs.

The mezzanine was a busy and noisy place even when Belk was not in town. Store manager Frank Matthews had a desk there, as did H. A. McLaurin, Belk's auditor, and W. I. Smith, who managed the traffic department, which was responsible for shipping goods to Belk's wholesale customers. Cashiers who handled sales for the entire store also were tucked into this space. In all retail establishments, sales clerks did not handle cash. Instead, they placed the sales ticket and the customer's payment into a wire basket that was carried along greased wire guidelines directed by a series of pulleys to the cashiers, who made change and returned the basket to the clerk. Called the Lamson system, the contraption provided a constant background noise of whirring and clicking as the baskets zipped along through various intersections. The system had certain efficiencies in large stores in the days before cash registers. It protected the owner from dishonest employees and centralized the accounting, and it freed the clerks to concentrate on selling, not accounting. But it had its drawbacks, principally the occasional derailment of a basket that would bring everything to a halt until a clerk climbed high on a ladder to right the misdirected carrier.

A prolific letter writer, Matthews kept a team of stenographers busy with correspondence to resources, business associates, and wholesale customers. Most of the typists Matthews hired faded quickly under a work load that included typing as many as 120 letters a day. Not long after Sarah Pharr had come to work in 1923, to help in accounting, another of Matthews's secretaries quit. Matthews offered her the job, and she accepted the position over the objections of her brother, who did not think it proper for a single girl to be working so closely with bachelor businessmen. Matthews liked her spunk, energy, and determination. Three months after she came to work, the store was damaged by a nighttime fire. The blaze was extinguished before the building was too heavily damaged, but when Pharr arrived for work the next morning, the electric power was out and even the telephone company was waiting for a safety clearance before reconnecting the lines. Frank Matthews was not waiting. He had damaged goods that he needed to move, and he wanted letters out to his customers before the day was through. Sarah Pharr, with the help of firemen, recovered her typewriter and set up shop in the men's store in an adjacent building and had Matthews's announcement of a fire sale in the evening mail.

Belk's frequent travels provided one-on-one opportunities for his young managers and his partners. There also was a need for group meetings, "to get the men together for exchange of information and ideas," John Belk said in opening the first meeting of the Belk Stores Association in September 1925, and "to get the men to have confidence in themselves, confidence in the stores they represent and to use good judgment in the management of them." At this first meeting, the brothers also admonished their partners to pay their bills on time; Henry Belk said he had had complaints from manufacturers. According to the minutes, "Belk emphasized very strongly that the stores who had been overbuying must stop the practice or else it would be necessary for some further steps to be taken." Young men anxious over their careers needed to hear nothing more.

Much of the meeting was spent talking about stocking the stores properly. J. G. Parks said he used a system of customer "want slips." If a customer did not find what she wanted in the store, then she completed a small form listing the item the store did not have in stock. Frank Matthews endorsed this idea and said the overstocking at the Greensboro store, which had prompted removal of a manager, would not have occurred if someone had been keeping a sharp eye on the business. Matthews also warned the managers to watch the competition closely. The minutes of the meeting report Matthews observed that "some of the mail-order houses and some of the other chain stores were making some progress in our territories and . . . it would be well to watch them carefully and be prepared to meet them on any of their special priced items."

The Belk brothers furnished the forty managers and Charlotte store officers with an evening meal at the Selwyn Hotel and reconvened the meeting at 7:35 to talk about a change in the New York buying services. As the group settled into their chairs, Henry Belk announced that he had severed connections with Alfred Fantl of New York as of September 1. Fantl had provided Belk with tips on market conditions, had located merchandise available at a good price, and had helped buyers when they arrived in New York City to shop for their stores. Through Fantl, the stores even had adopted a Paris address, claiming a European buying office at 5 Rue de Metz. Belk announced that he was replacing Fantl with a skeleton staff in the store's small office at 117 West 33rd Street, and he directed Frank Stevens, Karl Hudson, Frank Matthews, and Jim Williams to organize a proper New york office for the stores.

The more active New York office was needed to keep the stores closer to the changing fashions of the land. New York was no longer just a place to shop for bargains, closeouts, and discontinued lines. Belk customers in cities like Charlotte, Wilmington, and Winston-Salem were paying more attention to the season's new styles. Sarah Houston, whose experience in ladies' wear commanded attention from Henry Belk, no doubt argued for better arrangements. With an upturn in the economy, her customers now could afford more lines of ready-to-wear that were pouring out of cutting rooms in New York.

Belk's decision to invest in the stores' own New York staff reflected his confidence in the recovering economy and the strength of the business in the nearly forty stores he and brother John now owned. Belk had opened three stores in 1925, in Wadesboro, N.C., in Bennettsville, S.C., and, with Jim Williams, in Clinton, in eastern North Carolina. Three more opened in 1926, including a store in Charleston, S.C. In 1926, the brothers also announced another expansion in

Charlotte. The store would be extended back another seventy feet, and the East Trade Street front would be expanded to seventy-one feet. In addition, elevators would be added.

As the Belk brothers planned for further expansion of their business, the Leggett brothers were discussing their future. In the spring of 1927, they met in the shoe department of the Burlington store, where Will, Robert, and now Harold had managed the business, and talked about whether to build more business for the Belk brothers or set out on their own. The Belks had been good to the family. Will and Fred had been raised in John Belk's home. The Belks had backed Will when he opened the Burlington store and then had promoted him to the larger Durham business. Fred was doing well in Danville, where he had opened a store with the Belks' blessing, as was Robert, who had succeeded Will in Burlington. Harold was now manager of the Belks' Wadesboro store, which had opened not quite two years earlier. Despite this history, they realized that in years ahead the business would be run by the Belk children, not by the Leggetts.

After scouting the hills of Tennessee and Kentucky, two nearby states that did not have Belk stores, they settled on Lynchburg, Va., as the city where they would start their business. They had looked the old river city over and had found several department stores, but none presented overwhelming competition. If nothing else, they believed they could beat the existing businesses at their own game through better customer service. When they had stopped in the Lynchburg stores, posing as nothing more than customers, they had received cool treatment.

The brothers chose Harold Leggett as the manager for their store. Then they considered the next issue—breaking with the Belks. Again, Harold was chosen to carry the news because they figured he had the least to lose. Harold had just begun to work and did not own any shares in the Wadesboro store. Brother Fred owned 28 percent of the Danville store, and Will, who had made the Durham store profitable after money-losing years, owned all but five shares of the stock of the original owners. Robert owned a portion of the Burlington store.

Harold arranged for a Monday meeting with Henry Belk to announce the brothers' decision. The Friday before, however, he saw Frank Stevens and Henry Matthews step off the train in Wadesboro. They were soon in the store, and Stevens announced that he was there to relieve Harold of his duties as manager. The secret was out, and things had not gone according to plan, but Harold was thankful. Now, he told Stevens, he would not have to face Henry Belk directly. Harold cheerfully agreed to stay on long enough to get a new manager settled.

Frank Stevens also set out to fire Robert as manager of the Burlington store, but he got quite a different response when he arrived with Robert's replacement in tow. Robert refused to leave, particularly without payment for his stock, which was worth $9,000. Stevens was stuck. He did not have that much money. Tensions rose, and relations became quite strained between the Belks and their protégés. At one point, Henry Belk is said to have wanted to fire Will and Fred, in addition to Robert. John Belk, the more even tempered of the brothers, disagreed. He told his brother they would do well to keep the Leggetts in the fold. They were bright young men and would do well for themselves.

After some negotiations, the brothers struck a deal. Robert would leave the Burlington store, with his $9,000. Fred and Will would remain at their posts in Danville and Durham, and the Belks and Leggetts would become partners in any future stores. The stock distribution would differ from any other Belk partnerships, however. The Leggetts would own 80 percent of any stores they opened, and the Belks 20 percent, almost the exact reverse of the Belks' previous arrangements.

While the Belks were settling affairs with the Leggetts, Frank Stevens in Winston-Salem was eager to make changes in the brothers' wholesale business, which had grown substantially but haphazardly over the years. What had begun as a cooperative venture between a handful of stores before the turn of the century now required the services of a full-time shipping department, and bargains Belk buyers had stocked for sale occupied much of the space on the upper floors of the Charlotte store. Under the direct care of J. G. Parks and Frank Matthews, who also had stores to manage, the cooperative service for Belk stores now served more than forty Belk stores and another thousand small dry-goods stores throughout the region.

In March 1927, Frank Stevens called on Sam Scott, who was managing a competitor's store in Winston-Salem, and asked if he would like to develop a central purchasing operation for the Belks. Stevens knew Scott as a good merchant, and the two shared good-natured ribbing about the success of their stores. Scott was working for Gilmer's Department Store in Winston-Salem, but he was considering other possibilities. Stevens's offer piqued his interest, however, and on Stevens's instructions he took the train to Charlotte and talked to Henry Belk.

"When I came over to talk with Mr. Belk," Scott later recalled, "I found him up on the fifth floor sitting on a case of goods. I told him Mr. Stevens had sent me to see him. He said, 'See Frank Matthews.' So I went back to Winston-Salem and told Mr. Stevens what had happened. He said, 'Well, he was all mixed up.' Mr. Stevens had gotten a letter from him asking what kind of a salesman I would make in the retail store."

Next, Stevens asked him to go to Monroe to see John Belk. Scott had seen Belk before, when he and three Belk partners had come to Winston-Salem to buy goods at a liquidation sale of the store Scott was then managing. Stevens told Scott not to say anything, just to let Belk do the talking, "as he was a big talker. When I got there, I told him I had come in regard to opening a buying office in Charlotte, and he said, 'Mr. Scott, we have more buyers now than we know what to do with. I like to buy goods from my traveling friends. Frank Matthews sends out a list on sheetings and things of that kind every week or so.' I said, 'Well, doctor, all I know about it is that Frank Stevens asked me to come down here to talk with you about it.' He said, 'Come on back to the office.' I guess I was in there an hour and did not open my mouth." When he left, however, Belk told him, "Mr. Scott, you are the man we have been looking for all these years."

Scott concluded his affairs in Winston-Salem and reported to Henry Belk for his first day of work. "I am looking for a man who can buy anything from a sewing-machine needle to a white elephant," Belk said. "Are you that man?" Scott said he was not sure, explaining that the only lines he was really familiar with were shoes, britches, work shirts, cheap dresses, hose, and other small items. Belk replied, "I think you will learn."

Scott arrived just as the brothers were opening their new store. The $750,000 expansion included, in addition to more space for the established lines, a new furniture department on the third floor and more space on the fourth and fifth floors for the wholesale business. Altogether, the new store had more than 120,000 square feet of space. No store in Charlotte or the rest of the Carolinas was larger.

More than 25,000 people jammed East Trade Street at the "informal reception" on the eve of the opening May 1, 1927. People crowded through the large front doors and quickly collected the 12,000 souvenirs purchased for the occasion. They listened to the music of an orchestra hired for the evening and strolled through the wide aisles separating handsome counters of dark wood and display tables, looking over Belk's special grand-opening purchases. One report compared it to earlier excitement at Belk's "Bargain Day" sales that Henry Belk had organized years before. "Bargain day at Belks," the *Charlotte Observer* reported, "was a big day, and old timers say that it was not unusual for it to become necessary to have an extra squad of police to handle the mobs who gathered to take advantage of the bargains offered."

Belk's bargains now were displayed in what W. L. Wallis, the store's advertising manager, called his "million-dollar basement." He said the basement business would generate that much in sales of serviceable hats, shoes, dresses, stockings, and other low-price clothing. Also stocked in the basement store were housewares, kitchen utensils, and toys.

The Belks presented the latest in merchandising to Charlotte. The new Trade Street show windows had been designed by a Chicago company, and the store now had a full-time window dresser. The *Charlotte Observer* reporter was overwhelmed by the new cash-handling system. Belk had replaced the Lamson system of baskets with three and a half miles of pneumatic tubes. They served the same purpose but carried the cash and receipts more quickly, more quietly, and without the nettlesome derailments. The shiny brass carriers could carry their cargo from most any point in the building to the mezzanine cashiers and back in thirty seconds flat.

On the main floor, Belk had replaced the rows of display tables with handsome wooden and glass counters arranged in squares to create islands of counter space. Clerks in the center could handle customers on four sides. The store interior was brightly painted and better lighted than before. More and larger light fixtures hung from the high ceilings. Gone was the look of a cluttered country store, with goods stacked a foot or two high on crowded display tables and hand-lettered signs hawking specials dangling from the ceiling.

Sarah Houston, calmly efficient and businesslike, as respected a merchant as any man in the building, reigned over the store's second floor. She had been with Belk since the turn of the century, and her knowledge of the business was known from the Carolinas to New York. Young buyers off to market with the Belk crowd were told by their managers to "watch Miss Sarah Houston. Be guided by what she buys." For the opening, she had new shipments of gowns, lingerie, and dresses, some priced as high as $148.50. Belk might have winced at the price when he saw it, but he had long since relinquished control of the women's wear world to Miss Houston. He trusted her implicitly.

While fashion had become a more important part of the business, the main floor remained dedicated to domestics,

Belk's primary stock-in-trade. On opening day, Belk offered special prices on imported voiles, sheer and colorful; organdies brought from Europe; and "real imported Swiss in fine hand tied dots." Bolts of silks, satins, and crepes, and linens, damask napkins, and embroidered pillow cases were stacked neatly on the counters. Rayon bedspreads produced in Henry Belk's own mill in Ellenboro, N.C., sold for $3.95; bath towels from Cannon Mills were six for a dollar.

Henry Belk's rolltop desk on the mezzanine remained the business hub for the Charlotte store and forty-two others throughout the Carolinas and Virginia. By the time the new Charlotte store opened, most of those in North Carolina cities and towns were linked together by the 3,738 miles of paved roads. Cameron Morrison had made good on his promise to connect the lost provinces of North Carolina, and the highway system, second only to that of Texas in size, now included 7,551 miles of state-maintained roads.

Belk was not quite sixty-five, and he had a young, growing family at home. But he was not thinking about slowing down. If anything, the future was more promising than ever. Business was booming in the South, and Cam Morrison's pavement presented a clear, smooth highway to the future.

6. Thomasville Rockers and Red Camels

Partnerships built Belk stores. Henry Belk called the stockholder–store managers his partners, and through them he opened the largest network of dry-goods and department stores in the Southeast. He invested with other partners in numerous businesses, including insurance, textiles, and banking, and increased his wealth so that during the depression his personal accounts often saved a failing business. But the story of the early years of the Belk stores was the story of one partnership, that between Henry and John Belk.

In the spring of 1928, the Belk brothers were perhaps the best-known pair of businessmen in the Carolinas. Their name was on forty-two stores in three states, and their devotion to one another drew comments from their admirers. The two had not only established a remarkable business, but they had a long record of philanthropy, particularly in support of the evangelism and missionary work of the Presbyterian Church.

Despite their success and wealth, the brothers remained men of simple tastes and wants. John Belk's only extravagance was travel, which he did frequently and extensively, often with one or more of his daughters in tow. Henry Belk's grandest gesture was the large beige brick home on the hill overlooking downtown Charlotte. The house was completed in 1925 for Mary and Henry's family of five sons and one daughter and the family moved out of the old Elizabeth College president's home into their new residence.

The massive brick structure was built to last. It had all the finest conveniences available. Rich, dark walnut lined the walls of the library, and Italian marble was shipped in to construct the fireplace in the living room. White, blue, and pink tiles covered the floors and walls of the five large bathrooms and three half baths. Belk installed an intercom system so the family could communicate throughout the eighteen rooms, and a built-in vacuum system helped the servants keep the place tidy. At a time when most houses in Charlotte were selling for between $6,000 and $7,000, Belk spent more than $76,000 to build the mansion.

The two brothers had worked hard, had invested well in business and in people, and were widely respected. The depth of affection from those who knew them was no more apparent than on March 22, 1928, when all of Monroe and much of North Carolina turned out to help Henry Belk bury his brother.

John Belk's death came as a surprise. Both brothers were robust and hearty men; their mother was still living at age ninety-three. But on the Friday before he died, John Belk began experiencing chest pains and left the store. It was a busy time. Spring sales were just about to get under way. He spent the weekend at home, resting, but was back in the store on Tuesday, working there into the evening. At 4:00 A.M., Wednesday, March 21, Dr. A. F. Mahoney was summoned. Belk was suffering from serious chest pains and had spent a very uncomfortable night. The doctor arrived and was there when another attack occurred at 7:00 A.M. At 8:45 A.M. John Montgomery Belk died. He was sixty-two years old.

Monroe came to a stop. The schools closed, and mourners filled John Belk's large home on South Hayne Street, the crowd spilling out into the spacious yard. People came from miles around to pay their respects, their automobiles filling the streets around the Belk home. More than five hundred floral displays were delivered for services at Belk's home. Two large trucks were needed to carry the flowers to the grave. Newspapers across the Carolinas noted his death with editorials full of praise for John Belk's contributions to the South.

The death fell heavily on Henry Belk. He had lost not only a brother, but the business partner whose advice he valued above all others. In later years he said: "Brother John and I always got along mighty well together. He had fine judgment about things, and he always considered both sides of a situation before he made up his mind. Whatever he did always suited me, and I think whatever I did generally suited him. I suppose we were much closer than the average pair of brothers. Brother John was a good man, and a great man. I still miss him."

Until his own death twenty-four years later, Henry Belk kept his brother's picture atop his rolltop desk.

John Belk was irreplaceable. Henry Belk had many capable partners, men he trusted to represent him across the South. As the business grew, he had come to rely on them more and more, but none was ever as close as his brother. The two had complemented one another perfectly. Henry was often bold, even impulsive, and quick to act. He was willing to set off to Texas because of small-town rumors. John had the comfortable nature of the country doctor. His pace was slower, his decisions more thoughtful. He was the only one in business discussions who could completely change Henry Belk's mind, and he spoke up often to do that. This unique chemistry of brotherhood, more than anything else, had produced the vast mercantile enterprise that Henry Belk now faced alone without John's wise counsel.

The reading of John Belk's will settled the matter of who would assume responsibility for John Belk's interests. As expected, Belk left his affairs, including a stipulation that 15 percent of any profits from his businesses be donated to charity each year, in the hands of his brother. He was to manage the trusts established for John's daughters out of their partnership and stock owned in the forty-eight Belk stores the two had opened together. John expressed his complete trust by giving Henry the authority to settle any disputes over the estate, without question. "I have utmost confidence in his ability and integrity," John Belk said in his will.

John's will named his daughter, Mabel, and son-in-law, A. Frank Stevens, to succeed his brother in managing affairs of the estate. Henry Belk shared his brother's confidence in Frank Stevens and soon after his brother's death he began referring more and more business decisions to Stevens.

Stevens had already shown an ability to get things done and had begun to assume more responsibility than the average partner. He had given the three Leggett brothers training and support from his Winston-Salem and Burlington stores and then handled the delicate job of their departure. In addition, Stevens had shown he had an eye for good men. Henry Belk was pleased with Sam Scott and others that Stevens had sent to his office. Stevens could pick good locations for stores. His stores in the North Carolina towns of Burlington, Reidsville, Fayetteville, High Point, and Mount Airy were all doing well.

Frank Stevens and Henry Belk were alike in many ways. Both had an uncanny knack for sizing up a man and picking the right person for the right job. Stevens was not nearly as tall as Belk, nor as portly, but like Belk, he had a commanding presence. Stevens's mustache gave him an air of sophistication though he was a simple man who, like Belk, preferred his farm in Union County to the bright lights of New York. Stevens was outspoken, direct, and unpretentious. Compliments from him were genuine, not meaningless flattery. And, of course, he was a solid Presbyterian, dedicated to hard work and strict adherence to the faith. What some mistook for formality was simply his straitlaced religious upbringing that had no patience with foolishness or off-color remarks. Stevens also had demonstrated a keen business sense, and he was full of energy and new ideas.

The Belk organization needed someone like Stevens. The loose confederation of stores operated independently by partners had been adequate for a rural marketplace where fashions changed little, where stores stocked basically the same goods year in and out, and where the competition was another independent owner who shared the same philosophy. But the department store had revolutionized retailing since the Belk brothers had opened their first real department store in Charlotte.

The twenty years after 1910 had been the most prosperous in the history of retail business in America. Modern communications, a world war, and miles of newly paved highways had changed shopping habits that were generations old. Very few department stores did not grow during that time.

Prosperity had brought extravagances to stores in the larger cities, where their doormen dressed like palace guards of a Balkan prince. Even in smaller towns, merchants competed fiercely for business, offering free home delivery of purchases as small as a spool of thread. The charge-account customer was commonplace in big cities, as merchants showered every convenience on customers eager to buy.

Competition also brought change to the side of the business that customers could not see. As more and more departments opened in a single store, and as each department offered an ever-expanding range of goods for sale, more organization and support were needed to make sure that madam had the right item at the right time for the right price. The business was leaving behind the day when the owner checked in the stock, marked it up, waited on customers, kept the accounts, and wrote his own promotions and advertising.

Most Belk stores were small stores with a limited stock of goods, but the Belk operation was no longer a simple string of country stores. Competition was increasing the demand for a broader range of goods at lower and lower prices. Larger Belk stores now carried home furnishings, and some, like the Charlotte store, had expanded into infants' wear. Henry Belk's friends said he realized the potential infants' and children's wear market after he began to raise his own family. Experienced, sharp-eyed buyers were needed to comb the market constantly to find more new lines. Radio was beginning to tie the towns of the Carolinas together, opening new possibilities for advertising and promotion. In Wilmington, the Belk-Williams Company Male Quartet was on the air weekly, singing to southeastern North Carolina over WRBT. The quartet had its own theme song, a jaunty tune entitled, "Belk Stores Belt the Carolinas."

Most important, the buying service now had someone to spend full time developing new lines of supply for Belk's stores. Sam Scott's first job had been to organize the buying service. When he arrived in Charlotte in 1927, he found that buying was haphazard, that overstocked goods simply gathered dust on the fourth and fifth floors of the Charlotte store. Some shipments were as much as ten years old. Scott plunged ahead, with little help. He had no secretary to write and track orders and no assistants to handle the purchasing of goods. He did not have much of a guarantee that the job, which he had taken a pay cut to accept, would even work out. But he was confident that he had made the right decision in signing on with Belk.

Scott had a solid background of more than twenty years in the retail business, and he could see the potential in the Belk organization. He had been a salesman on the road, (one of his customers had been Belk's early Charlotte manager, Herbert McDonald), and he had worked the other side of the counter as well. Scott and Stevens had been friendly competitors in Winston-Salem. The two would exchange street-corner banter in the evening as they closed their stores for the day. "One day," Scott once recalled, "I was going by as he waved his hand at his window and asked 'What do you think of your competitor's window?' I looked, and he had a window full of cheap merchandise, sheets for eighty-eight cents, ninety-eight-cent overalls, and fifty-cent work shirts. I told him that I didn't know he was in business. I was interested in making money for my firm." Scott's response made an impression on Stevens, who made a note to hire him away when he had the right job.

At Belk, Scott first got rid of old stock. He slashed prices and found buyers among Belk's wholesale customers and Belk managers for merchandise that had been out of style for years. Some store managers said later they took the piece goods, table cloths, and clothing, including button shoes that would never return to style, out of an obligation to Henry Belk. They knew they were going to lose money on some of the dated goods. Scott also renewed his contacts with manufacturers in the area and salesmen who had sold him goods in Winston-Salem, and he began scouting the markets.

Scott soon got his chance to prove himself for the Belks. Shortly after he started work, he traveled to New York to attend a sale of water-damaged stock of the New England Dry Goods Company. Goods worth about $1 million were up for auction. It was the kind of sale that Belk and hundreds of other merchants followed to pick up goods at cheap prices. Scott bid often and well. But he was nervous about the $45,000 worth of merchandise he had shipped to Charlotte. He wrote Henry Belk in advance of his return that he might have paid too much.

"When the goods arrived in Charlotte," Scott later recalled, "it looked like the Southern Railroad had loaded one of its biggest trains with this merchandise. Mr. Belk checked every piece of goods that came into the Charlotte store, and he started checking at nine in the morning and finished at 6:30 that evening. And Dr. Belk had come up from Monroe to see what I had bought."

John Belk had told Scott not to buy for him. He said he liked to buy most of what he needed from traveling men and then fill in with stock he would get at cost from his brother.

"About five times while Mr. Belk was checking his merchandise," Scott said, "Dr. Belk came back to ask if I had shipped him a case of goods like that and I would always say 'no.' Finally, he said, 'Why didn't you?' and I reminded him of his instructions. He said, 'Next time you see anything you think enough of to ship Brother Henry, ship me the same thing.'"

Henry Belk did not speak to Scott while he checked in the crates, opening each one and running his hand over the fabric or checking the construction of the weave. Finally, when all was accounted for, he said, "Mr. Scott, I can't find the goods that you thought you paid too much for. We are going to double our money on this entire shipment." At that moment Scott was the happiest man in Charlotte.

By 1930, Sam Scott had not only won Henry Belk's confidence but was gaining the support of the partners. The managers who shopped with Scott were not a captive audience, obliged to stock their stores with goods from Henry Belk's warehouse. Belk firmly believed that the store managers should buy from whoever offered the best price or best deal.

If a salesman showed up at the store in Anderson, S.C., with a lot of blankets or hosiery for sale at a cheaper price, then Erskine Gallant was expected to buy from the salesman. Gradually, as Scott's reputation grew, more and more managers made their way to Scott's sample-laden desk on the fifth floor.

Karl Broome, Belk's partner in Hickory, who had expanded to other towns in the mountain foothills, was one of Scott's first regular customers. He placed thirty-two orders on his first visit and came back for more. A few months after he started checking with Scott and buying from him instead of salesmen on the road, Broome stopped by Scott's office. "Mr. Scott," Broome said, "I have been around to quite a few of the Belk stores. It used to be that no two of them looked alike, but I can see in all of the stores I have been in items that you are offering up here."

Scott's ambition was to increase the sales volume through the buying service. With the buying power of all stores combined, Belk managers would get the best price, good deliveries, and better discounts. The opportunities for special arrangements were abundant. North Carolina textile mills led the nation in production of denim, damask, towels, underwear, hosiery, yarn, and blankets. Most of these mills were in easy reach of Scott's base on East Trade Street, and mill owners and sales managers knew the Belk business well. For Scott's plan to work, however, he needed Belk stores to begin coordinating special sales and promotions, something they had not done before.

Scott tried his first promotion with a supplier who had sold to him at Gilmer's Department Store in Winston-Salem. Scott ordered 100,000 yards of silk fabric, paying ninety cents a yard. It was to sell for $1.69 per yard in the stores. The orders arrived and were shipped to the stores, and Scott waited for the outcome of his experiment. The original shipments sold out in a day and practically every store reordered. Scott was in business.

A year later, Scott took this project one step further. Rather than arrange a one-time sale on a special purchase, he set up a rebate plan for an entire line. He arranged with Veldown Corporation to deliver one free sanitary napkin for each one the stores purchased at twenty-five cents. At the end of the year, the company would rebate to Belk stores the price of each one sold, as advertising expense. On this promotion, Scott collected $15,500 in cash for Henry Belk.

Slowly, but perceptibly, Scott's planned purchases were making a difference in stores across the Carolinas. And his job became easier as confidence in his abilities grew among Belk managers. Henry Belk was watching Scott work with Will Leggett and some of his young buyers and finally called him aside to ask a question. "Mr. Scott," Belk said, "you don't show any samples. How in the world do you sell these men all the goods you are selling them?" "Mr. Belk," Scott replied, "I just tell them the truth." Belk turned around and walked away without saying a word.

As business increased, Scott expanded the office, hired a secretary, and added other buyers, several of whom were sent to him by Stevens. Like any shrewd merchant, he found a way to pay for the additional staff. On his buying trips to textile mills and manufacturers in the region, Scott arranged for suppliers to pay rebates on quantity business. Soon, these rebates amounted to enough to cover the expenses of operating the buying service.

Scott's money-saving purchases, his scramble for cheap goods, and his contacts among resources arrived at just the right time. When Henry and John Belk closed the books on business in 1927, they ended one of the best sales years of the decade. Only 1926 had been better. It would be nearly a decade before the growth the Belks had known in the mid-1920s would return. Hard times were at hand.

Long before the rest of the nation, the South began experiencing the economic problems that would become even more severe and be known forever as the Great Depression. By the time of the stock market crash in 1929, Belk's stores were ending their second year of little or no growth in sales, despite the addition of fifteen new locations. Cotton prices had fallen from their 1927 high, tobacco prices were down, and

Southern textile mills, rocked by violent strikes and declining demand, were slowing production. Everywhere Belk looked, there were fewer dollars available for people to spend in his stores. The governor even encouraged North Carolinians to live off their own land as much as possible, by planting vegetable gardens.

Bad weather, particularly a drought that dried up the South, complicated matters. Eggs dropped to twelve cents a dozen, and every merchant in town had two or three bales of cotton in front of the store marked, "Buy a bale—5 cents a pound." Watermelons sold for fifteen cents, butter was twenty-five cents a pound. The few mills that were in production paid subsistence wages. As agricultural prices plummeted, businesses found themselves in trouble. The collapse of Asheville's Central Bank and Trust Company, a casualty of the failure of the booming resort development business, was the first of the 215 bank closings that hit the state between 1929 and 1933.

Henry Belk was first and foremost a merchant, but he had invested in many other businesses as well, including the Charlotte National Bank, which in 1938 merged with Wachovia Bank and Trust Company. When Sam Scott told Belk he had recently heard from a friend in Lynchburg, Va., about traveling bank examiners checking banks in the Southeast, Belk had confidently replied, "Mr. Scott, there is not a bank in Charlotte that is not in excellent shape." He expressed full confidence in the future.

Some weeks later, however, Scott was in the store when Belk, his blue chambray shirt dripping with perspiration, came running up the steps, taking them two at a time. "Come on back to my office," he told Scott. "I want to talk to you." In the office, Belk said he had just come from the witness stand and a grilling by the same bank examiner Scott had told him about. "He even had Cameron Morrison on the stand," Belk said. The bank survived a run by customers, but others did not. Of the eight banks in Charlotte, four closed.

Like everyone else, Belk and his employees took in their belts as conditions grew worse. Salaries were cut, and man-

agers watched every penny to keep bills paid. They struggled to meet payrolls. Karl Hudson in Raleigh, N.C., had to
postpone payday when the bank with his deposits closed
and never reopened. Hudson called employees together and
told them they would have to generate enough sales during
the week to raise the money for their salaries. Hudson made
the payroll, though several days late.

Some Belk managers found themselves having to sell goods
at less than they had paid for them. Their customers just did
not have any money, and the refrain salesclerks heard most
often was, "Don't you have something for a little less?" Store
managers postponed repairs and renovations of their stores,
despite the cramped quarters and dated appearance. It was
hard to think about the future when there were only a few
dollars left in the box each day.

Despite the severe conditions, Belk stores remained open.
In fact, Henry Belk soon was taking over new locations from
owners who could not weather the storm. Belk opened twenty-two stores in 1930 and 1931, most of them in small North
Carolina towns connected by the state-financed road system
begun by Governor Morrison.

With sound credit and available cash, Belk was in a position to buy goods at cut-rate prices. Just before the federal
government's first round of economic recovery legislation
went into effect, Scott went to New York, scoured the market, and returned home with first-class merchandise for one-
fourth to one-third the original price. Back home, he made a
2,000-mile swing through the South, visiting mills. When he
returned to Charlotte, he had put together the largest purchase of goods that he would ever see. "Shortly afterwards,"
Scott later recalled, "we went under the NRA and the value of
the goods doubled overnight."

By 1933, the store sales showed the first increase of any
significance since 1927, but the growing number of stores
accounted for most of that. Workers in the Carolinas were
still on short shifts or could find no work at all. Mills and
factories were begging for work or had closed indefinitely.
On at least one occasion, Sam Scott's orders for Belk stores

were all they had. Take the example of a rocker Scott ordered from Thomasville Chair Company in Thomasville, N.C.

While visiting his sister in Lynchburg, Va., Scott saw a rocker that struck his fancy. Though it had originally been priced at $79, she had bought it on sale for $39. Scott turned it over to find out who had made it, and he copied Thomasville's name and the model number. When he returned to Charlotte, he called the company and asked them to send a salesman by. The next day, a man was there to take his order for the chairs at $14.75 apiece. That salesman thought he had "met the biggest fool he had ever seen in his life," Scott said later. The salesman returned to the factory and told his boss, "We have never sold more than twelve of these chairs to anybody, and he gave me an order for 400 and said he probably could use 1,000."

Scott added just enough to cover freight and the expense of handling these chairs and advertised that any woman who could show she had bought $50 worth of merchandise in a Belk store could get one of these chairs at cost. By the time he finished the promotion, Belk stores had ordered 7,500 of the chairs.

No one was happier about the success than people in Thomasville. With the Belk order in hand, the factory reopened. Townspeople and workers were so happy they marched in a group to the Thomasville store to thank the Belk organization for putting them back to work.

On another occasion, Belk and Scott heard about yards and yards of gingham available at a mill near Charlotte. They bought all the owner had and asked if he could produce more of the gingham and other yard goods that Scott would send samples of. The man "broke down and cried like a baby," Scott said, recalling the visit. "He said he was broke and did not have enough money to buy groceries for the family." Starting production was out of the question in his financial condition. "Mr. Belk told him, 'I want you to go today, and I don't mean tomorrow, to Charlotte and buy enough looms to fill this mill to make the kind of goods that Mr. Scott will send you samples of.'" The plant went back into production, and Henry Belk joined another board of directors.

Though he left most of the buying to Scott and buyers in the stores, Henry Belk occasionally accompanied Scott on trips to New York. He had three or four old friends that he would visit, including a manufacturer who sold him ties for $4.50 a dozen and Thomas Merritt, a merchant from whom he had purchased auctioned goods since the turn of the century. "Mr. Belk would start in at one end," Sam Scott later recalled, "and when he left he would have bought practically everything Mr. Merritt had."

Bargaining with rag merchants was part price and part guile. Yates Laney, then a merchandise manager at Hudson-Belk in Raleigh, was with Belk on one trip when Belk could not get a merchant to agree on a price for 70,000 yards of cloth. The two merchants were a quarter of a yard apart. Someone in the group suggested that each man toss a dime at a nearby crack in the floor. The one whose coin came closest would name the price. Belk tossed and won. As he and Laney left the merchant's warehouse, Belk turned, smiled sheepishly, and said, "You know, that's almost gambling."

In 1934, Belk opened the most stores ever in one year. By Christmas, there were Belk stores in twenty-seven new towns. The 1934 list included locations in the Carolinas as well as Virginia, where the Leggetts were expanding; in Tennessee, where John Parks had left retirement to return to the business; and in Georgia, where Erskine Gallant was expanding his operations. (Gallant had opened the first Belk store in Georgia in Hartwell two years earlier.)

Belk often heard about new business opportunities, particularly about towns where a Belk store might thrive, through his contacts in the Presbyterian Church. Belk was a leader within the Mecklenburg Presbytery, which covered the counties around Charlotte. When he went to synod meetings, one former associate said, a preacher would tell him about a town where a merchant was going out of business or where a building was available for a new store. Belk would follow these leads, traveling to the town on Saturday to measure the volume of the trade and then remaining for church services with the preacher's congregation on Sunday. If both the depth of the business and the depth of the religion were to his liking, then he would arrange to sign a lease or purchase a building on Monday.

Some new locations were the result of sheer chance encounters. In 1934, Belk was returning from a Florida vacation when he stopped in Ocala, Fla., to cash a check. He went to a bank that he thought was managed by an acquaintance from the Presbyterian Church, but he got the wrong one, and the teller refused to take his check. He left the bank and was walking down the street when he bumped into Colin Lindsey. Lindsey had once worked for Belk in Charlotte, selling shoes and serving as Belk's chauffeur in his off hours. The two men fell into conversation, with Belk telling Lindsey about his troubles at the bank. Lindsey finally helped Belk get his check cashed at the right bank, and during their chat, Belk asked Lindsey if Ocala would be a good spot for a store. Lindsey said he thought there was a building available, and the two set off to find it. By April of the following year, Belk-Lindsey was open for business on $18,000 in capital. Belk put up $12,000 and Lindsey $6,000. Belk had added another state.

Belk frequently visited in Florida, where members of his mother's family had resettled around the turn of the century on land Belk had purchased. He had heard as a young man that a grower could make $1,000 an acre from orange groves, and he had snapped up fifty acres at a ridiculously low price. The groves proved to be a source of income for the Walkup branch of the family, who managed the property for Belk, and a source of oranges for Belk, who shipped them to his favorite partners and relatives. The Belk family always stopped in Macintosh, a small town not far from Ocala, where he always paid a lengthy visit to his cousin, Ginnie Robinson. She was disabled with arthritis, and the Belk visit offered the only relief for her daughter to get away for some time to herself. The Belks, with their maid and chauffeur, would perform the chores.

During the stay, Henry Belk would sit on the porch of his cousin's house and visit at a nearby country store. M. C. Quattlebaum's father owned the store. As a teenager, Quattlebaum always liked to see the Belk family arrive because he knew he would have cash in his pocket by the end of the day. Belk gave children a dollar if they could recite the abbreviated version of the Presbyterian catechism. If a youngster could recite the Shorter Catechism—named for its writer, not its length—then he would pay five dollars. Quattlebaum learned them both and, he said years later, "I'd hit that old man up for six bucks every year." In 1941, when Lindsey brought Quattlebaum to Charlotte to check with Belk before setting him up in a store, Belk gave his complete endorsement to the new manager. "He's OK," he said. "He knows the catechism."

Lindsey was a nimble merchant. He filled his store with the standard order of goods for a small town store and with items not often found in Belk stores farther north. Lindsey sold venetian blinds, for example, installing them himself. He also established a delivery route of sorts, taking orders in his hometown of Macintosh and filling them weekly when he returned for the weekend to visit family.

Lindsey and other managers expanded into new lines with Belk's blessing. Belk had few rules, virtually none if a man was making a profit and keeping his expenses down. Sarah Pharr, who now was secretary to Belk as well as to Frank Matthews, prepared weekly summaries of the stores' previous week's sales. She arranged the numbers in spreadsheet fashion on a legal pad, and then added an accordion fold so Belk could follow the tabular information across the page. His rule of thumb was that operating costs should not exceed 18 percent. When a manager's costs climbed near that figure, or went higher, he was sure to hear about it, either from Belk personally or by letters that Sarah Pharr typed. Belk was stern in his reproof, but he always closed with an encouraging word.

Belk also stayed on the road, often dropping in unannounced for visits with his managers. He was not trying to catch his men unawares; he simply preferred the informality. When he was known to be in the area, however, store managers telephoned ahead to tell the next manager down the road Mr. Belk might be headed his way.

Managers enjoyed seeing Belk, but they also wanted to have the store looking its best when he arrived. He would review their stock, talk about the community, and offer suggestions for improvement. If Belk was coming, the manager would see that the windows were properly dressed, the stock was straight, and the floor clean. The floor cleaning often had to be repeated when Belk left. Belk chewed tobacco constantly and frequently left a reminder of his visit at the corner of a stairway or behind a counter.

Archie Hampton was the manager in Laurinburg when Belk came calling shortly after Hampton had taken over the new store there in the early 1930s. Hampton had worked for John Hensdale, first in Fayetteville and then in Dunn and Rockingham, before moving to Laurinburg, a farming community near the South Carolina line. Belk was not in Hampton's store long before he noticed some shoes that Hampton was trying to get rid of. They had come with the initial shipment of opening goods, perhaps from Scott's fire sale, and had not sold well. He had marked them down to get them out of the store. Belk told Hampton he thought leather prices were on the rise. "I believe a good merchant would keep that price up there. I don't believe I'd reduce," he said. "I'll tell you what you do. You mark those back up, and the next time you're in Charlotte, you tell me how many you've sold."

"I didn't sell a single pair of those shoes at that price," Hampton recalled years later. The next time he was in Charlotte, for a meeting of managers, Hampton heard Belk tell others about the store he had visited where shoes were priced lower than he thought wise. "He didn't mention names, but if anybody looked at me, they would have known who it was." Hampton said he did not dare disagree with Belk's strategy and tell him about his sorry sales. "That was his way of trying to keep you from overdoing something. He was smooth about that kind of thing."

Belk usually did not direct his managers to do something. Instead he offered "suggestions" as he had to Hampton. But he did not mince words either. On another occasion, Sam Scott and Henry Belk had stopped in a newly opened store to check on progress. There were only two customers in the place. In addition, Scott recalled, "they had nothing that Mr. Belk liked to see in the windows as he went around, such as fifty-cent neckties, ninety-eight-cent overalls, the biggest pair of shoes in the house for ninety-eight cents, and sheeting for five cents a yard. He told this young manager that he didn't believe he knew how to run a Belk store."

Scott said a few days later, after the two had returned to Charlotte, Belk spotted a Leggett store manager who looked much like the young manager they had seen a few days before. "Mr. Belk got him down and commenced telling him what a poor window he had," Scott recalled. "Finally, I went up to Mr. Belk and said, 'This is not the man we went to see. This is one of the Leggett store managers.' He apologized to him profusely."

While a store manager would certainly know Belk on sight, sometimes his help would not. When Belk walked into the Spartanburg, S.C., store one day, a salesman approached him before the manager could get to the door. "What can I do for you today?" the salesman asked. Belk said he had been thinking about a serge suit, but he did not believe the store had his size. The clerk reached for Belk's collar to check the size and said, "Well, you sure need a suit as this one has faded." Other clerks in the store knew Belk but did not tell the clerk, who proceeded to sell the old man a suit, a shirt, and a hat. He then looked at Belk's feet and suggested a pair of new shoes.

While the salesman was fitting the shoes, he said, "My name is 'Red' Fain, and I'm glad you came in to see us." Belk reached for his hand and said, "Well, my name is Henry Belk, and you keep working like this and you will be manager of one of my stores." O. N. Fain did succeed to manage a store. In fact, he was later responsible for five stores, called the Leader Stores, that he opened in South Carolina towns to sell specially priced, marked-down merchandise, particularly piece goods. The Leader Stores claimed to have the largest selection of fabrics in the country.

Frank Stevens often traveled with Belk. They shared the same conservative philosophy of merchandising. A Belk store should be a farmer's headquarters, Stevens told the managers he posted in towns like Mount Airy and Shelby. He wanted in every manager's inventory an ample supply of unbleached sheeting, cheesecloth, an array of piece goods, and sturdy work clothes. Five-cent shoestrings, ten-cent socks and ninety-eight-cent plow shoes must always be in view. He did not make a fuss about nice fixtures. Recalled Archie Hampton, "Mr. Frank believed that if you fancied a store up too much you might run some of your customers off."

While Stevens's approach to merchandise matched Belk's, he was more concerned about streamlining the operation of the stores and consolidating common services. The buying service, for example, had helped the Belk stores pool their buying power and get better prices. The New York office helped local managers find bargains and keep track of fashion changes. Stevens had other things in mind, too.

In 1935 E. A. Anderson, Belk's accountant and internal auditor, was called in to see Stevens and Belk, who were concerned about fire-insurance coverage for the stores. Fire was a merchant's constant worry. Most store buildings were old. Wiring was inadequate. Wooden floors soaked with cleaning oil and piles of fabric and dry goods burned quickly. Sprinkler systems were unheard of, and the smallest flame threatened to reduce the dry stock inside a Belk store to ashes well before firemen could respond. Belk's own Charlotte store had been damaged several times. The last blaze, in 1931, had nearly closed the doors on the recently renovated store. He had collected on the insurance and reopened, but Belk knew nothing could repay a merchant who lost his customers during remodeling or relocation because of fire.

From time to time, store managers had called on Anderson

for help in settling insurance claims. Based on that experience, he told Stevens and Belk that coverage of Belk stores varied from town to town, partner to partner. Some carried too much insurance, driving their operating costs up, and in other stores, managers trying to improve their balance sheets scrimped on insurance and gambled that fire would not close them down. Anderson had advised managers of what he found and made recommendations, but his involvement in their affairs encountered objections. They did not like interference of any kind from Charlotte store officials.

Despite these objections, Anderson left the meeting with instructions from Stevens and Belk to consolidate insurance and provide uniform coverage for the stores. It was a mammoth task, requiring review of carloads of existing insurance contracts for more than one hundred stores. Anderson moved into space on the fifth floor and went to work. When he had finished, he had saved enough in premium charges to cover the cost of operating both the New York and Charlotte buying services.

After successfully combining insurance coverage for the stores, a year later Anderson worked with Sam Scott to introduce a group insurance program for store managers and buyers in the Belk stores. Cutting costs helped stores stay in business. Group insurance coverage also helped attract good people to the business.

Stevens's success in consolidating these services was not his first. Four years earlier, in 1931, Stevens had introduced Belk's first private-label merchandise in response to the tough competition in Winston-Salem. The rapid growth of Winston-Salem, which was full of tobacco workers and was an important farming center, had attracted many merchants besides Frank Stevens. Particularly troubling was the added advantage that the J. C. Penney store had with its private-label goods. Penney's could sell work clothes and other merchandise cheaper than Stevens could buy them from traveling salesmen, and the Belk buying service could not provide a steady supply. Farmers in town for the tobacco markets might take the Belk-Stevens pencils Stevens's boys gave away to attract attention at the warehouses, but customers headed straight up the hill from the tobacco markets, past Stevens's store to Penney's, to buy their overalls.

Denim overalls, cut high in the front with straps over the shoulders, were the workingman's uniform. Factory workers and farmers alike wore them daily, changing into dressier clothes only for special occasions. When Stevens saw Penney's drop the price on their Payday overalls to one he could not possibly match, he called on Frank Matthews. They worked out a plan to fight back. Working with Matthews, Stevens found a Tennessee manufacturer who would make blue denim overalls for him for less than a dollar a pair, a price that would let the stores beat Penney's price and make a small profit to boot. He placed the first order and gave his new merchandise the name of Red Camel. He got the idea from R. J. Reynolds's Camel cigarettes, the brand many of his Winston-Salem customers owed their paychecks to.

The first shipment arrived and Stevens beat his competition. Before long, other Belk managers were placing large orders. They had a quality piece of clothing, at a price they could use to draw customers into their stores. And, best of all, if customers liked the Belk brand there was only one store to shop for another pair.

A tobacco farmer in town to sell his crop could walk up the street to Stevens's store and pick up a pair of overalls for a dollar and pay twenty-five cents for a blue chambray work shirt. The following year, Stevens and Matthews had a second overall label, called Bloodhound, a name borrowed from a popular plug of chewing tobacco, which they sold even cheaper than Red Camel. And within a few years, Belk had the Red Camel brand on a variety of denim work clothes and a work shoe manufactured by Craddock-Terry Shoe Company.

Stevens's creations were born of necessity, but the private-label business, combined with Belk's fast-growing network of stores, moved the business into another dimension. Within a few years, before the outbreak of World War II, the private-label market would grow and help carry the business into the postwar expansion of the retail business. In time, even Stevens's Red Camel label would reach popularity among a group of customers he never knew. Red Camel, the label he created for farmers and factory workers, emerged in 1987 as a label on women's and girls' sportswear.

Thomasville
Rockers
and Red
Camels

On August 15, 1937, an announcement by Belk Brothers Department Store in Charlotte captured the headlines of the *Charlotte News*. In its largest machine type, spread across the full front page, the newspaper reported that Belk had signed a contract for a $300,000 extension of its East Trade Street store through to East Fifth Street. The Charlotte store was expanding again just ten years after the last major addition. The newspaper article was accompanied by an architect's rendering of the new Fifth Street front. The facade featured clean art deco lines, quite a contrast to the curlicues and flourishes on the other end of the block on the East Trade Street front. J. A. Jones Construction Company said it would complete construction in six months.

The addition would add about 20,000 more square feet, eight times the space Henry Belk had in his first store. With 186,000 square feet, the enlarged store would have ample room for an expanding line of goods and features that fully qualified Belk as a department store. New departments were planned, and Sam Scott and his staff in the buying service on the fifth floor would have more room for their growing business. Scott's buyers were now purchasing merchandise from 150 or more mills and factories in the two states. In one year, Belk bought more than $25,000 in men's and boys' caps from one manufacturer alone. Three to five railcar loads of Charles Cannon's towels were shipped to Belk stores each year, and Belk buyers were even importing linens directly from Ireland.

Charlotte, the South, and Belk stores had survived the worst of the depression, the longest period of economic stagnation the nation had known. Piedmont textile mills were running full shifts. "The sound of the spindle is sweet," a Gaston county minister told his congregation of mill workers, "if we can but realize that we are helping to clothe the people of the world." The region showed signs of pulling itself back together again. Charlotte was building its way to a population of 100,000 citizens by 1940, and the city's boosters claimed Charlotte to be the textile center of the world and the trading center of the Carolinas. The city had its own center of art and culture, the Mint Museum, and supported a symphony orchestra. It also had the highest homicide rate in the Carolinas.

Buses were about to replace streetcars downtown. Eastern Airlines provided service through the small Charlotte airport, which had opened through the determination of Mayor Ben Douglas. The city's daily newspapers, the afternoon *News* and the morning *Observer*, were fighting for circulation, and radio had become a permanent part of everyday life. WBT, the South's first radio station, founded in 1920, was a full-fledged member of the CBS network and carried the latest in national programming, including *The Lone Ranger*, *The Romance of Helen Trent*, and late-night concerts of classical music.

Henry Belk was seventy-five when workers began tearing down the small buildings on East Fifth Street to make way for his very large one. Normally vigorous and active, always on the move visiting store managers in towns across the South, Belk was housebound, crippled by arthritis. His wife, Mary, and his eldest son, Henry, stood in for him when store officials posed beside a steam shovel for a newspaper photograph when construction began. Despite his disability, Belk kept abreast of business in his stores. Sarah Pharr forwarded weekly reports on sales from the more than 150 Belk stores. If store managers and others from Belk's operations needed to see him, they conducted business in the living room of the Belk home, just a few minutes' drive from the store.

Belk Brothers Company, Belk's leading store and the largest department store in the region, was in the charge of George Dowdy, who had assumed the management of the store in 1933. Dowdy had developed a reputation as a bold merchant, eager to try new things. Trained by the Belks, he had begun his career as a teenager working as a clerk in menswear in the Durham store. He had subsequently been promoted to manage a variety of departments in the store. Before coming to Charlotte, he had been assistant manager in Danville under Fred Leggett and then had managed the Concord store.

Dowdy had been raised on a farm outside of Durham. He had the build of a field hand—he stood six feet five inches tall, weighed about 225 pounds, and wore a size 14 shoe—but had the style of a gentleman. He was clever and quick thinking and often told a story on himself about an early encounter with Henry Belk. As a young clerk, he had slipped off to the stockroom in the Durham store to rest and recover from a late date the evening before. In the quiet of the back reaches of the store, he fell asleep with his head in his hands. He awoke and recognized the toes of the shoes in front of him as belonging to Henry Belk. He remained in his pose for about ten seconds, then said a quiet "Amen" and looked up to speak to Belk. Belk returned the greeting, noting the prayerful gesture, and commented on Dowdy's reverent nature to the store manager.

Dowdy arrived to assume management of the Charlotte store when the business was recovering from a disastrous fire. Just before 2:00 P.M. on July 13, 1930, a Sunday, a man in a car on East Trade Street spotted smoke coming from the windows of the Belk store. He sounded the first alarm, and firemen arrived to find the basement ablaze from a fire feeding on linoleum squares stacked for sale and automobile tires stored in the basement. Soon, flames and heavy black smoke spread through hollow interior columns to the third floor. The columns, steel beams covered with wood, became chimneys for the blazing basement, sucking heat, flames, and smoke up through the center of the building. The thick smoke billowing from open windows in the upper stories could be seen clearly from the homes in Elizabeth Heights. Belk's family watched in awe from their home on Hawthorne Lane.

Charlotte Fire Chief Hendrix Palmer left only a small contingent of his force in reserve and called virtually every available man and piece of equipment downtown. As news spread, he received calls from departments in outlying towns which volunteered support. Onlookers filled East Trade and College streets. The *Charlotte Observer* reported that 50,000 people—half the city's population—turned out to watch. It was Charlotte's worst fire in years. Ten firemen trying to control the burning rubber and tar-based linoleum were injured when the first floor of the building collapsed into the basement. Damage was estimated to be about $300,000. Charlotte and the Carolinas had been roasting under unusually hot summer temperatures. The chief speculated that fumes from a recent repainting of the interior had been ignited by a spark.

This was not the store's first blaze. Fire had heavily damaged a warehouse of the Charlotte store in 1910, and a fire had broken out in the store in 1913. In 1923, the main store had been heavily damaged by a blaze that broke out in an adjacent hardware store. Smoke and water damage had been extensive. In 1930, Frank Matthews stood with Henry Belk on the street and watched their store burn again. When it was over, the basement was four feet deep in water. The adjacent buildings occupied by the men's store and shoe store were intact, as was the bargain store on College Street, but goods throughout all the buildings were damaged by water and smoke. Sam Elliott, a young clerk, was one of those assigned to lay out salvageable goods for drying. He and others carried soggy clothing and bolts of fabric to the flat rooftops of downtown buildings, where the hot sun and high temperatures that had wilted Charlotte and much of the state for weeks now helped prepare goods for the fire sale. Until the merchandise could be collected, Elliott stood guard at night, nervous about the pistol he had been given to protect Mr. Belk's property.

The store reopened almost immediately and operated out of the College Street location and the building housing the men's store and shoe store, while workers reconstructed the main store.

The Charlotte retail competition was much tougher than

that George Dowdy had known in Concord. J. B. Ivey and Company, Mellon's, and smaller speciality stores for women and men catered to the wealthier customers in town. Belk's was locked in daily combat with Efird's, a longtime rival in Charlotte and more than thirty other towns in the Carolinas. Efird's and Belk's had hopscotched across the Carolinas following each other to one small town after another. One day Belk's would have fabric on special and then feature summer frocks the next day. Efird's, located just around the corner in its large new building on Tryon Street, would respond in kind. Both kept a worried eye on Sears, Roebuck and Company and Montgomery Ward, whose national buying and manufacturing power gave them an automatic price edge.

During the depths of the depression, the two national chains offered goods at prices that Belk found difficult to match. In 1930, when one-quarter of the nation was out of work, Ward won customers by extending credit to those who purchased twenty-five dollars or more in merchandise, except groceries. "Basically, the American public is honest, meets its just obligations," declared a full-page advertisement that Ward placed in 650 newspapers across the country to announce the plan.

Despite the challenge from Ward, Belk remained on a cash basis. Some Belk store managers allowed their best customers—the bank president's wife or an established businessman—to run a tab, but managers needed their cash and limited any credit. Managers fought competition with price, when they could, and relied on service and their own reputations to keep customers. Belk had now become an old friend to many shoppers. The slogan "Home of Better Values" was more than a decade old when Ward and Sears opened their doors.

If the Monroe store, now managed by George McClellan, husband of Belk's half sister Bessie Simpson, was the mother store for Belk, the Charlotte store was her favorite son. The focus of the Belk organization, it was far larger than most stores and had a wider selection of goods. In addition to Belk's traditional line of inexpensive clothing, piece goods, and household items, customers could find portrait photography services at St. Johns Studio, one of the first lease departments in a Belk store. And the store offered ladies' clothing and millinery a cut above that found in most Belk stores. The Charlotte men's and boys' departments, the undisputed domain of Frank Matthews, also had more flair and fashion.

Matthews cultivated Charlotte clientele like a careful gardener. He had been in the store more than thirty years and was well known in the city, active in church and civic affairs. Children whose parents had shopped at Belk's were now having children of their own, and Sarah Pharr watched the newspaper for birth announcements. She passed the notices along to Matthews, who would see that a new mother received a free pair of size one Red Camel overalls for her newborn, along with an invitation to shop at Belk's. Attention to detail and customer service were Matthews's trademark.

Those who trained under Matthews never forgot their lessons. Sam Elliott, a Matthews protégé, knew the clothing sizes and color preferences of young men from some of the city's best families as well as their mothers did. In addition to boys' clothing at low to moderate prices, Elliott kept his shop stocked with fashions for the young men heading off to Chapel Hill or Duke University. Elliott, who had begun a Belk career of nearly fifty years in the Charlotte store, said Belk did not care much for that, or him, at first. Elliott smoked a cigar, a habit Belk strongly disapproved of, and he was something of a dapper dresser. Elliott's display of pricier men's and boys' clothing nettled Belk. He would stop by the boys' department and ask to see Sam Elliott's five-dollar suits. "He knew I didn't have any and that the cheapest thing I had was ten dollars," Elliott recalled. But that was Belk's way of letting him know he preferred the lower-priced goods in the store and it reminded Elliott to look out for all customers.

Matthews was the reason Belk enjoyed its reputation as a store with a strong menswear line. Matthews and Belk had trained young managers to attract the man of the house to their stores. If the store was in a farm town, then it should

have an ample supply of sturdy work shoes and denim overalls. When a farmer found value for his dollar, Henry Belk
and Frank Stevens reasoned, he would return to outfit the
rest of the family. In the city, Matthews believed the same

was true for a businessman who found a good suit or inexpensive ties and shirts. As a result, early Belk stores were
stronger in the men's lines than in ladies' ready-to-wear or

lingerie. A woman's shopping interests were secondary, except, of course, in piece goods, which curiously did not carry
the lower status of ladies' wear.

As shopping habits changed, particularly in the cities, that
strategy was less effective. By the 1920s, Charlotte ladies
were keen on the latest fashion and the city's stores prominently displayed newspaper advertisements about their most
recent purchases. Mellon's, for example, called its Gray Shop
the "Fifth Avenue Shop of the Carolinas." George Dowdy
had to look no further than his Sunday newspaper to see
that Charlotte women were making more and more buying
decisions and Belk stores must cater to women as their prime
customers.

Dowdy's answer to this growing trend rested, in part, with
Frank Stevens, who was reorganizing Belk's New York office.
After Henry Belk had severed relations with Alfred Fantl,
Stevens had sent one of his men from the Winston-Salem
store to manage the New York office. Stevens, usually a good
judge of men, this time had misjudged. When the new manager, who had been there only a short time, returned to Winston-Salem for a meeting and arrived wearing spats and a
silk hat and holding the leash of a small dog, Stevens knew
he had made the wrong choice. He needed someone who
could relate to Main Street, not Fifth Avenue. The man was
fired, and for several years the office was managed by Emma
Weiss, who had been the secretary hired for Stevens's first
manager.

Sam Scott had spent many of his early years with the
stores in New York and had helped Stevens look after things
there. As Scott's responsibilities in Charlotte increased, Stevens went looking for a new permanent manager. His choice

was R. D. McCraw, who had managed the Winston-Salem store for two years. Stevens had hired McCraw on Scott's recommendation. McCraw, who was then managing a store in Lynchburg, Va., previously had worked at Gilmer's in Winston-Salem, Scott's old store. Stevens liked McCraw's merchant's sense, his flair for writing in-store promotion cards, his energy and ideas, and, particularly, his memory. Stevens kept his business "under his hat," and he wanted someone else who could manage details and figures. The New York job required a person who could deal in odd lots for a variety of merchandise, from piece goods and basic stock to ladies' dresses and millinery.

When Stevens first approached McCraw about the New York assignment, McCraw declined the offer. He had his eye on a partnership interest in the Greensboro store, which was planning a large new building. Stevens insisted and McCraw accepted, but only after making a tour of the state for long discussions with the major partners and a brief visit with Henry Belk. "I had seen Mr. Belk only once before," McCraw said. "He came into the store in Winston-Salem, and it happened to be on a day that I had a big shoe, priced at a dollar and stuffed with paper to make it look better, displayed in the window. He thought that was great."

"When I got to New York," McCraw recalls, "Ray Cline and George Dowdy were with me." The offices were on the third floor of 450 Seventh Avenue, at the corner of 34th and Seventh. The quarters were small, and the staff dealt more in information than quantities of goods. Buyers in the New York office had no money of their own to spend on goods. They simply collected a few samples to show store managers and department heads from the stores when they came to New York to see the fall and spring lines. The New York staff also steered Belk buyers to vendors with the best prices, passed along fashion tips, and helped them place their orders.

When the trio arrived at the office, Ray Cline, manager of the Concord store, opened the door and George Dowdy pushed McCraw through and said, "Now, Bob, get in there and make yourself a job." McCraw was not a welcome sight to the New York staff, who had not been told he was coming to displace Mrs. Weiss. It took nearly six months before he had won the confidence of the staff, and it would be years before he had all the people he needed to handle the additional services he wanted to provide Belk store managers.

McCraw's changes in the New York office meant Dowdy's buyers in Charlotte received faster, easier access to the growing variety of fashions and merchandise in the nation's garment district. But if Dowdy was going to take advantage of the new lines, he needed a store large enough to accommodate goods for the basic Belk customers, plus Charlotte's growing fashion tastes. The announcement in August 1937 revealed the solution to that problem. The new store would be Henry Belk's largest and most contemporary, in both merchandise and styling.

Workmen began construction immediately after the addition was announced. J. A. Jones was eager to meet a May deadline, symbolically important as the fiftieth anniversary of the opening of Belk's first store in Monroe in 1888. The new store would extend 400 feet directly through the center of the block, from the East Trade Street entrance to the new shiny steel doors on East Fifth Street. Every department would be expanded and improved when the revamped store opened.

The plans called for a new dimension for a Belk store. In addition to more sales space, Dowdy also added more comforts for shoppers. Store aisles would be wider and the interior brighter. The mezzanine office area, where Henry Belk had kept a lookout on his main sales floor below, was to be transformed into a comfortable ladies' lounge, with sofas and easy chairs, telephones, writing tables, and a lavatory. An air-conditioned tearoom, with seating for two hundred people, was planned for the basement. And "high-speed" elevators would carry people to the upper floors.

Jones's workers did not make the deadline. It was August 25 before Henry Belk turned the key on the new East Fifth Street entrance and opened the Carolinas' largest department store. Charlotte shoppers, and many a manager who had started with Henry Belk years before, were dazzled by what they saw inside. Gone were the hardwood floors and dark interior and any notion that shopping at Belk was not a woman's prerogative. The new store was well lighted; a new floor covering called Compolite shined with polish. In addition, Belk's now had a French Room, where shoppers could find better dresses and outfits nearly comparable to fashions on sale at Ivey's or Mellon's. At the sides of the main aisles, stylish new store fixtures separated the vast openness of the sales floor into discrete departments. A new china department was added. An expanded line of house furnishings was on the third floor, along with something entirely new, a beauty salon, featuring both "budget" service and an "exclusive" shop. "An expert was employed to plan it," the *Charlotte Observer* reported. "She used her own knowledge and that gained from visiting some of the best known salons in New York." Cosmetics received center-aisle attention on the main floor, a spot previously held by piece goods, which now had a new enlarged location away from the front door.

While shoppers, city officials, and other dignitaries roamed the aisles, Henry Belk stood in the middle of his new store shaking hands and chatting with well-wishers. He stood near the stairway to the lounge on the mezzanine, his old vantage point overlooking the main floor. Architects had provided a new office on the fourth floor with space ample enough for his rolltop desk and a conference table. Just more than ten years earlier, when he and brother John had invited Charlotte to see the new Belk store, three hundred employees had been on hand to greet visitors. This morning, in the largest department store in the Carolinas, six hundred employees helped eager customers take advantage of the opening-day sale bargains.

Not far away from the spot where Belk chose to greet visitors on opening day was something that had eluded him for years—an entrance to his store from Tryon Street. When Henry Belk had chosen his location on East Trade Street in 1895, Tryon Street north of Trade had few businesses. By

1937, however, Tryon Street north and south of Trade had become the state's busiest retail thoroughfare. Prior to remodeling, Belk's had arranged for a store entrance through Woolworth's. Shoppers would no longer have to go halfway around the block to reach the store. Henry Belk's store now had access, however modest, to Tryon Street.

William Henry Belk could not have picked a better alternative to Texas than Charlotte when he chose the new home for his business in 1895. While his decision had been based largely on convenience, he certainly had not been disappointed. The promise of growth and a bright future that Belk had seen in Charlotte had been fulfilled. By the time he opened his new addition in 1938, Charlotte was the leading city in the Carolinas and one of the busiest in the Southeast. The depression had slowed but not stopped the growth of the Piedmont's textile industry, which was recovering to the level of production it had achieved ten years earlier. Charlotte, a city of commerce and finance tied closely to this industry, reflected the renewal of the region and the optimism shown in Belk's new store. Stylish and contemporary, Belk's was a jewel in the Queen City's crown, the largest department store most Carolinians would see in their lifetimes.

Now fifty years old, Henry Belk's mercantile empire was more than a mammoth store in Charlotte. In the intervening ten years since the Charlotte store had last been remodeled, Belk had more than tripled the number of his stores. The original Belk logo, a star with points representing each store, now had so many points that it looked more like the sunburst that eventually would become a familiar symbol on Belk signs and shopping bags. While the Charlotte store was the pride of the company, Belk's customers were more likely to associate the Belk name with their hometown stores, all of which were smaller and generally less sophisticated. Though far from elegant, they were no less valued by local citizens who considered a Belk store (and Belk himself) an important member of their community.

Making every customer feel special was the theme of Stanton Pickens, who spoke to about 450 store employees gathered November 22, 1938, for the annual Thanksgiving dinner. This was a special event, as it marked the fiftieth anniversary of the business. Asked how he had accomplished so much, Belk, in his modest, humble style, said he had observed "the rules of honesty, friendliness and treated all customers with consideration. Kindness is worth a million dollars and it doesn't cost a cent."

The hometown feel of a Belk store was preserved largely as the result of Belk's decentralized style of management, a marvel by most any measure. In 1938, Henry Belk was doing business at 162 locations in seven states; his stores were paying weekly wages to more than 5,000 employees, who by year's end would help generate more than $27 million in sales. Despite the size and range of the business, the Belk network had no more senior management than that necessary to run an operation one-tenth the size. Belk did not have a single vice-president on the payroll; he had no personnel department, no central administration or billing departments; he did not even have a name for this large enterprise. Except for the buying services provided by the New York and Charlotte offices, where store participation was strictly voluntary, the only link from one Belk store to the next was the common bond of William Henry Belk.

The Belk system succeeded because of the faith and responsibility that Belk placed in his partners. They were his handpicked disciples, and he called on them, instead of assistants or vice-presidents, when he needed someone to revive a troubled store or when he found an opportunity to expand and needed an experienced overseer close by. They shared his merchandising philosophy and his Christian values, and they had helped enhance the Belk reputation throughout the region. When a partner opened his first store, the Belk name appeared beside his own on the store signs and sales tickets. By lending his name to the business, Belk helped introduce his partner to the community, giving the business instant credibility. Afterwards, however, Belk's senior partners built their own reputations for honesty, integrity, and fair dealing in their business. They now held positions of trust in the church, in the business community, and with their customers.

Belk's senior partners were strategically located across the Carolinas and Virginia. Belk had not planned the arrangement or the subsequent development of informal territories of operations. This simply had evolved like most things in the Belk operation; a partner would just move on beyond the last outpost of a Belk store to the next promising city. Accordingly, each of the partners had expanded from his first store into smaller towns. Frank Stevens looked after the central part of North Carolina from his Winston-Salem store. He had satellite stores in Reidsville, Mount Airy, Burlington, High Point, Thomasville, Lexington, and Fayetteville. Karl Broome, one of J. G. Parks's protégés, had expanded to towns in the foothills of the Blue Ridge Mountains from his home store in Hickory, N.C. Erskine Gallant had opened first in Anderson, S.C., and expanded to other nearby South Carolina towns. In 1929, he had begun stores in small towns of northeast Georgia. Within ten years, he had more than a dozen stores carrying his name. Parks, after selling out his interest in his North Carolina stores, had established himself in east Tennessee. In 1938, after only seven years with Belk, Arthur Tyler, from his base in Rocky Mount, had opened his ninth store in eastern North Carolina.

When these partners expanded, they usually chose someone they had trained to open and manage their stores for them. Parks had launched several new partners from his Concord store, including Cyrus White and Karl Broome. Frank Stevens had helped train Will Leggett and then assigned him to supervise his new Burlington, N.C., store. In 1926, Stevens had asked John A. Hensdale, whom he and Leggett had trained, to open a new store in Fayetteville in an available building that Henry Belk had heard about from two ladies he had met at a Presbyterian church meeting.

The Leggetts had been the most successful partners with their expansion. By 1939, they had twenty-three stores in which they owned the majority interest, as well as the Durham, N.C., and Danville, Va., stores, where Belk owned the majority of the company stock. They opened stores on borrowed money, bought goods on credit, and turned over merchandise fast to generate cash to buy more inventory.

On occasion, the Leggetts took goods from an existing store to stock a new one. Whenever the stack of merchandise got three feet high on one store's counters, it was said the Leggett boys would level it off and start another store. Henry Belk backed them on each new location and seldom bothered to check on them personally as he did with other partners. "We'd tell them [the Belks] where to send the check," Harold Leggett said, "and they would."

None of Belk's partners had been with him longer than the Matthews brothers. They exemplified the loyalty of the partners to Henry Belk and the family style that characterized the Belk operation. Frank and Mac Matthews were officers and stockholders in the Charlotte store. They had been there almost from the beginning. Frank had come to work in 1899 and had held just about every job in the store, from helper to store manager. He now supervised the men's and boys' departments and handled menswear buying for Belk stores using the buying service. Mac was company treasurer. Brother Houston Matthews had built Matthews-Belk in Gastonia into the largest department store in the county. He had one satellite store, Matthews-Belk in nearby Belmont, and an interest in one more, Belk-Schrum, in Lincolnton. Another brother, Henry, was assistant manager in Gastonia and was looking forward to having his own store. Houston's older sons, Eugene and Houston Jr., were clerking in their father's store, and young Frank, not yet a teenager, distributed advertising circulars after school. On Saturdays he helped at the store and often brought in his father's lunch from home. Houston Matthews would slip off the sales floor on a busy Saturday just long enough to eat a sandwich in the basement.

Houston Matthews's Gastonia store was one of the early stores the Belk brothers had opened. There had been two managers before Matthews moved there in 1910. Gastonia had just changed its charter to read "city" instead of "town" when Will Kindley opened the business in 1901 as Kindley–Belk Brothers Company. The county fathers were disappointed in the 1900 census count—only 27,903—but still Kindley found enough customers to report an early profit to the Belk brothers. Within a few months after he took over, he had expanded his sales force from three to eight.

Kindley stayed in Gastonia three years, then left the company, returning later as a department manager in Greensboro. John W. Kirkpatrick, one of Kindley's salesmen, succeeded him, but he left in 1910 to open Belk-Kirkpatrick in York, S.C. Houston Matthews, recently married, and personally trained by his older brother, Frank, and by Henry Belk himself, came to Gastonia to stay.

The Gastonia store had a prime location on West Main Street. The railroad station was just out the back door, across a vacant lot where farmers and rural folk parked their wagons for Saturday shopping excursions. When Belk chose a building for his store, he wanted ample parking for customers who had come from out of town. The store was small, but it was a challenge to young Matthews.

Not long after he moved to Gastonia, Houston showed up at Belk's desk one morning, discouraged and disappointed with his performance. He could not do any good with the store, he told Belk. Belk was not going to give up on his protégé. As he had with Karl Hudson a few years before, he sat Matthews down and restored his spirits, offering encouragement to the young merchant. Belk had seen what the Matthews brothers could do, and he believed Houston was made of the same stuff. If he tried hard enough, Belk told Matthews, he could make a go of it. Now, Belk said, get back to Gastonia and go to work. Belk's counseling helped. By 1919, Matthews was a familiar figure in town, and when the Belk brothers offered him stock in the company, he eagerly accepted. The first sign reading "Matthews-Belk Co." went up over the store's display windows.

Gastonia's future looked promising. More than one hundred cotton mills were operating in the county, and more were on their way. In the 1920s, local boosters adopted the slogan "Organize a mill a week." They fell short of the mark, but by 1929 Gaston County was the leading textile county in the South and third in the nation. Houston Matthews's store grew right along with the town. As business increased and Matthews ran out of space in one building, he would expand to adjacent buildings as they came available. By 1930, Matthews-Belk occupied much of the block on Main Street. (The Danville stores would in time occupy as many as nineteen separate buildings, all linked together as one unit.)

Like all Belk managers, Matthews was resourceful, and he was a careful shopper. He knew businessmen in the area who could give him good deals on fabric and finished goods such as hosiery, sheets, and blankets. Traveling salesmen called regularly from Belk suppliers like Craddock-Terry Shoe Company. Gastonia was located on the main railroad line, and Matthews's store was within sight of the Arrington Hotel, where salesmen put up for the night. Piedmont and Northern Railway's regular trolley service to Charlotte made it convenient for Matthews to monitor Sam Scott's merchandise on the fifth floor of the Charlotte store.

When the Belk protégés left to open their own stores, they carried with them a special interest in the part of the business in which they had received their training. Houston Matthews's background was in shoes. He had sold them in the Charlotte store and had bought them when he accompanied Henry Belk on buying trips. In time, Matthews-Belk became widely known as the place in Gaston County to buy shoes. Arthur Tyler's interest was housewares, and his stores had more furniture and household items than most Belk stores. John Hensdale had supervised Frank Stevens's ladies' wear departments in the Winston-Salem store while he attended night school. His stores reflected that early responsibility. Down the rail line in Anderson, S.C., Erskine Gallant's store had one of the largest selections of piece goods in the state. Gallant had spent more than ten years selling fabrics in the Charlotte store under the watchful eye of Henry Belk before Belk suggested he find a place for a store. In fact, Gallant had spent so many years reaching high on the shelves to pull the heavy bolts of cloth that one arm had developed more than the other and his wife had to take a tuck in the sleeve of his shirts to give him a proper fit.

The independence Belk gave his partners produced small, large, and medium-sized stores that had much in common but also were very different. All Belk stores carried the same sorts of clothing and goods, but there was no guarantee that a blue chambray work shirt purchased in Concord, N.C., would be the same brand as one purchased in Danville, Va. Even after Belk's own buying service evolved, Henry Belk encouraged his managers to shop around. Never throw a salesman out of the store, he told his men. Even if you do not buy something, you should hear him out. You might learn something, he told them.

Other merchants had tried Belk's strategy of sharing ownership in expansion stores. J. C. Penney had used a similar system in the years before World War I when he took on "associates" to manage the Golden Rule stores he was opening in the West. Penney's sytem was discontinued and corporate ownership became the rule in the 1920s, however, just at the time of Belk's early expansion.

Belk's philosophy set his managers apart from the chain-store managers who often rotated in and out of towns with no time to establish any relationship with a community. A Belk manager was not merely accepting a temporary assignment when he left Belk's office to take over his first store; he was expected to extend the same service to the community, particularly the church, that Belk practiced himself. In 1939, Belk dispatched Norman Scott to Columbia, S.C., with more instructions on the affairs of the Presbyterian Church in South Carolina than on store management. "After I came here, he kept asking about the presbytery," Scott told a group of churchmen years later. "I thought I was sent here to run the store." He said he really did not find relief from Belk's repeated questions and directions for churchwork until the local presbytery was reorganized and the church hired a full-time executive secretary.

Belk partners cared about the towns they lived in and

looked for opportunities to improve them. It might be a small gesture, like Erskine Gallant's determination each year to be the high bidder on the first cotton bale sold in the county, or something with deeper meaning and lasting val-

ue. Houston Matthews was a leader in the Gastonia Merchants Association and the Kiwanis Club and an elder in the Presbyterian Church. Karl Hudson spent much of his spare time spreading the gospel according to the Presbyterian church in rural Wake County. Hudson had been raised a Presbyterian, and three years after he moved to Raleigh, he married the daughter of a Presbyterian minister. The denomination was not strong in Wake County when Hudson moved there. A product of the evangelism the Belks supported in Union County, he decided to do his part to spread the faith. On Sundays and Wednesday nights, Hudson was usually in southern Wake County helping teach Sunday School or organize a church. Hudson's son Karl said years later that his father's work in the church is one of the reasons the store enjoys support among customers from that end of the county.

Belk matched his partners' commitment to the communities and was willing to help when called upon. In 1936, Belk was in the Raleigh store meeting with Karl and Will Hudson when Karl told him that Pilot Mills in Raleigh had closed and mill workers were standing in soup lines. "This is a disgrace," Hudson said. "The capital of North Carolina should not have the Salvation Army feeding people of this mill." Belk agreed to investigate, and the group left immediately to drive to the mill, located just outside of the city. Belk found the superintendent and learned that the owners would sell the entire operation—plant, spindles and forty-two houses— for $80,000.

Within a few days, Belk, the Hudsons, and other investors drawn from the Raleigh staff pooled their resources, bought the mill, and within two weeks had it in production, turning out plaid gingham that was shipped straight to Belk stores and other customers. Belk also arranged for the New York buying office to market the mill's cloth. One investor, Yates

Laney, then merchandise manager of the Hudsons' Raleigh store, used the $3,000 he made on the deal to pay for stock in his own store in Chester, S.C., a few years later.

Belk and his partners survived the depression, largely because their stores carried the kind of merchandise that people needed in good times and bad. The stock-in-trade of any Belk store was piece goods, work clothes, and shoes, all at the lowest prices that could be had. While some stores had upgraded their stock during the heady days of the 1920s, managers had not wholly exchanged basics for fashion. Piece goods, for example, remained a fourth or more of the typical Belk manager's annual sales. When customers turned from fashion to economy, Belk managers trimmed prices to suit their customers' pocketbooks. And any stocks of fancy ribbon, expensive fabrics, and stylish clothing they might have would simply gather dust.

Profits were slim, but Belk did not lose a single store during the nation's worst economic disaster. He came close in some communities, however. In September 1932, the store in Goldsboro, N.C., was about to shut its doors because of an impossible increase in rent. Belk called Arthur Tyler in nearby Rocky Mount and asked him to meet in Goldsboro. "I found him on the street in front of our building," Tyler later recalled. "The store was plastered with going-out-of-business signs."

"Mr. Tyler, ain't this a shame!" Belk exclaimed. "You know I open stores, not close them. I have never closed a store in my life." Belk offered the store to Tyler if he would get it back in business.

"After that we looked the town over," Tyler said, "and finally found a very desirable large building, which was formerly a furniture store. We negotiated for this at a very low rental. We opened this store with practically no fixtures, using kitchen tables, plumbing pipes for hanging, and most any type of shelving we could put together without much cost." As manager of this ramshackle start of a business, Tyler assigned Sam H. Hocutt, assistant manager of the Rocky Mount store.

While Belk had not lost any stores, many were in need of repair and remodeling. Belk stores, particularly those located in small towns, were narrow and cramped. Managers used every available inch of floor space to make the most of their rent payments. When they needed more room, they stacked boxes up the wall, hung socks from the ceiling, and stacked luggage high above the showcases along the walls. Merchants had little incentive during the depression to plan a fresh new look for their stores or to consider expansion. Fixtures got a new coat of paint rather than being replaced.

As the economy began to improve, the challenge to Belk stores was whether this network of independently managed stores could continue to compete in a changing market. The level of competition was growing along with the cities and towns of the region. National chain stores like Montgomery Ward, Sears Roebuck, and J. C. Penney were in the larger cities. Small five-and-dimes like Penders or Eagle Stores had raised the level of competition in small towns across the South. The chain operations purchased in large lots, remained close to the markets in New York and elsewhere, and often presented a more contemporary look than local merchants. To compete, Belk managers needed a steady supply of merchandise and the marketing skills to attract the attention of customers who now expected more than the country-store style of business. And they needed larger, more up-to-date buildings.

The Belk partners' first move was to shake some of the country-store flavor from their stores. With new vigor, they began spending more money to create as much talk in the community about the "new" Belk look as about the old Belk prices. One of the first large projects was in Durham, N.C., where Will Leggett remodeled his 50,000-square-foot store and installed the city's first escalators. Another remodeling followed soon in Spartanburg, S.C., at the store managed by partner Grier Hudson. Hudson had left his brothers Will and Karl behind in Raleigh to open his own store in 1932. He had weathered the economic storms, and as the economy improved, he was one of the most active businessmen in town.

Hudson helped organize a new bank for the city and put down the money for the first property transaction on Main Street since the onset of the depression. In 1938, with the addition of the adjoining building, he opened a newly remodeled and expanded 25,000-square-foot store. A year later, Frank Stevens remodeled his Burlington store, now under the management of partner Vance Beck. Gallant, whose Anderson, S.C., store was the largest department store in the state, with 65,000 square feet, expanded to Athens, Ga., and Seneca, S.C., where the newspaper reported that the arrival of a new Belk store was a sign of good times ahead. "The Belk organization is a large one—of 160 stores located in nine states. Executives of the organization are men of broad vision who through years of experience make selections of locations with care. For Seneca to be selected as a site by such a group is a signal honor."

After reopening the Goldsboro store, Tyler opened another in Tarboro that same month, followed by one in Elizabeth City in 1935 and stores in Kinston and Washington in 1936. He opened two more in 1937 and another in 1938.

In 1939, Belk replaced his small store in Greensboro with a stylish three-story building located at the very crossroads of the city. With 88,000 square feet on three floors and the basement, the Greensboro store was the largest and finest of the Belk stores outside of Charlotte. Greensboro architect Charles Hartmann, who also had designed the elegant 17-story Jefferson Standard Building across the street, gave the Belk building a contemporary look. The focal point of the building was the Belk name, set in bold art deco letters placed one atop the other on the northwest corner, overlooking the Square in downtown Greensboro. The building's smooth modern exterior and corner focus gave it the look of the prow of an ocean liner.

Belk spent more than $400,000 on the new store, which had three times the floor space of the old location. Though smaller than the Charlotte store, the Greensboro store included many of the additions to Belk's traditional lines that George Dowdy had introduced in Charlotte. The store featured a beauty shop, photographic studio, shoe repair shop, gift and glassware departments, and more stylish women's fashions than customers could find in smaller stores. And this store was fully air-conditioned. Hartmann even put opaque glass block in place of the usual double-hung sash windows along the north and west sides of the building.

Less than a year later, in June 1940, the Hudsons opened a $500,000 store in Raleigh. Three stories tall, the building extended a full city block from a main entrance on Fayetteville Street, the city's finest retail address, to Wilmington Street. Ten years earlier, the Hudsons had scrambled to meet their payroll. Now, their department store was the largest in eastern North Carolina.

Local newspapers emptied their type trays when a new Belk store opened or an old location was remodeled. Complete sections were published, replete with stories about the improvements to the building, the backgrounds of the manager and his department heads, and a long story detailing the rise of Belk's business from the humble beginnings of 1888. No paper gushed more over the opening of a store than the Elizabeth City, N.C., *Daily Advance* in 1938: "To say that the new Belk-Tyler store is the most modern and attractive of any east of Raleigh would fall short of describing the building in its entirety, say dozens of persons who have passed it by and marvelled at its striking appearance." The story then enumerated the store's modern conveniences, such as its concealed awning, the venetian blinds in all windows, and right and left doors so two customers could enter and exit at the same time.

For the first time, the stores' ambience and appearance were important to Belk managers. And Belk's partners made the most of their innovations. They supplied information to the local newspapers that described the new buildings down to the fuse boxes. Indeed, some improvements were exceptional for small towns. The Belk store often was the first in town to have elevators and the first to be large enough to require entrances from more than one street. Stores in small towns now had Lamson pneumatic tube systems for handling cash transactions; some had carpeting over the wooden floors darkened with years of oiling; others added comfortable smoking lounges for men and women. As stores grew larger and more modern, Belk stores were often the first to be illuminated throughout with fluorescent lights.

As the decade of the 1930s ended, the new face of Belk stretched from the coast of North Carolina at Tyler's Elizabeth City store to Gallant's stores in the heart of north Georgia. Sales in Belk's stores had doubled; Belk and his partners did nearly $30 million in business in 1939. Except for 1930 and 1932, sales had increased every year. Belk's eldest son, Henry Jr., had joined his father as an assistant in his fourth-floor office in Charlotte and was busy helping his father's partners open stores. Yet, despite the new locations, the expanding variety of merchandise, and the growing complexity of the business world, Henry Belk's entrepreneurial style of business was the same as forty years before.

The Belk organization defied understanding by most outsiders. Many retail observers of the day thought the multistate confederation of stores should not be successful, at least not by the standards of big business. The inefficiencies of multiple corporations and the dispersed decision making should have proved fatal years before. What most outsiders did not understand was that the Belk organization was a system of family businesses that, though independent, belonged to a larger family called Belk.

Belk's system has been called a "merchant's democracy" because Belk's partners all started from the same point and aspired to large or small operations depending largely on their own interests and abilities. Regardless of the size of his store, each partner received regular encouragement and support from the Belk brothers. They treated their partners as part of their own families. When the operation was small, they sponsored an annual event that subsequently grew into a system of communication and cooperative learning that continues today. It all started around John Belk's dinner table in Monroe. In 1900, the brothers invited their partners and their employees to John's large and spacious Monroe home for what the newspaper called a "social-industrial" meeting. Held just before Thanksgiving, it was an evening of good food, conversation, prayerful thanks for the blessings of a good year, and recognition of individual accomplishments.

By 1912, the Belks had ten stores, and the annual ingathering had outgrown even John Belk's large home. The banquet now required seating for 375 people—store managers, department heads, and salesclerks—all of whom traveled to Charlotte at the Belks' expense for what at that time was called the "Belk Convention." The Belk people were greeted by an orchestra at the Hotel Selwyn, were served a five-course dinner, and then settled into an evening of inspirational messages from the Belk brothers and others from the Charlotte store. Nearly a dozen speakers, including one who tied the success of the Belk business to the future of the Democratic Party, rose to address the gathering before the evening's agenda was complete.

In the 1920s, Henry Belk organized the Belk Stores Association, and store managers gathered quarterly to share ideas, discuss problems, and, occasionally, receive gentle scoldings from Belk, who was not reluctant to point out potential trouble spots. By the late 1930s, with more than 160 stores in the organization, even this had become too unwieldy. So, annual managers' conventions were organized.

These meetings were both family reunions and business meetings and were put together by Frank Matthews who, in 1940, prepared for the gathering of more than two hundred managers, assistant managers, partners, and others. In typical Belk style, Matthews drew upon the strengths of the members of the Belk management family in preparing his program. Karl Hudson of Raleigh, who had just opened his new store, spoke on the outlook for the future; George Dowdy and Belk's auditor, E. A. Anderson, talked about the importance of keeping proper records; R. D. McCraw from the New York office talked about market trends; and Charlotte attorney D. E. Thigpen talked about tax laws. Managers also heard presentations from buyers in piece goods, shoes and hosiery, bargain-basement merchandise, men's and boys' wear, and ladies' wear.

In addition to the annual conventions, Matthews also organized individual associations for buyers of boys' wear, menswear, and infants' and children's wear. The first was for boys' wear, one of Matthews's favorite departments in the store. In May 1939, Matthews and about twenty boys' wear department managers met at a family-style country restaurant on the shores of the Catawba River near Charlotte. Matthews explained that the idea of an association for Belk buyers had come to him when he attended a national meeting of boys' wear buyers. Why not do the same for Belk people? Together, he said, buyers could share ideas, selling tips, and information on trends and fashion. A year later, Matthews formed a similar group for menswear buyers. When the two groups met together in September 1940, more than one hundred store people joined him at the river restaurant for a day-long business meeting.

Matthews had arranged for a fashion show—with live models wearing the upcoming fall fashions—motion pictures depicting proper and improper selling methods on the floor, and a talk by Rebecca Elliott from the Charlotte store, who supplied tips on selling to young men. "The boy as he grows older," Miss Elliott said, "prefers a young man to assist him in selecting his outfit, while his mother in shopping for her small son prefers a young lady to help her with problems." She continued, "If we are to make a friend of the boy and continue to sell him, we have to be able to see things in his light—in other words, to speak his language."

A month later, the infants' and children's wear association met in Charlotte. J. C. Williams of Belk-Williams in Wilmington was the luncheon speaker. "There are three types of customers," Williams told the group. "The first is 'Mr. and Mrs. Rockefeller.' Many salespeople make the mistake of paying undue attention to this type of customer, to the point of ignoring the other types. Mr. and Mrs. Rockefeller have the purchasing power, but they are not our type of customer.

They are not the ones we are going to make any money out of." The average customer, Williams said, is "the type that is trading in our stores. And they are more important than the rich customer." But, he warned, don't forget the "below-the-average customer. Of all the groups, it is the latter group that we need to pay more attention to. Try to make them feel welcome in our stores."

Henry Belk could not have said it better. After fifty years of growth, the Belk philosophy remained unchanged despite the social and economic changes in the region that had reshaped the South from a predominantly rural society to a region of cities and towns. Belk's stores were still for the average person. However, this no longer meant just farmers and mill hands who bought the same denim dungarees and work shirts year in and year out. Fashion and style were now taught as being of equal importance with courtesy, personal service, and attention to a customer's needs. With merchandise in good supply, Belk's stores increased their stock and, instead of waiting for closeouts and end-of-season specials to become available on the markets in New York, as they had once done, Belk buyers were asked to follow Miss Elliott's advice to be "the first in town to show a new item."

A decade before, the onset of the depression had stalled Belk's growth throughout the region just at the time Belk's partners were beginning to establish themselves. Now, World War II threatened to halt the upgrading and improvements in the stores begun since the economy had begun to recover. When America retooled for war, fashion and style were exchanged for basic needs.

The nation's wartime expenditures did not flow proportionately to the South, but it seemed that wherever the dollars for the war effort were being spent, a Belk store was close by. America's young men poured into the region to be trained at large installations in Columbia, S.C., and Fayetteville, N.C., and other smaller posts located throughout the region. And the men that were not training were building. Military installations grew from sleepy Southern outposts to major depots in the military's archipelago, almost overnight.

Of equal importance to Belk was the increased demand on the textile industry and other industries, which returned people to regular paychecks, adding more dollars to the cash boxes of many Belk stores. Altogether, the war meant an additional $2 billion in business for North Carolina's industries.

More than one hundred Army, Navy, Marine, and Coast Guard stations were established in North Carolina alone. They ranged in size from a small airfield near Maxton, which was turned into a glider base with a 6,000-foot runway, to nearby Fort Bragg, which swelled from 5,000 to 100,000 men virtually overnight. Many of these newcomers were construction workers who came to build barracks, training areas, and classrooms for the world's largest artillery base. Fayetteville nearly collapsed under the pressure. Housing was impossible to find. Local citizens rented rooms in their homes, at times putting four to six workers in a bedroom.

To meet the demands of workers who needed dungarees, work shoes, and shirts, John Hensdale cordoned off a section of the men's department in the Belk-Hensdale store in Fayetteville and posted special store hours just for the men who came to the city to help build Fort Bragg. Hensdale's sales clerks could not keep enough Red Camel dungarees, jeans, cotton chambray shirts, and heavy work shoes in stock. Resupply orders were placed weekly, after the store closed on Saturday night, to insure that another shipment would be in town for the Wednesday specials.

On the eve of America's involvement in the war, R. D. McCraw in the stores' New York office had urged Belk's partners to increase their purchases. If the United States joined in the world war, an allotment system was sure to be imposed, restricting the supply of all materials, particularly textile goods, which were a store manager's bread and butter. Without a steady supply of piece goods, Belk stores would be in trouble. As 1941 rolled to a close amid war fever, McCraw talked some managers into taking all the money they had available, including cash banked for year-end dividends, and placing the largest orders they could. Many like Wyche Horton, manager of the Belk-Leggett store in Durham, and Karl

Hudson in Raleigh, took his advice. When restrictions were imposed limiting orders to no more than what customers had received before the war, those Belk managers who had listened to McCraw were in better shape than those who had not anticipated the changes.

In the years that followed, McCraw scoured the New York markets to keep Belk's stores stocked. One part of his job was to make sure that manufacturers fulfilled orders placed by the stores. The other was finding merchandise to buy. "You worked both sides of the street and tunneled under, if you could," he recalled later. "A lot of times I used to go out about 9:30 A.M. and stay out all day. It's amazing the amount of goods you could pick up as you went along."

Back home, Belk's managers and buyers, who had been shopping the area mills for years, used their personal contacts with mill owners to stock their stores. Some mills, like Springs Mills Company, made sure the Belk stores in their area had sheets and other items made at home. Col. Elliott Springs, head of Springs Mills in Rock Hill, S.C., told Yates Laney, then managing the Belk store in nearby Chester, to place his orders and they would be filled without question. Springs said he did not want the stores where his workers shopped to be without the goods they were making.

Sometimes a sharp-eyed buyer would find material in search of a buyer and trade one lot of goods for another. Laney once located 2,000 yards of unsold cotton pocket material, enough to finish one hundred men's suits. He bought the pocket material and then swapped it to a New York manufacturer who had suit material but nothing to make pockets from. "I swapped one yard of mine for three yards of theirs," he recalled.

The war stripped stores of experienced managers and salespeople just at a time when Belk and his partners were expanding again. Yet they managed to find enough people to open thirty stores between the Pearl Harbor attack in 1941 and the end of the war in the Pacific in 1945. The war had not dampened spirits or promotional zeal. When Henry Matthews reopened his expanded and renovated store in Macon,

Ga., a store he had opened in February 1942 after working with his brother Houston in Gastonia for ten years, he advertised airplanes for sale. Customers could pick up a new Luscombe Silvaire, a 19-foot metal plane with a wingspan of thirty-four feet, at the store. The plane cruised at a speed of 100 miles per hour. There is no record of any sales.

Managers who were not called to duty, or who remained at home for medical reasons, handled the extra work load. In the Dillon, S.C., store, the manager's wife replaced her husband when he left for the service. Belk also found a supply of help in salesmen who had once called on the stores. Their companies no longer needed salesmen; they could sell anything they had to customers like Belk, who were begging for goods. Besides, there was no gasoline available to keep a sales force on the road.

The war years strengthened the Belk business. Henry Belk had tripled the number of stores in the 1930s, and his sales had doubled. By the end of the war, sales were two and a half times what they were at the end of 1941 though the number of new stores added during this time was only one-sixth the number in 1941. The war helped partners pay off long-standing debts from the depression and put money in the bank to use to continue expansion through the rest of the decade, when goods were more plentiful and a new generation of managers had returned from the war.

When Henry Belk held his stockholders' meetings in the years after the war, the sons of many of his senior partners joined their fathers in this annual accounting. A second generation of Hudsons and Matthewses and Gallants was preparing to enter the business, just as Henry Belk's own sons were returning to take up positions in the company. Beginning in January, as soon as the books were closed for the year, the meetings took several weeks as the formal business of all of the corporations Belk owned was conducted in front of his rolltop desk in Charlotte. By 1950, three hundred such meetings—one for each store corporation—were held, one right after the other. Partners and their managers formed lines outside Belk's office, waiting their turn to be called to account for the year's business. They would meet with Belk, and if their stores had been formed before 1928, with Dr. John Belk's heirs, Frank Stevens and his sisters-in-law.

Though Belk was approaching ninety years of age in 1951, the meetings followed a routine unchanged over the years. Belk, alert as ever, kept track of financial details of each store, scribbling penciled notes in a ruled notebook that in earlier years he was likely to have pulled from a stack of school pads in stock in the store. When a store had had a difficult year, a manager could expect a grilling; the man with a sorry record approached the bar with dread. If there was time, Belk often questioned his partners and their men about business affairs in their communities, local politics, and the condition of the Presbyterian Church. These reports provided a reasonably accurate survey of consumer confidence and the strength of the economy and, though informal, were a useful planning tool for the business. Finally, Belk would pronounce judgment for a manager who had passed the test. "Well," he would say, "it looks like the sheriff won't have to close you up." Then the manager was excused as the stockholders declared their dividends and set the manager's salary and bonus, if there was to be an increase in pay.

In 1952, Belk's partners held the annual meetings without Henry Belk. The year before, Belk had concluded the series of meetings and, as was his habit, had gone to Florida to vacation and visit relatives in Macintosh. He had developed influenza and on his return to Charlotte had undergone surgery at Presbyterian Hospital, now one of the city's leading medical institutions. With the help of Sarah Pharr, his long-time secretary, and a nurse, he had returned to a regular schedule of visits to his office in the new Belk Stores Services building. Even into the harsh winter months, he had shown up for policy meetings and had attended the store's 1951 Christmas party. His sons, who were assuming more responsibilities, and his partners had continued to take major decisions to him.

Early in the third week in February, however, Belk developed a bad cold. When his condition worsened, his doctor tried to find a bed for him in a Charlotte hospital. None was available for the man who had endowed medical facilities throughout the South. An oxygen tent was set up in his home, and he received attention from nurses and doctors at Presbyterian Hospital located just next door. On Thursday, February 21, when a bed became available, he was moved to Presbyterian, where, a few hours later, at 3:30 in the afternoon, Belk died. He was eighty-nine.

Despite Henry Belk's age, his death surprised even those who had been close to him. Belk stores closed the following Friday and Saturday. At first, funeral arrangements remained indefinite as the family awaited the arrival of John Belk, a captain in the Army, who was trying to return home from Japan. He was unable to make the necessary flight connections and would not arrive until two weeks after his father's death, much the same as in 1928 when Dr. John Belk's two daughters, who were traveling abroad, had failed to reach Monroe in time for their father's funeral.

Funeral services were held Sunday at Belk's home on Hawthorne Lane. The Reverend Charles G. McClure, pastor of Caldwell Memorial Church, conducted the services. He had just come from a funeral service for the Reverend John G. Garth, who had been Henry Belk's close friend and fellow laborer in the Presbyterian vineyard. McClure's service for Belk was impressive, but not as elaborate as some expected for a man who had given so much to his church and his community. The theme McClure used in his brief tribute was the lament of David on the death of Abner: "Know you not that there is a prince and a great man fallen this day in Israel?" Belk's partners, men he had trained and brought into the business as teenagers, served as his pallbearers. The service concluded at Charlotte's shaded Elmwood Cemetery, where Belk's grave was marked with a simple headstone.

Newspapers across the state followed with tributes to Belk. The editorials recalled the remarkable growth of a business based on simple principles of honesty and fair dealing, the depth of Belk's commitment to the church and his community, and, the *Charlotte News* said, "the example of his own life, full to overflowing with a certain steadfastness that serves as an anchor in this turbulent age." As many citizens had grown up not knowing another president besides Franklin Roosevelt, many in the South had spent a lifetime with Henry Belk.

The vast mercantile business Henry Belk left behind was unparalleled in the development of the South. He had started small and had grown with the region, building on the products of local industry and, perhaps most importantly, on the people of the South. If anything, the newspapers failed to notice an important legacy. None knew Belk's story quite as well as the young men who had followed him into the small stores in Monroe and Charlotte and who now, years later, were responsible for the day-to-day operation of the business. Belk's merchandising philosophy, and the Christian values he applied to business, would survive well beyond his years because at his death his business remained, as always, in the hands of his partners.

William Henry Belk had resisted designating in his will one of his children to oversee his department-store domain after his death. Henry, the oldest, was the heir apparent, but none of the Belk children had been raised as heirs to one of the largest fortunes in the state. They had received no weekly allowance and had earned their spending money at jobs in the store. The boys had begun working in the store as checkers, wrappers, and helpers as soon as they were able. Tom Belk and Henderson Belk, the two youngest, were busy young merchants at the age of eight in the basement bargain store. They sold overalls, shirts, rose bushes, and other bargains, earning a dollar a day, with an extra dime if they sold their quota of a thousand dollars in merchandise a day. Tom used his to buy sodas at the store's tearoom.

Life for the family revolved around their large home on Hawthorne, the store, and the church. The brothers played football, basketball, and baseball on the large lawns surrounding the house, even forming neighborhood teams to compete with teams from other Charlotte neighborhoods. They sold lemonade from stands in front of the house and played with the family pony, Bobby, and a goat named Billy. There also was an assortment of dogs and cats, and mules were kept in back to cultivate their mother's garden. The children were occasionally a rowdy bunch, but seldom when their father was around. "We were taught to work and not to play," Henderson recalled. Their father was more often at the store than at home, and occasionally Henderson followed him back to the store in the evening when he returned after supper to review store reports and work late. The child frequently curled up for a nap on a counter on the main floor while he waited for his father to finish for the night.

As the oldest, Henry Jr. was the first to take an active part in running the business. When he was in his early twenties and between semesters at college, he returned home to help his father, who then was disabled by arthritis. Henry worked at his father's desk in his office at the Charlotte store. After the elder Belk recovered and returned to his daily routine, the two shared office space. Henry Jr. was primarily his father's chief assistant, but early on he saw the need for more organization within the growing support staff for the Belk stores and began assuming more responsibilities. His father had little use for people or departments that did not turn a profit, but Henry's plans called for more than simply a buying service where store managers visited Sam Scott's sample room and placed orders. More coordination of effort was needed, and Henry saw ways to consolidate common services.

In 1938, Henry, with his father's endorsement, expanded the duties of E. A. Anderson, the company's chief accountant, to include preparation of the corporation tax returns for individual stores rather than leaving them to accountants spread across the South. In 1940 he brought Gibson Smith into the buying office to oversee Belk's large personal and corporate property holdings.

Real estate was an important measure of success to William Henry Belk. He often told his partners that the only money he ever lost on real estate was property he did not buy. Belk encouraged managers to buy their store buildings and to remain on the lookout for adjacent or nearby locations that would be available for expansion. When managers brought a lease in for his signature, he often asked, "Wonder if they would sell?" As a result, when Smith came to work, many of the 150 Belk stores often owned several parcels of real estate and buildings in a variety of shapes and sizes. The paperwork and records for each corporation were in offices and file cabinets in four states. Smith's first task was simply to prepare accurate descriptions of each. In addition, Smith was asked to look after a number of farms in Union County and across the line in South Carolina that Belk had acquired.

World War II interrupted Henry's plans for further development of what was now much more than a simple buying office. Henry left for the Navy, and one by one his brothers joined the war effort. John picked up his Davidson College diploma in 1943 and in less than a week was wearing army fatigues. Tom left Davidson College and joined the Navy; Irwin and Henderson also left college to enlist in the Army. Even if the Belk sons had remained at home, it is doubtful that many more changes would have taken place. Store managers and Belk buyers in New York and Charlotte stayed busy merely finding goods to sell.

William Henry Belk was in his mid-eighties when the war ended and his sons returned home. As they had twenty years before when Belk approached normal retirement age, Belk's senior partners asked who would succeed him as the leader of their organization. Belk was noncommittal. When one group of senior partners paid him a call and asked about the future, Belk simply pointed to the photograph of his five sons and daughter that sat atop his rolltop desk and responded confidently that they were his board of directors.

Henry Belk had no specific plans for his children, although Henry Jr.'s ascension to the top position was an accepted fact. As he had with his partners in the early days, Belk expected his children to find their own places in the business. Not long after John was back in civilian clothes, he met with his father to talk about the future. "Well," Henry Belk said, "what do you plan on doing?" John recalled, "I had a bad habit of smoking, and he saw a cigarette and said, 'You know I don't hire men that smoke.' I said, 'Well, you quit chewing and I'll quit smoking.' And he said, 'Let's go to work.' And that was all that was said. We just came down to the office, and he never did say anything else about it, so I think I was hired." (John did not stop smoking and his father did not quit chewing. His spittoons remained beside his desk at the office and his chair at home until he died.)

John began working in personnel in the Charlotte store, helping store manager George Dowdy and real estate manager Gibson Smith on projects, including the $300,000 air conditioning of the Charlotte store and the construction of the new buying offices on East Fifth Street.

Henderson Belk telephoned his father when he returned from overseas to let him know when he would be home. His father asked him to stay right where he was, in Charleston, S.C., and report to the Charleston store for duty. The manager needed help, the elder Belk said. Stay and do what you can, he said. As it turned out, Henderson did not return to Charlotte to live for several years. After working for a time in Charleston, he returned to college to complete his education and later took store assignments in Columbia, S.C., Asheville, N.C., Henderson, Ky., Thomasville, Ga., and Texas before returning home to Charlotte.

Henry Jr. resumed the lead position when he was discharged and picked up where he had left off, developing the buying office and services to stores. In 1946, he brought in David McConnell, a South Carolina native and Harvard-trained lawyer to organize a legal department. McConnell was a tax specialist with political contacts in Washington. He not only handled company business but helped the senior Belk organize his substantial estate. That same year, Henry tapped people like Sam Elliott, then a leading salesman in the Charlotte store, to join Sam Scott's staff of buyers, and he looked for other opportunities to improve the ranks of the buying office staff now working harder than ever to keep up with demands of the stores. Real estate management was expanded to include construction and maintenance of buildings.

The real task facing Belk store managers in the postwar years was not selection of merchandise but simply finding something to sell. Production could not keep up with demand. Americans were impatient to recover from the rationing and shortages of the war years. When a shipment of cotton fabric arrived for sale at the Belk's Charlotte store, the crowd of women clamoring to get to the counter was such that it prompted a report in the *Charlotte News*. "There was a home-front battle for yardage on the first floor of Belk Bros. Co. yesterday afternoon," the *News* reported April 14, 1945, "as an army of women fought for four yards of pique or dotted Swiss or chambray or most any of the cotton materials that haven't been in evidence on store shelves for quite a spell." Customers grabbed bolts of cloth and cornered sales clerks until someone would take their money. One customer was quoted as saying, "You know, this is bad. You have to grab and run, stand and guard, wait and wait, then pay full price for what you get, only to have someone look at you as if you were stealing."

Though his sons had assumed more responsibilities, the elder Belk remained the central figure in the business and was as interested in details as always. One day, Henderson drove his father to Concord to check on construction of a store expansion. Belk, in his eighties, climbed through the building debris to the third floor level and walked out onto a bare steel girder. Henderson reached to steady his father, who turned and warned him away.

"Leave me alone," the elder Belk said. "You are going to make me fall."

Despite his age, Belk had as sharp a head for numbers as he had had when he was calculating the cost of a sale in his first store in Monroe years before. His secretary, Sarah Pharr, prepared weekly store sales reports by store number, folding the sheet so different balances and sales figures would line up with individual stores. When Belk saw store managers, he would pull the sheet from his coat pocket and, without hesitating at the more than three hundred rows of numbers, quickly refer to their sales for the year and compare them against the last year's results. Young managers, who approached Belk in awe anyway, marveled at the old man's remarkable quickness at connecting store numbers with their towns and with their names.

Even relatively minor changes were cleared first with the elder Belk. When Henry wanted to add Elliott to the buying staff, he called Elliott into his father's office and, with Elliott standing by, asked about moving him from the store, where he managed the boys' department, to the buying service.

"Mr. Belk turned to Henry and said, 'Mr. Matthews depends on this boy,'" Elliott said, recalling the exchange. Elliott was Matthews's best salesman, though he was no "boy."

He had been working in the store for twenty years. Henry persisted and his father agreed. Elliott joined Matthews in the buying service and began shopping the market for boys' wear for all the stores—at a salary increase from $70 to $80 per week.

On the occasion of the fiftieth anniversary of the opening of the Charlotte store, the Charlotte Chamber of Commerce honored Belk with a celebration dinner. At one point in the evening, the elder Belk was asked if he had plans for any additional stores. He replied that he did not, but his sons might. In 1946, Belk and his partners opened twenty-five stores, or an average of one every two weeks. Altogether, the Belks opened more than sixty stores between the end of World War II and the close of the decade. Most were in small towns, including places like China Grove, N.C., a textile town of about 2,000 citizens about thirty miles north of Charlotte. The China Grove business district was little more than one block long.

Any town was a likely target. Henderson Belk was driving his father to Florida in 1949 when the two happened to stop in Thomasville, Ga., in the southern part of the state near the Florida line. "I wanted to run a store myself," Henderson recalls. "So, I said, 'Dad, here's a little town that doesn't have a store in it. Why don't you let me try it?' So we looked around, found a vacant building, and he said, 'Okay.'" Henderson got married, took his honeymoon, and moved with his new bride to Thomasville to run the new store.

Henderson did not stay in Thomasville long. He scouted new locations and eventually made his way to Louisiana and Texas. Henderson Belk found a company looking for a buyer, and he tried to interest his father's partners, the Matthewses in Gastonia and Ogburn Yates in Asheboro, in moving into Texas. Finally, on one trip west, Henderson bought the company's building and fixtures and then returned home to find a partner group to take it on. Henry, his older brother, greeted him saying, "Henderson, if you would go to China, you would end up buying a store building and coming back and wanting to open a store there." The Matthewses later took the building and fixtures and opened Belk's first Texas store in the small town of Paris.

After repeated store openings and hours of preparation for new stores, manhandling bulky counters into place, Henry Jr. had developed a design for store fixtures that made them easier to assemble and more portable, saving time and money. The fixtures were manufactured by Young Manufacturing Company in Norwood, N.C., which had been organized in the late 1930s to build counters, display tables, and other wooden fixtures for Belk stores during the rash of openings before World War II. The business was run by two brothers, one of whom had worked in Stevens's Winston-Salem store. When Stevens had opened a store, he had dispatched Kermit Young to help store managers build counters and display tables.

Most of the initial stock for the new stores was bought through the Charlotte buying office, which had changed little since Sam Scott opened his "sample room" twenty years earlier. The office had a bargain-basement atmosphere. Scott and his small group of buyers worked behind a chicken wire enclosure amidst samples of merchandise and piece goods. Before the store was air-conditioned, the summertime heat cooked employees working on the fifth floor. Salesmen who called on Sam Scott and others in the office were forced to wait on crude wooden benches that often left splinters in the seat of a visitor's pants as a reminder of the visit.

Despite the discomforts, the buying service was a busy place. When store managers received word that Scott had a good deal on merchandise, they would often carpool to Charlotte, with the manager from the most distant store picking up his colleagues on the way in. They looked over Scott's samples and placed their orders. On a given day Scott might have piece goods or a supply of diapers, rocking chairs, or blankets—and all usually purchased in lots of 7,000, a number Scott favored for some eccentric reason. Managers, particularly those from the small stores, depended on Scott for piece goods and also placed orders for menswear with Frank Matthews, who looked after Belk's own private brand, Red Camel shoes and overalls. Abe Craddock, part of the Craddock family that once owned the large shoe-manufacturing company in Lynchburg, Va., helped managers with shoe lines.

While the Belk buying service had remained much the same, the stores and the region it served had not. At the beginning of World War II, most Belk stores were in small, isolated towns. During the 1940s, many of these small towns had grown into small cities. By 1948, Belk customers no longer were just rural folk, farmers, and factory workers who shopped for a good price on a piece of gingham or were attracted to the store by a bargain price on blue denim overalls. A growing number of Belk customers now worked in offices and lived in the suburbs. For Belk to compete, stores needed to stock for fashion, not just price.

In 1948, John Belk assumed responsibility for the buying office and began improving strained relations and rebuilding credibility between the buyers and the new aggressive crop of young store managers impatient with Sam Scott's style of buying for price, not the latest style. The New York and Charlotte offices added buying departments for accessories and ladies' ready-to-wear and lingerie, and expanded their coverage of blouses and sportswear. In 1948, Tom Belk, just graduated from the University of North Carolina, returned home and joined John in the buying office. At about the same time, Guy Byerly, Jr., whose father was a partner in the Mount Airy, N.C., store, left his job there and came to Charlotte to learn the piece goods business from Sam Scott. Sarah Belk also became a buyer for women's wear, dividing her time between Charlotte and the New York office.

New blood and new attitudes did not bring success immediately. The Belk stores had to prove themselves and work into new markets growing in importance in the fashion industry. Belk stores were not generally known among New York manufacturers of fashion merchandise. In the California markets, where the women's sportswear and beach fashion business was developing rapidly, virtually no one had heard of the company. Even if manufacturers knew of Belk, it was not always a plus. Belk buyers were preceded by the company's half-century-old reputation as a group of small bargain stores in conservative Southern towns. While manufacturers might consider putting their goods in some of the larger stores, like Charlotte, Raleigh, or Gastonia, they preferred to do business with Ivey's, which had a more fashionable image. Most simply had a notion that the small Belk stores they had seen in country towns in eastern North Carolina were the Belk stores they would see anywhere. "When I went out to California the first time," R. D. McCraw of the New York buying office recalled, "some of the resources would hardly let us in. They told us, 'You don't have anything but a bunch of country stores over there on the East Coast.'"

Working with George Dowdy, who was eager to upgrade the Charlotte store to compete with growing fashion-conscious stores in the city, McCraw called together managers of twenty-five of Belk's largest stores in the late 1940s. He had found a California buying service, Harry and Sidney Arkins, willing to work with Belk, but he needed the endorsement of the stores to share the cost of the Arkins' services. The stores agreed, and for two years Belk's used the Arkins as sources of buying information and as an entrée to California manufacturers. Later, the buying service absorbed the cost.

When manufacturers and others from outside the region called Belk stores "little country stores," they were not far off the mark in some cases. Even the stores that had improved their appearance and upgraded their merchandise still operated much as they had for years. Belk's auditors helped store managers prepare their accounts, but this large, multistate operation had no uniform systems, even for keeping track of merchandise on the shelves. Managers used a variety of systems, if they had any at all. Most had not progressed much beyond using gross sales as a measure of their daily or yearly business. The problem was that the dollar amounts did not discriminate between lingerie or overalls.

Shortly after he took over the operations of the buying office in 1946, John Belk attended the first school that IBM conducted for merchants. He came back to Charlotte with the outline of a system to help managers, and the buying service, organize inventory by departments. The numbering system could accommodate large or small stores by adding one or two digits. It was well suited for the variety found in the Belk operation. When the system was installed, the Belks, for the first time since their father set up business with a partner, had something more than gross sales to use to follow the flow of business in their stores.

As Belk's sons expanded the operation of the buying service, its offices spilled out of the quarters on the fifth floor of the store into offices in nearby buildings in downtown Charlotte. Henry convinced his father a new building was needed, and the elder Belk picked a site a block east of the store, just beside the railroad tracks. He rebuffed John's arguments to move to a more distant location, which John argued would help distinguish the growing buying service from the store operation. The $450,000 building, outfitted with offices for executives and show space and storage for buying service samples, opened in April 1949. Construction was delayed because of the shortage of structural steel, and the building was put up hastily, creating problems for those who would use it for the next forty years.

In 1950, John turned his responsibilities in the buying service over to his brother Tom and left for Korea, one of thousands of American soldiers President Harry Truman recalled for duty with United Nations forces. His father came to Augusta, just north of Fort Benning, Ga., on the eve of his departure, and the two shared a long visit. It was their last, although the two exchanged letters during Belk's years in Korea.

Tom Belk had been out of college only two years when he succeeded his brother at the buying office. He was young, but Sam Scott had taken him and Guy Byerly, Jr., on as special students, introducing them to the trade. One of the first assignments Scott handed Tom when he came to work in the buying office was to get a Mississippi textile manufacturer to deliver on his contract for a supply of gingham. Scott had a contract for deliveries, but the mill owner would not ship the order unless Belk agreed to pay an additional premium. He dispatched Tom to get the goods.

Belk's first attempts were rebuffed. The man wanted Belk to pay more because he now could get more than when he made his deal with Sam Scott. Belk made no more progress than Scott had made, however. Then Belk learned the man was a sports fan. "I finally heard that he was a big Mississippi State guy," Tom Belk recalled, "and Clemson was playing Mississippi State. So I bet him on the football game. Clemson won, and he delivered the contract."

The same year John Belk left for Korea, one of the country's largest department store chains, Allied Stores Corporation, opened a 200,000-square-foot store in North Gate, the nation's first regional shopping center, located about seven miles north of Seattle, Wash. Built by an Allied subsidiary, North Gate was something quite different from the neighborhood centers, with small shops and a grocery store, that Americans had become accustomed to in the 1930s and 1940s. First, it was big. The center offered parking for 5,000 cars, featured two of each kind of specialty shops inside, sponsored a children's nursery for mothers busy shopping, and had a totally controlled environment. The anchor was a large department store. In addition, the center was located outside of the city and was not associated with any particular neighborhood. The builders placed it on a site convenient to shoppers who would rather drive to North Gate than drive downtown to do their major shopping.

Allied had chosen Seattle after several years of watching the nation's suburban communities grow together, fusing into larger and larger metropolitan areas as subdivisions opened on the perimeters of the nation's large cities. The GI Bill and expectations of a home in the suburbs, both products of four years of war, combined to launch the exodus from the cities to the suburbs. People moving out of the cities were taking their shopping dollars with them. In the decade of the 1940s, before North Gate opened, downtown retail sales had increased by 177 percent, but sales in suburban stores had increased by 226 percent. During the same period, only one department store was opened in any major Southern city. Suburban merchants and shopkeepers, who offered friendly service and front-door parking, made it easy for women to forsake the tradition of shopping downtown, where congested stores and streets were making shopping more of a chore than a pleasure.

Shopping centers had actually been part of American city life for some time. The first was Roland Park Shop Center, which opened in 1907 in a Baltimore, Md., neighborhood five miles north of downtown. The first tenant was a drug store, and the center featured off-street parking. It was small; its six stores combined had less space than the Belk brothers' 1910 store. But Roland Park was a convenient shopping spot for the comfortable neighborhood located nearby.

By the 1920s, men's and women's specialty shops had begun to leave the center city and some major department stores in New York, Boston, and Chicago had opened suburban branches. These were generally smaller stores that did not carry the full line of merchandise. America's first planned, one-owner shopping center did not arrive until 1923 when J. C. Nichols Company opened Country Club Plaza in Kansas City, Mo. The center, located on a forty-acre tract astride a major highway five miles south of downtown, featured small specialty shops and catered to automobile traffic and residents of a nearby subdivision, which Nichols also had built. Before World War II, these small neighborhood centers offered convenience and provided a home for small specialty shops, a restaurant or cafe, and perhaps a movie theater. They appeared to pose no threat to retailers downtown.

The postwar building boom and America's move to the suburbs combined to produce changes that would greatly affect large downtown stores. Americans now were more mobile. Cars and gasoline, in short supply during the war, were available. By 1947, more than half of America's households had automobiles, making shopping centers more accessible than stores in the cities. Suburban stores were also getting larger and beginning to offer a greater variety of goods, thus relieving shoppers of a trip into the city. Often, returning veterans used money from the GI Bill and a few years experience clerking in a store before the war to open their own specialty shops in the small suburban centers. It was relatively easy to get into business, and the centers offered relatively inexpensive space to open a store.

City merchants began competing for shoppers' attention not only with price but with convenience. Stern Brothers, one of Allied's stores in midtown Manhattan, offered customers half-price round-trip tickets into the city from Westchester and Connecticut if they would shop their Forty-Second Street store near Grand Central Terminal. The move to regional centers and the change of American shopping behavior was not widely accepted as inevitable. One writer, with blissful optimism, reported in the early 1950s that, "though a visit to a regional shopping center can serve a very useful purpose, it can never take the place of the 'day in town' with all that that implies to the suburban housewife—shopping, a show and dining out."

Most of Belk's partners took comfort in such optimism and remained assured of their downtown locations. In 1948, the Hudsons in Raleigh had considered opening a store in Cameron Village, the state's first shopping center, located near a residential development close to the state college, and decided to remain where they were. "We probably never realized how important a decision it was," Karl Hudson, Jr., recalled years later, "and didn't feel impelled to make a great effort."

Rather than forsake their downtown location, the Hudsons made improvements to their Fayetteville Street store. In 1948, they installed the city's first escalators. The event attracted live radio coverage and left Karl Jr. with a day he would never forget. On opening day a reporter with a live microphone accompanied Karl as the escalator carried its first passengers to the second floor. Midway up, the moving stairs stopped, dead. Improper wiring had blown a circuit. Electricians made repairs quickly, and in the next few days more than twenty-five thousand people came to Hudson-

Belk just to take a ride. One young customer was quoted as saying, "It's like going right up to heaven, ain't it?"

The Hudsons and other Belk partners had more to worry about. The South had been a fertile field for expansion of national chain stores for years. Thirteen national chains included in the Fairchild Publications' *Daily News Record* survey in 1948 reported that 1,276 of their 6,797 stores were located in the South. Expansion had slowed in recent years, except for two companies, Franklin Stores, a variety chain, and J. C. Penney, soon to emerge as a leading competitor for Belk. Penney opened eleven stores in the South that year alone. Sears, Roebuck & Company opened a major distribution center in Greensboro, N.C., in 1947 to help serve its 126 stores in thirteen Southern states.

"In Sears' scheme of operation," the report said, "the South is highly important and has been considered so for a number of years." While Sears did not open many new stores, it began to expand its smaller stores, including some in Belk's own backyard, the North Carolina cities of Asheville, Greensboro, Winston-Salem, and Fayetteville. Other companies were expected to follow Sears's lead, and the result would be "competition for the retail sales dollar in the South that will be more intense than ever before. As a matter of fact, what is going on today is the effort of each individual store and organization to jockey itself into the best possible position for that era of intensified competition which everybody expects."

Henry Belk, Jr., had spotted what he thought was a chance to position Belk for the anticipated growth. He saw Florida as the state of opportunity. Six months after William Henry Belk's death in February 1952, Belk opened the family's first shopping center store, in St. Petersburg, Fla. The Belk-Lindsey store had 23,400 square feet in Central Plaza Shopping Center and was located adjacent to the city's downtown business district. The timing may have been coincidental. Belk's father had opened stores in many different locations, and he might have chosen a shopping center site had there been any in the South. But this store included many features that never appeared on any plans that William Henry Belk had approved. The changes quickly put Henry at odds with his brothers and sister.

The St. Petersburg store was like no other in Belk's history. Henry hired a New York design firm to plan the store, which featured contrasting flamingo and chartreuse oriental designs. He installed speakers and an audio system to provide background music throughout the store. Instead of selecting a manager with years of experience in the Belk ranks, he promoted A. Tuttle Smith, who had been with the Belk-Lindsey group for about a year. Smith previously had been with J. C. Penney, Belk's leading rival in markets across the region. The store stocked Belk staples such as piece goods and notions, but ladies' ready-to-wear was its primary stock-in-trade. The most striking change from previous stores, however, was on the sales floor. Nearly all the merchandise was presented for sale as self-service.

Henry's ideas were novel, even revolutionary for a business whose founder barked at salesclerks who would let a customer roam the store unattended. The younger Belk had promoted the idea of self-service drug centers during buying office shows, but no store had adopted the self-service concept that ten years later would be a primary marketing strategy for successful retailers.

Belk's family had objected to these changes for a Belk store, but Henry had proceeded anyhow. The St. Petersburg store was a success. A year later, without consulting with his family, Henry and Colin Lindsey opened a second, similar store in Tampa's Ybor City. Unlike the St. Petersburg store, which had captured the cover of *Busy Bees*, the Belk organization's new company magazine, the Tampa store got nary a mention. Meanwhile, Belk opened traditional department stores in West Palm Beach, Fla., and Palestine, Tex., within a month of the Tampa opening. They received lavish attention in the bimonthly publication.

Henry's decision to open the Tampa store and other unilateral actions severely strained his relations with the rest of his family, except for Henderson, who along with Lindsey owned stock in the store. When buyers from the store arrived at the Belk buying office in Charlotte for merchandise shows in the spring of 1955, their order books were taken from them and they were ejected from the building. Henry and Henderson filed suit against John, Tom, Irwin, and Sarah, and the enmity building within a very private family became public. After a series of legal moves and countermoves, the suit was dropped. Two months later, Belk Stores Services Incorporated was formally organized. To outsiders, the organization of BSS was simply the formal recognition of what already was in place. In many respects it was, but the incorporation of these services into one legal entity was more than an organizational overhaul. The most dramatic change was at the top. The BSS board, composed of family members and the senior partners, installed John as president, not Henry Jr., who left for Florida where he remained president of the Belk-Lindsey group.

In November, Belk Stores Services released a statement cutting all ties with Belk-Lindsey Company. "The Belk-Lindsey Company stores in Florida are not members of Belk Stores Services Inc., and these stores are not authorized to use the services of Belk Stores Services Inc." The statement went on to say that manufacturers should not ship any merchandise bearing Belk trademarks to the dozen or so Florida stores or disclose any information to these stores. Belk-Lindsey subsequently established its own buying offices in New York, across the street from McCraw's offices.

In just a few months, the company had received more publicity about its private affairs, particularly family matters, than at any time in its nearly sixty years of business. Newspapers carried detailed accounts of the legal maneuvers and financial difficulties of the Florida store, which spawned rumors that a Belk business was bankrupt. Even *Women's Wear Daily*, a leading national retail trade publication, carried reports on the lawsuit and subsequent settlement.

During the summer of 1956, John Belk had to be careful about appearances. He had begun talking with Paul Efird

Christmas in the Belk home on Hawthorne Lane. Standing, left to right, are sons Tom Belk, Henderson Belk, Henry Belk, Jr., and John Belk. Seated, left to right, are William Henry Belk and his wife, Mary Irwin Belk, their daughter, Sarah, and son, Irwin Belk.

In 1949, William Henry Belk and James Cash Penney met and shared an evening together. Penney's early Golden Rule stores were established in much the same way Belk set up his partners. Penney's system did not survive changes during the 1920s, however.

The shelves and drawers of William Henry Belk's rolltop desk contained the weekly sales figures from his stores. Belk received visitors and counseled store managers seated within arm's reach of any information he needed about his business. Callers knew when an interview was over when Belk reached for his hat and turned back to his work. The photograph on the right corner of the desk is of Belk's brother, John. The spittoon at his feet was another permanent fixture.

A. Frank Stevens, Dr. John Belk's son-in-law, assumed more responsibility for the management of the buying service, particularly in the New York office, after Dr. Belk's death. He lived in Winston-Salem, N.C., where he also supervised a group of stores in Piedmont North Carolina.

An early store promotion in Charlotte, in which a cow carrying a Belk placard through the streets of town with a sign reading, "This Is No Bull," drew just as much attention nearly forty years later for the Marion, N.C., Belk-Broome store.

One of the strengths of the Belk organization was its deep roots and established presence in the communities it served. By the late 1940s, the Belk store in Statesville, N.C., already was celebrating its 37th anniversary.

The Belk showcase was the Charlotte store, which by the 1950s had
expanded to several adjacent buildings along East Trade Street. The Belk
shoe store was one of the few that advertised a fluoroscope that, like an
X ray, could show the bone structure of a customer's foot.

about bringing the fifty Efird department stores into the
vast Belk organization. One of the difficulties in the negotiations was where to meet. Both men were well known in
Charlotte and, of course, within their own stores. They had
to arrange their sessions so they would be away from their
offices, away from downtown Charlotte, away from those
who might question why the Efirds and the Belks, retail
competitors in the Carolinas for a generation, were suddenly
so chummy.

The business insiders on Tryon Street knew something
was afoot. Efird's was not financially healthy. The business
had been on the block for some time, and the Charlotte

When a Belk store expanded in the booming downtown business areas of the late 1950s, a manager simply acquired an adjacent building, put a door through the walls, and moved in. At one time, the Belk-Leggett store in Danville, Va., was spread throughout nineteen different buildings.

banks were anxious about their loans. Already, one had called a large note. The busiest retail season of the year, the fall and Christmas shopping season, was just ahead, and Efird's would need more cash for stock if the stores were to remain open. A group of influential Charlotte investors had talked to George Dowdy, general manager of Belk's Charlotte store, about leaving Belk and assuming the management of the Efird stores under their ownership. Dowdy, who had spent more than thirty years in the Belk family and achieved national recognition among the country's fashion retailers as head of the National Retail Merchants Association, had considered the offer, then turned it down. The future of the

One of the busiest departments in the buying service was piece goods. Sam Scott (second from right) built much of the business of the buying service from textile mills in the Piedmont, and their goods assumed a prominent position in many stores. Attending this piece goods meeting in New York in October 1953 are (from left) Henry Reichard, Tom Belk, D. S. Kimrey, Guy Byerly, Jr., J. D. Morgan, R. D. McCraw (head of the New York buying office), Scott, and R. D. Currance.

well-known Efird chain of stores throughout the Carolinas was in doubt.

Belk stores, on the other hand, were financially healthy and nearly at the peak of their territorial growth. The Belks were operating more than 325 stores in sixteen states. In the past fifteen years, Grier Hudson had expanded from his base in Spartanburg into Alabama, while the Matthewses had expanded into Georgia. The Leggetts had opened more stores in Virginia and expanded into Maryland. The Simpson branch of the family, children of Sarah Belk Simpson's second marriage, now had stores in Ohio, Missouri, and Arkan-

Store windows and displays drew more attention when customers strolled the downtown sidewalks of major cities like Greensboro, N.C. The Greensboro store, featured in this Founder's Day display, was the first to be completely air-conditioned. It's art deco design was the work of Greensboro architect Charles Hartmann, who designed other large Belk stores.

sas, as a result of the recent purchase of a small group of stores in the Midwest. Henderson Belk had raised the Belk flag in Tyler, Texas. North Carolina was virtually saturated. Belk stores could be found in almost every North Carolina county, no matter how small.

The department store was in its heyday in the South. North Carolina's downtowns remained vigorous, alive, the

The Belk organization communicated with individual store managers and buyers through annual shows and conventions at which Belk Stores Services promoted its private-label lines like Archdale. BSS merchandise managers purchased cloth and designed apparel for sale under dozens of Belk names.

major retail centers, but changes that would reshape American cities—and retailing—forever were more obvious. Retailing as most of the senior partners had known it was at a major turning point. Cameron Village, the large forty-store neighborhood center in Raleigh, N.C., featured off-street parking, underground wiring, and covered sidewalks. Charlotte's first center, Park Road, was scheduled to open in No-

Belk executives frequently invited representatives of the companies that supplied their stores for tours in the Carolinas. This group gathered outside the Belk Stores building in Charlotte in 1954.

Evangelist Billy Graham, a Charlotte, N.C. native, grew up around Belk stores and as a young man sold shoes in a Belk store in Tennessee. In 1958 he returned to the downtown Charlotte store, along with members of his crusade team, for a visit with Mrs. Belk. Pictured are (from left) Tom Belk, Graham, Mrs. Belk, Grady Wilson, Irwin Belk, George Beverly Shea, Henderson Belk, Charlotte store manager George Dowdy and BSS executive Grant Whitney.

In 1938 the Charlotte store expanded again and Belk promotions drew customers from miles around. Store manager George Dowdy already had begun to emphasize fashion and style more than his counterparts in the smaller stores in the towns of the Carolina Piedmont.

The development of North Carolina as a dairy state owes something to Horton Doughton, Belk's partner in Statesville, N.C., and Sam Scott, who encouraged William Henry Belk to support a calf-raising program. An unidentified onlooker stands behind Scott, the calf's owner, Doughton and Belk in Statesville in 1944.

vember 1956 and Greensboro's Friendly Center was planned for the summer of 1957. Store managers still catered to their local hometown customers—the folks who came to Main Street to shop—but television was beginning to create markets that reached beyond the home city of the broadcaster, linking cities and towns on the periphery to growing metropolitan areas like Charlotte. Between 1951 and 1953 alone, the number of households with television sets in the Charlotte area had grown from 160,000 to 400,000. And the discount-store phenomenon was off to a strong start in the Northeast. It had not extended throughout the South and Kmart was still Kresge's, but some local entrepreneurs were experimenting with this style of merchandising, particularly in Florida.

National department store groups like Allied Stores and Federated Stores had not discovered the South as a potential market, leaving Efird and Belk stores to fight each other for the dominant position in their communities. The founders of the two organizations had competed with one another during the expansion in the early half of the century. One might beat the other to open a store in a growing textile town of the Carolinas, but the other was never far behind. When J. G. Parks opened his store in Concord, a major competitor was Efird's. When Frank Stevens opened in Winston-Salem, the Efirds' store had been doing business there for four years. The Efirds opened their Durham store before the Hudson brothers could expand in that direction from Raleigh. They had a store in South Carolina's capital city of Columbia in 1915. Belk did not arrive until nearly twenty years later.

The Belks and Efirds sought the same customers. Both were trying to attract middle-income shoppers. Neither was a fashion store. Both battled for the shoppers' attention against the national chains like J. C. Penney's, Kress, W. T. Grant, and Sears, Roebuck, as well as local merchants. In towns where they both had stores, the two were pretty evenly matched.

What Efird had that Belk did not, however, was a front door on Charlotte's Tryon Street, the Carolinas' most prestigious retail location. Efird's Charlotte store was one block north of the square, at the corner of Fifth Street and Tryon in a handsome five-story building directly across Tryon from Ivey's, Charlotte's most fashionable store. Like Belk's store, it was the flagship of the chain and had caused considerable excitement when it opened on September 7, 1923, with the first escalator in the Southeast, beating even Macy's in New York with a "moving stairway."

The massive Belk store covered the heart of the block on the northeast corner of the square in Charlotte, but shoppers had to leave Tryon to get to Belk's main entrances on Fifth Street and East Trade. When Belk and Efird talked in 1956, a $4 million renovation and expansion of Belk's Charlotte store was well under way. Work was to be completed in time for the busy fall season. Only an alley separated the rear entrances of the two stores. A merger would produce a combined store of 600,000 square feet, the largest in the Southeast outside of Atlanta, and, finally, a Tryon Street entrance for Belk's.

The final terms for the sale were worked out at Paul Efird's home on the Catawba River outside of Charlotte. When they had negotiated a price, John Belk picked up the telephone and called Joe Robinson, then head of Charlotte operations for Wachovia Bank and Trust Company. Would Wachovia lend Belk's what was needed to close on the purchase price of $3.5 million? The hour was well past midnight, but Robinson gave Belk quick approval and told him to close the deal. Belk did not know that Wachovia had already investigated Efird's for another prospective buyer and Robinson knew as much about the company, its assets and liabilities, as John Belk did. The real estate alone was worth as much as the Belks were prepared to pay. Robinson did not need any more information to tell Belk to proceed.

Paul Efird and John Belk had plenty still to do. Both had to secure agreement from family members. Belk also had to win the endorsement of the senior partners, men like Arthur Tyler in Rocky Mount, Frank Stevens in Winston-Salem, and John Hensdale in Fayetteville, before he could commit their corporations to the necessary loans and guarantees. Belk needed their consent as stockholders of the various store corporations that would absorb the Efird stores. One by one, John Belk picked up their endorsements.

Finally, late in the afternoon of September 20, 1956, after most workers at the Belk Stores Services office on East Fifth Street had gone for the day, John and Tom Belk and their chief lieutenants—Assistant General Counsels Leroy Robinson and John L. Green, and General Counsel David McConnell and the company's controller, Nat Howard—began calling the Belk partners who had stores in the forty-nine towns where an Efird store was located. That accounted for all of the Efird locations except Erwin, a textile town south of Raleigh in eastern North Carolina. Each Belk manager was to meet his Efird counterpart first thing in the morning and assume control of the store. The Efird manager, and all of his staff, would report to the Belk manager immediately.

The Belk network was efficient not only at selling goods, but also at dispatching important management decisions. "We made all our calls in a matter of hours," John Belk recalls. "Paul Efird was still calling the next day." In fact, some Efird managers had not received the news when the Belk managers arrived to pick up the keys to the stores. Charles Gardner, the Belk store manager in Lumberton, N.C., walked across the street the next morning and met the Efird manager on the sales floor of his store. When Gardner realized the Efird manager did not know what was afoot, the two went to the Belk store, where Gardner explained the new arrangement.

The Efird manager in Laurinburg was waiting for Belk manager Archie Hampton. "That was the happiest man I ever saw," Hampton recalls. Like most, the Efird store had a limited inventory of merchandise because the company was short of cash and credit to place advance orders for goods. On some lines, Efird managers were showing samples to customers, who then placed orders that were relayed back to Charlotte, where deliveries were arranged. Other Efird managers were delighted about the change because they knew the Belk managers had the independence to manage their own stores with little central control. Efird's founders had operated like this, but their children had exercised more control, including centralizing buying and other operations in Charlotte, a change that had led to the decline of the once-vigorous business.

The details of the sale took six months to conclude. Nat Howard, the Belk controller, spent so much time tying up all the necessary financial details that John Belk finally dubbed him "Mr. Efird." Howard moved into the Efird corporate offices above Martin's Department Store, an Efird-owned store in the old Bee Hive location at the corner of College and Trade streets. He worked against a deadline to come up with a final accounting of the deal. In addition, Howard helped arrange for ownership of the Efird stores to be brought under the individual Belk companies in the towns where they were located. In some cases, partners immediately doubled their number of employees and amount of floor space and business. With the Efird stores short of stock, the Belk managers had to hurry to arrange for the cash to get merchandise on the shelves in preparation for the fall selling season.

Some wags criticized the purchase, saying the Belks paid a steep price for a Tryon Street address, but there was more to the deal than prestige. In one stroke, Belk consolidated its position in important markets in the Carolinas and Virginia, picked up a sizable share of the retail sales dollars being spent in those towns, and added real estate to the books that would return a handsome profit in years to come. Most important, the conclusion of the Efird purchase was a successful test of the emerging new leadership of John and Tom Belk. When he negotiated the Efird purchase, John Belk was only thirty-six years old and had been president of the newly organized Belk Stores Services Incorporated for less than a year.

That same year, the company and the family were back in the news, but this time the subject was more pleasant, more familiar. The Belks' Charlotte store, the largest in the group, was reopening after another extensive face-lift and expansion that added 200,000 square feet of new space. The Belks' store-opening skills, practiced across the land in the ten years following the end of the war, were all brought to bear on the celebration of the opening of the $4 million addition to the Charlotte store. What had begun as 35 feet of street frontage on East Trade Street now was a massive building five stories tall that covered more than half a city block.

The addition featured a new front with marble columns on East Fifth Street and a newly constructed section that extended along College Street midway to the corner of East Trade. In bold letters on the high solid front was the name Belk's. The arrangement of the new store was explained in elaborate detail in twenty-four page sections that appeared in both the *Charlotte Observer* and the *Charlotte News*. Shoppers found a gourmet shop, a bakery, a self-service Drug-o-matic for "non-prescription drugs and salves," a cafeteria with dual serving lines, a Teen shop, a Sleep shop, a bookstore, expanded areas for all existing departments from ladies' wear to household furnishings, a full-time bridal consultant, and a first-aid station with a registered nurse on duty. Thanks to the recent purchase of Efird's, the store also had easy access to Tryon Street. The rearrangement included a subtle, but telling change. Piece goods, the backbone of the early Belk stores, the department that had been the training ground for many of William Henry Belk's partners, was no longer on the store's main floor. Fashion accessories, cosmetics, lingerie, and sportswear would now greet Belk's current generation of shoppers.

On Monday, November 12, under a brilliant morning sun, Mrs. W. H. Belk handed Mayor Philip Van Every of Charlotte a pair of scissors, and he snipped the ceremonial ribbon and officially opened the store. The Belks' guests for the day included hundreds of manufacturers who supplied the merchandise that filled the big store, Gov. Luther Hodges, Sen. Sam Ervin, Jr., and New York banker David Rockefeller. A luncheon for North Carolina bankers—paid for by Union National Bank, of which Irwin Belk was a board member— followed at Myers Park Country Club. Simultaneously, the Belks provided a luncheon for their manufacturers and other vendors. Both groups gathered for dinner that evening at the

Carmel Country Club. There was not a spare hotel room in the city of Charlotte that night.

It was a glorious day in the evolution of William Henry Belk's retail dream. It also was the beginning of the end of an era. Three days later, another group of excited retailers and developers opened Charlotte's first regional shopping center on former pasture land just down the hill from evangelist Billy Graham's homeplace. On Thursday, some of the same city officials who had helped the Belks celebrate watched as a button was pushed to activate chemical isotopes that burned through a ceremonial ribbon to open thirty-two stores at Park Road Shopping Center on the southern edge of Charlotte's expanding suburbs. Plans called for fifty or more stores on the forty-acre tract anchored by the city's first Penney's store. Even J. C. Penney himself attended. The last time he had been in Charlotte was when he visited Henry Belk a few years before Belk died. The two had spent an evening together, sharing stories about their humble beginnings and philosophies of business.

Cold hard numbers, not sixty years of tradition, had brought the crowd of dignitaries to the end of the asphalt near the city's corporate limits. Developers of the Park Road Shopping Center announced that they had placed their center in easy reach of 30,000 customers whose average annual incomes—just more than $6,000—made the south Charlotte location ideal for the area's first regional shopping center.

Two tall cranes backed up to the east front of the large Belk store in Charlotte one evening in the spring of 1968 and hoisted a 12-foot Belk sign with stylish new letters to workers who anchored it into place on the side of the building. Several weeks later, the cranes reappeared. Workmen pulled down the first sign, which was turquoise with black highlights, and replaced it with one in white with a black outline. The new sign featured the now-familiar bold *B* in crisp white letters with a curling return. The exchange created little notice beyond Charlotte, but it was the first step toward a major transformation of the South's largest mercantile business.

The new signature represented not only a new image for Belk stores, but the beginning of a new direction for the business as well. During the 1960s the company reflected the changes taking place in the Southern towns and cities where the old order was passing. A new generation of blacks and whites broke color barriers and opened new job opportunities in Belk stores and across the land. Southern wage earners, once concerned about supplying the necessities for their families, now had more money to spend and expected modern merchandising in the old, familiar stores now becoming isolated in declining retail areas of downtowns. To meet these challenges and others meant a new way of thinking and working for those responsible for Belk stores.

Before the New York marketing firm of Lippincott and Margulies created the "Big B" and a companion "Big L" for the Leggett stores, it had given the Chrysler Corporation its five-sided star and created a new look for RCA. The firm had redesigned the interior of a nuclear submarine and designed the Golden Rondelle, better known as the Johnson's Wax Pavilion at the 1964 World's Fair in New York. And the company had plotted the marketing future of a myriad of products, from wine and beer to cake mix and lawn fertilizer.

Names, logos, interior design, marketing strategies, and corporate imagery were the company's stock-in-trade.

Corporations didn't call on L&M for the routine, and Belk's request certainly was unique. The leaders of Belk stores were embarked on changing the stores' public image after being the familiar neighbor for nearly eighty years. They wanted a common symbol, a stylish Belk look, that would unite the network of nearly four hundred stores then operating in nineteen states and Puerto Rico.

Rarely, Harold Margulies admitted, had his company tackled a problem quite like this one. His challenge was to find a graphic identifier for a family of stores that had almost as many personalities and faces as there were children. There were large stores, like the flagship store in Charlotte, and many smaller ones in towns and hamlets across the region. Belk merchandise included everything from bargain-basement work clothes to contemporary fashion and accessories. Store names varied from town to town, and even from one side of a single store building to another. The Belk name, and the names of the Belk partners, appeared on signage and billboards in a variety of type styles, some of which were unchanged since the 1930s. Even the company's de facto sunburst logo, printed on advertising displays and store promotions, appeared in different arrangements. In addition, store slogans came in as many shapes and sizes. The Charlotte store's was the old, familiar, "Home of Better Values." It had been part of Belk in Charlotte for more than forty years. At Belk-Tyler stores, the slogan was "where brand names reflect Eastern Carolina's preference for quality."

L&M's team of researchers packed cameras and note pads into their bags and rode the circuit of Belk stores. They talked to more than forty partners and store managers and visited stores in large cities and small towns. They studied newspaper advertising and reviewed the company's image on television. They snapped pictures of store fronts and store signs in the daylight and at night. They collected samples of shopping bags and wrapping paper, company stationery, sales tickets, match covers, packaging for Belk's private-label brands of merchandise—anything that had the Belk or Leggett name printed, stitched, or painted on it. In June 1967 they presented their report to a special committee of the Belk Stores Services board of directors.

The Belk organization enjoyed a number of assets that could never be duplicated by large chains or competitors, the L&M specialists said. The individual Belk companies were well known in the cities they served, and they enjoyed reputations for caring about their communities. Belk managing partners were Boy Scout leaders, elders in the Presbyterian Church, captains of local fund drives, the pillars of the community; their stores joined in community projects and supported civic ventures. Henry Belk's early reputation for running stores that offered honest value for fair prices still lived; customers trusted Belk stores. And Belk's own private-label brands were so ubiquitous that many customers accepted them as national brand merchandise. Customers were disappointed when they relocated out of reach of a Belk store and found that Belk's own Heiress hosiery was not available. They placed orders by mail. These were the pluses.

The marketing specialists then gave the Belk executives the bad news. People in the South were on the move; one out of five relocated to a new city every year. In addition, shoppers in small towns also were willing and able to travel to a large city to spend their money, forsaking their local stores for the greater variety and styles found in larger stores in cities twenty, thirty, or fifty miles away. Belk stores, meanwhile, were still local institutions that had a limited unifying image. The autonomy that Henry Belk had granted his partners had created a confusing array of stores ill-suited to compete in the modern marketplace that now was regional, not local, and that showed no respect for traditional community boundaries. The mixed identities of Belk stores meant that each Belk store had to reacquaint a newcomer to its town. Their prescription: the company must position itself so it would no longer be four hundred separate stores serving local customers, but one very, very large network of stores serving the nearly 32.5 million people who lived within 100 miles of a Belk or Leggett store.

Further, some stores remained out of touch with customers seeking contemporary style and fashion. Renovation of store interiors and upgrading of the merchandise mix had not reached every community. Some store interiors were dark, unattractive, and just plain old-fashioned. Poorly done, hand-lettered signs in some stores suggested that Belk was a cheap operation. Some store managers still presented merchandise as their predecessors had a generation before, despite increased emphasis on display and marketing from Belk Stores Services.

Finally, the L&M report showed that Belk was not immune to outside competition. After conquering the West Coast, major national department-store chains, fashion conscious and aggressive, already were eyeing the South as the next great opportunity for growth. Macy's, which owned Davison's in Atlanta, was branching out. Rich's, based in Atlanta, also was expanding. Belk needed a new identity, L&M reported, that was simple, strong, unique, appropriate. They recommended the "Big B," and the "Big L," for the Leggett stores.

Not since John Belk had assumed the presidency of Belk Stores Services in 1955 had the company leaders, men who had learned the merchant's trade from Henry Belk, so much to think about. The balance of power on critical decisions lay with these senior partners, most of whom were twenty to thirty years older than Henry Belk's children, who now owned the majority of the stock in their store corporations. These men had been hearing that their way of doing business, downtown on Main Street, was obsolete. The future lay in the suburbs, the young people said. And familiar hallmarks such as better values, low prices, and durability were being replaced by something from the "Pepsi Generation." Now, they learned, a new corporate image was needed to unite under one common identity the independent stores that carried the stamp of their own personalities and identities.

The most influential of the senior men was Arthur Tyler of Rocky Mount, a stocky, silver-haired, jowly dynamo with a delightful twinkle in his eye. He was chairman of the board of Belk Stores Services and had been since its creation in 1955. Tyler was not the partner with the largest number of stores. When he was elected chairman, he had fourteen stores, most of them in small towns in eastern North Carolina. The Gallant brothers, meanwhile, had more than twice that number throughout Georgia and South Carolina. Tyler was not the most senior of the partners. When he took over the Belk family's Rocky Mount store in 1931, the names of Matthews, Hudson, and Parks were already part of the Belk tradition. Tyler was respected as an accomplished merchant who had performed as one of Henry Belk's most reliable partners during the hectic days of expansion in the 1930s and 1940s.

Tyler was born in Virginia, the son of a railroad engineer, and grew up in Henderson, N.C., about fifty miles north of Durham near the Virginia state line. As a youngster, he worked in various stores in town, including a grocery where he earned fifty cents a day for a day that began at 7:00 A.M. and ended at 11:00 P.M. Before he signed on as an artilleryman in World War I, he had committed himself to a career as a merchant. Like Henry Belk, he forsook an education at the university at Chapel Hill; after one year there, he went to work to open the way for a college opportunity for younger brothers and sisters. By the time he was twenty-one, he had been a salesman on the floor, window decorator, and floor manager for the Anchor store in Henderson. By the time he was thirty, he had managed one of the smaller Anchor stores and had run the firm's New York buying office. In 1931, Tyler was managing the financially troubled Anchor store in Winston-Salem when Frank Stevens asked him if he would be interested in working for Henry Belk.

Stevens, who already had recruited several Belk men from

his competitors' stores in Winston-Salem, had taken a liking to Tyler and the way he ran his store. The two men kept close watch on one another, even to the point of sneaking predawn visits to the other's front display windows to compare prices on sale items by the light of a flickering match. On this visit, Stevens went right in the front door and asked Tyler to go to Charlotte and talk with Henry Belk about a position with Belk. On Stevens's recommendation, Belk asked him to take over the Rocky Mount store and run it as if it were his own.

The Rocky Mount store was well stocked and located in a lively, thriving tobacco market town. But it had not done well under the management of another of Dr. Belk's sons-in-law, John C. Daughtridge, who was suffering from failing health. Within a year, Tyler, the first manager Belk ever appointed who had not trained in a Belk store, had turned the Rocky Mount store around, giving Belk a 20 percent dividend in the depths of the depression. A year later, Tyler already had plans for a new store, in Kinston, when Belk called him to Goldsboro to take on that ailing store.

Throughout the 1930s and 1940s, Tyler opened up eastern North Carolina for Henry Belk, extending the company's name to the shores of the Albemarle Sound in Elizabeth City. His stores did well, and Tyler was well liked in the towns where he did business, a first-rate ambassador for Belk and his businesses. He was a lively promoter, and his stores were popular additions to the small eastern North Carolina towns. They usually were the best around, and Tyler kept making them better. When renovations were necessary, he was one of the first to introduce modern conveniences to his stores, even in the smallest tobacco towns in the coastal plain.

Tyler knew his territory well and had a strong sense of history and place. He was one of eastern North Carolina's leading boosters. Henry Belk liked what he saw in his protégé and was a frequent visitor to Tyler's territory, especially in the spring when the shad were running in the coastal rivers. Belk was fond of a meal of shad fried up in a batter.

Tyler frequently arranged for interviews with the noted merchant by local newspaper editors, who could count on a lively story.

Tyler's influence extended deep into the heart of the Belk organization. In 1942, he helped organize a profit-sharing retirement fund for Belk employees and chaired the first supervising committee. In 1954, when the Belks went into the insurance business, creating a self-insurance reciprocal to cover their stores, Tyler was named chairman of that. A year later, the N.C. Merchants' Association recognized him as one of the state's six outstanding merchants. That same year, when Henry Belk's children were divided over control of their father's estate, the new board of directors of Belk Stores Services, composed of senior partners like Tyler, the Leggetts, and the children of Henry and John Belk, turned to Arthur Tyler.

With the exception of George Dowdy, Tyler also was the most forceful of the senior partners. The partners respected Tyler's ability as a leader and his skill as a merchant. Moreover, he was a good bridge to the Leggett family, the most influential partner group in the organization. Tyler's territory was close to the Leggett brothers' operations in Virginia, and he was personally close to the Leggett brothers. And, the partners hoped, Tyler could resolve the differences within the Belk family.

These were the most uncertain times in the history of the business. The Belk organization needed the strong hand of Tyler at the helm. Henry Belk had left behind hundreds of privately held companies in which he had owned a majority interest. When he was alive, his partners had only their founder and inspirational leader to answer to. On his death, his stock was distributed equally to his six children.

The discord in the Belk family left many uneasy. Disagreement among Belk's children created concern among bankers, who for years had lent the Belk companies money based more on reputation and faith than on a balance sheet. In fact, Henry Belk had never provided a financial statement to a banker; if his signature was not enough, then he just took his business elsewhere. The divisions in the family put the partners in awkward situations. Belk's children were frequently divided on matters that needed stockholder approval—the location of a new store or renovation of an old one, for example—matters in which a partner's minority stock often determined the outcome. But, when a partner cast his vote, he was faced with choosing sides among Belk's children, who on another vote might be determining his annual salary or approval of a pet project.

The internal difficulties also came at the time when this vast cooperative network of stores was in need of more central organization and support. The department-store business had become much more complex than in Henry Belk's day. Store managers now had to comply with more government regulations, from personnel to pricing. New competition from neighborhood shopping centers was forcing managers to reconsider not only their mix of merchandise but how they ran their stores. A store needed more flexible hours to compete with shopping centers that offered evening shopping, and qualified sales people were harder to find. As job opportunities opened up in the South, clerking in a department store did not have the appeal it once held in small towns. No longer could a manager expect to find a man like Homer Cook who, by the time he retired from Matthews-Belk Company in 1958 at the age of seventy, had sold shoes at the Matthews's family store in Gastonia for thirty-seven years. Managers needed help managing work shifts and recruiting and training new salespeople, many of whom were not looking for a career like Homer's.

There also was the challenge of managing the various Belk Stores Services departments. When Tyler assumed the chairmanship of bss, the new, nonprofit corporation was much more than a buying service with a sample room. It was an insurance company that provided protection to hundreds of buildings and thousands of people. It was a shipping company that daily routed truckloads of goods to store loading

docks hundreds of miles apart. It was a real estate management company responsible for an inventory of more than
seven hundred pieces of real estate that included everything
from downtown buildings to working farms. It was a law
firm with a team of three lawyers. It was an accounting and
auditing firm. It was a financial clearing house for millions of
dollars in loans from banks all across the South. It was a
manufacturer with more than two dozen private-label items,
from sheets to shoes. And each was a separate fiefdom responsible to a committee of partners, Belks, and influential
store managers.

While the overall responsibility for managing BSS remained
with the board, the day-to-day duties fell to John Belk, who
was president. He shared the responsibility with his brothers
and sister, who by now had staked out their own areas of
work. Brother Tom had taken charge of buying and was
building a list of credible private-label goods that helped
partners increase their profits each year. Irwin, whose interests were in finance and banking, assumed responsibility for
the accounting and auditing departments, and he was in
charge of bank relations, supervising the files of loans outstanding for the various companies. Sarah, who had married
a New York investment banker and lived in Manhattan, continued her work in women's wear from the New York office.
She had recruited a design professor at New York University
to produce the company's first fashion reports. Henderson
took over management of the Charlotte Efird's store and pur-
sued his own business interests outside of the stores, including investments in stores with Henry Jr.

The ability of the Belk children as merchants was still to be
proven. To many of the senior partners and BSS executives,
they were still the Belk "boys." The partners had come up
through the ranks and believed in on-the-job training. Yet,
only Henderson had managed a store, and only for a brief
period. John had helped open a number of stores and had
supervised managers; Tom and Sarah's experience was in the
buying service. Irwin had concentrated his talents in finance

and business. Even if the Belks had been united, it is doubtful they could have made major changes. "If they had gotten real tough," recalls partner Tommy Leggett, "then the partners would have told them to get lost, and they wouldn't have had anybody running the organization."

If John Belk could not command, it did not mean he could not lead. He turned to persuasion as a way for getting things done. It helped that people just liked John Belk. Tall, handsome, with a shock of curling hair, he had a boyish, friendly look about him. A caricature drawn by Pulitzer Prize winning cartoonist Gene Payne and given him years later would feature a broad, toothsome grin. He enjoyed good company, was a dedicated sportsman, and quickly became the family's foremost ambassador to the public and the partners. A bachelor, Belk had plenty of time to devote to the business, and he poured himself into it. He drew upon his experience in opening the Savannah store and others ten years earlier, his work in the personnel department at the Charlotte store, his years in the buying service, and his own appreciation of people.

Ironically, while the unique structure of the Belk organization created problems in succession, it provided strength in a curious way. Despite the internal turmoil, the partners continued to run the stores and expand into new stores in downtowns and suburban shopping centers. By the end of 1956, the Belks' partners had suburban stores in Savannah, Ga., Greenville, S.C., and Memphis, Tenn. In late July 1957, John Belk was on hand to open the company's first North Carolina shopping center store in Friendly Center, which was located about three miles northwest of downtown Greensboro.

Developers announced that Friendly was the "Piedmont's First and Only Regional Shopping Center." This claim stood only if Raleigh's Cameron Village, open for nearly a decade, and Charlotte's Park Road were not included in the reach of the promoter's boast. Like these centers, Friendly was located on the edge of the city, near a growing middle- to upper-income residential area. All three centers were designed to accommodate about two-dozen stores, most of them small speciality shops. The stores were one level and lined up side by side in front of ample parking spaces. Customers strolled from one store to the next under a broad canopy.

These centers and others throughout the South were a step above the early strip centers, but they were modest in comparison to regional centers opening on the West Coast and outside of large Northeastern cities. Major national department-store chains now had stores in fully enclosed and air-conditioned malls, which seemed to have no limit to their size. The department stores in these large centers were ten times the size of Belk's Friendly store. Malls not only were getting larger and larger, there seemed to be no end to the opportunities. One large city reportedly was overbuilt with three suburban shopping centers in 1953. Six years later, fifteen more were under construction.

Friendly Center cost $1 million to build. It featured parking spaces for 1,300 automobiles, a children's playground, evening shopping hours on Mondays and Fridays, and twenty-four stores, including specialty clothing shops for men and women, a hardware store, Eckerd Drugs' first Greensboro store, a restaurant, and a small department store called Harlee's. Belk's store was the largest, and inside an artist had transformed one wall into a 12-foot-high mural of familiar Greensboro scenes. With 24,000 square feet of shopping space on one level, it was about a third the size of the Belks' main store downtown. It was still only a branch store, more a convenience for shoppers who simply did not want to go downtown.

John Belk invited two hundred Belk store managers and Belk people to the grand opening of the Friendly store, the company's 354th new location. Not all were as enthusiastic about it as Belk was. Frank Stevens, one of Belk's mentors and a believer in the traditional merchandising that had built the business, pulled his young protégé aside after the ceremonies and asked him where the store's stock of shotguns was located. Belk, surprised at the question, reminded Stevens that Belk did not sell firearms. Stevens, far from comfortable about the store's almost rural location, said he had just seen a rabbit run by the front door and he might want to do some hunting.

Belk's suburban stores had begun to receive a lot of attention within the company. Of the six new stores opened that year, two, including Friendly, were suburban locations. The Belk organization, however, had not forsaken its traditional location on Main Street. The same year the Friendly store opened, Matthews-Belk, now under the management of Houston Matthews, Jr., his younger brother, Frank, and his sister Elizabeth, opened a $1 million addition to the family's Gastonia store, creating a four-level store with more than 100,000 square feet of shopping space. The store also combined the Efird and Belk operations under one roof and was the first Belk store with escalators that carried customers both up and down.

The shift to the suburbs, though still a small share of the overall retail business, had begun to concern downtown store managers and department heads. They began looking for ways to entice shoppers back to their stores. During one brainstorming session at Belk's Charlotte store, employees suggested having employees call ten customers and invite them to shop at the store on Friday; someone else suggested originating radio and television broadcasts from the store. Other ideas included better lighting on the storefront, free bus transportation, exhibits of canned goods, baking contests, and hobby displays. None of these would work, of course. In small steps, with the opening of each new shopping center, the market for downtown stores was on the decline.

Shopping centers, a more mobile society, and an expanding Southern economy created pressures on the business that Henry Belk had not had to contend with. The biggest challenge facing his son John as president of BSS was how to unite the confederation of stores which was growing larger and larger each year. By the end of 1958, there were 380 stores located in seventeen states. More than 100 of those stores had been added in the previous ten years. Most were in the Carolinas, Virginia, and Georgia, but nearly 2,000 miles separated the front door of the Leggetts' stores in Maryland and the Paris, Texas, store run by the Matthewses.

As the number of stores increased, so did the competition among the Belk partners for territorial claims. There was no formal assignment of territories, no map on the wall at Belk Stores Services defining which partner was responsible for which area of the Southeast. There was nothing more than a general agreement among the partners about who did business where. Conflicts inevitably occurred, and part of John Belk's job was to mediate the disputes. Belk, in turn, often called on Tyler for help, as he did when the Simpson group in South Carolina purchased a small group of stores that included one in the Norfolk, Va., area, the territory claimed by the Leggetts. Tyler cooled off the Leggetts and Simpson remained out of Virginia. Tyler performed similar duties in Tennessee in territorial disputes involving the Parks group of stores.

John Belk was needed everywhere at once. As BSS president and president of the hundreds of store corporations, he presided over more than a dozen store openings in about eighteen months, from Louisiana to Indiana. He worried about the weak stores and their futures. Not all the Western stores had been successful. All but one of the Texas stores had closed within ten years after they opened. In addition, he supervised the details of the Efird merger and began planning the closing of some of these stores as shopping habits changed and downtown trade declined.

The strain of keeping peace within the family, building relations among the partners, and attempting to resolve the challenges ahead for the company took its toll. In 1958, a bleeding ulcer laid John Belk up in bed. Forced to slow down and unable to meet the busy schedule of the past few years, Belk made a personal resolution to take problems one at a time, dealing with those he could and leaving others for the future. He also realized that he did not have the training he needed to handle the job. Neither a Davidson College degree, the U.S. Army, nor assorted assignments in the buying office had prepared him for the task of managing such a unique company.

Belk's schedule changed. He began spending more time studying management and attending seminars sponsored by groups like the National Retail Merchants Association and the American Management Association. He signed up for an AMA session designed specifically for company presidents and found among his classmates other young businessmen trying to manage businesses in a rapidly changing society. One was a former IBM whiz named Ross Perot, who was looking for new ways to market computers.

Seminar materials, management texts, and other books began to spill over from piles accumulating in Belk's small office on the first floor of the BSS offices on East Fifth Street in Charlotte. Located just down the hall to the right off the lobby entrance, the best that could be said of John Belk's office was that it was serviceable and convenient. Like their father, none of the Belks paid much attention to large offices, large cars, or the usual amenities associated with millionaire businessmen. John Belk continued to live at home with his mother, bought his clothes off the rack in the store, and drove a moderately priced Buick. His only indulgences were golf and team sports. A college basketball team captain, John Belk did not mind spending more money than the average sports fan for box seats at stadiums and coliseums from Washington to Atlanta.

If John Belk was waist deep in management, brother Tom was equally immersed in merchandise. On the BSS building's second floor, the dozen or so departments that composed the buying service were separated from each other by pegboard partitions and racks of clothing samples. Part showroom, part warehouse, and part office, this was the home of the buying office. Tom Belk's "office" was separated from the rest of the employees by nothing more than a waist-high divider; guests entered through a plainly painted swinging door. He shared a secretary with Sam Elliott, whose desk was nearby.

The youngest of the Belk boys, Tom worked like a man in a hurry to catch up. He expected nothing but perfection from his staff of buyers. In the imprecise world of retailing, where virtually every order is a gamble, he wanted to know why a buyer had bought so conservatively when stores ran short or had been extravagant when markdowns were higher than normal. He demanded no less of himself. Even though he and his wife, the former Katherine McKay of Charlotte, were raising a family, he borrowed his father's habit of working long after others had left for the day. Unlike his father, however, he found time to become active in the community and was a frequent civic volunteer.

Tom Belk faced many of the same challenges in the buying office that John found in the stores. The legacy of store independence had pervaded the buying office when Tom took his brother John's place in the early 1950s. Tom Belk and his buyers had limited control over the buying practices of the stores and were left with persuasion and gentle but persistent pressure on store managers to upgrade and improve the merchandise mix that Belk believed was necessary to keep the stores competitive.

Nothing underscored the laissez-faire operation of the buying office more than Belk's introduction in 1954 of a housewares show. Rather than offer items piecemeal, Tom Belk had organized a show around this one department. His buyers had prepared displays of piece goods, linen, bedding, curtains, draperies, summer furniture, rugs, and housewares. Belk and his chief assistant in this area, Guy Byerly, Jr., also offered to demonstrate to managers how to display and advertise these lines, and they had arranged for a home decorator to be available to advise store managers on what to expect from customers. Some manufacturers set up displays.

It was a complete package, far different from the cluttered sample room and variety-store atmosphere of Sam Scott's old operation. A store manager could walk out of the show with a complete new department where he had had but a stack of piece goods before. Most chain retailers would have demanded attendance by their store managers. Tom Belk had to lure store managers and buyers to the BSS show with promises of door prizes and other gimmicks.

The housewares show was one of a series of shows that attracted store buyers and managers to the Charlotte office more frequently each year. If Tom Belk could not control the kind of merchandise in Belk stores, he could influence buying decisions by offering a better deal on merchandise than they could find elsewhere.

By 1954, the company's private-label business had expanded well beyond overalls, work shoes, and hosiery. The buying office now offered two lines of men's dress shirts and ties, men's suits, hats, sweaters, and pajamas. Sam Elliott had produced a line of boys' wear under the label Dixie Lad, and the Belks' own hosiery mill, Belvedere Hosiery Company in Charlotte, was turning out the Heiress and Reigning Beauty lines as well as socks under the name of Belbro and ABC. Craddock-Terry Shoe Corporation produced the stores' twelve brands of shoes for men, women, and children, including the Virginia Bond, named for Virginia Bond Robinson, a ladies' shoe buyer in the Charlotte office. The office estimated that by 1960 more than 10 million items would be manufactured under a Belk label.

That estimate was low, largely because of the State Pride label that Tom Belk and Byerly, who had succeeded Scott in the domestics department, introduced at the 1954 housewares show. Like Frank Stevens's Red Camel overalls twenty years earlier, the State Pride label was born out of competition from J. C. Penney Company.

With the opening of each Penney store in Belk towns, Belk and Byerly were hearing complaints from store managers that they could not touch the price Penney put on its own Nationpride brand of sheets. No matter how good a deal Belk buyers made with manufacturers, buying in large lots for the stores, they could not get a price to compete with Penney. Penney's stores could cut their private-label brand to within a thread of actual cost. To meet their competitor and make any profit at all, Belk managers would have had to sell brand name sheets at a loss.

Tom Belk and Byerly had first approached the elderly Scott, still the dean of domestics in the Belk organization, with an idea of producing a Belk brand sheet. Scott was not receptive and would not listen to his two former understudies. They persisted and called on major mills in the area, anyhow. After rejections from most of the major manufacturers, who sniffed at what appeared to be a small order, they finally found a plant in Durham, N.C., that wanted the business.

Byerly had a supplier. Now he needed a name. Most Belk brand names reflected the region, such as Sam Elliott's Dixie Lad boys' wear, a work shoe called Old Hickory, and an inexpensive men's dress shoe called the Southerner. Byerly and Tom Belk traded ideas and finally settled, halfheartedly, on Pride of the South. One night, shortly before the packaging was printed, Byerly awoke about 2:00 A.M., sat bolt upright in bed, and announced to his startled wife, "State Pride. That's it. It's short, it indicates we're tops where we are in each state." The next day Belk endorsed Byerly's suggestion, and one of the most successful private-label lines in the company's history was born.

Byerly's first order to the Durham mill was for 10,000 sheets. The buying service paid $17.10 a dozen, the best price they would ever get, and gave managers a low-priced sheet they could use to beat Penney. The sheets sold out to the wall, and the stores clamored for more. A month later Byerly introduced State Pride rayon and nylon blankets and in the following year a plaid bedspread. A year later, he added feather pillows, mattress covers, pillow covers, mattress pads, Dacron curtains, Heirloom spreads, and corded bedspreads. Next to come were bath sets, cotton rugs, a luxury line of sheets, more blankets, more bedspreads. When Byerly retired from the company nearly thirty years later, John Belk suggested the State Pride name someday be chiseled on his tombstone.

By 1959, the private-label business at Belk stores accounted for a major share of the buying office's inventory. Its catalog offered clothing lines for boys and men, home furnishings, hosiery, shoes for all ages, infants' wear, girls' wear, and lingerie. The buyers shaved prices on Belk labels by combining purchases into larger orders to get the best advantage from the mills, sometimes buying more than 250,000 yards of some fabric to be shipped to a variety of manufacturers who cut and sewed the pieces. Not infrequently, the Belk shipment was the largest some manufacturers would receive during the year.

Tom Belk had plans for more. He moved Sam Elliott out of boys' wear and put Elliott's desk beside his own at the back of the second-floor buying office. Never fussy about job titles, Belk gave Elliott the fuzzy assignment of merchandise relations manager. His job was to expand the private-label business and help Belk coordinate the work of buyers in various departments.

Within a year, Belk and Elliott had doubled the private-label business in the menswear department. Belk was stretching its manufacturers to produce well-made, durable goods at rock-bottom prices. One knitting mill in Belmont had been making Belk's T-shirts and briefs for years, and the owner told Elliott that he could handle the larger orders Elliott said would be coming. When the orders began to roll in, however, Elliott realized the small mill could not handle the expected demand. He quickly mailed a sample of the shirt he wanted duplicated to a larger mill, Washington Mills in Winston-Salem, where a salesman confidently took the order at Elliott's price of seventy-nine cents each.

A few days later, Elliott paid a call on Washington Mills, where he found that the salesman had not closely examined the shirt and was unaware of the quality Belk demanded for its goods. After Elliott arrived, the man finally pulled the shirt from the package, measured it and looked at the close weave of the cotton yarn. "Mr. Elliott," the manufacturer said, "this is a dollar T-shirt in anybody's book."

"I know that, but you didn't know that, and you said

you'd be glad to make it and I want to buy some," Elliott told him. The mill filled the order for a few thousand dozen, but balked at making more at the low price. By that time, however, Belk's main supplier had built up enough of a supply to catch up to the demand at the regular, lower price.

A large part of the success of the private-label program in the late 1950s was simply timing. The Belk brands of clothing for boys and girls arrived just as the postwar baby bulge was growing up. Mothers already accustomed to shopping at Belk for themselves found sturdy play clothes, little girls' dresses, and outfits for their children at prices well below what they could find elsewhere. They bought and returned to buy more.

In addition, Belk's young, energetic merchandise managers, working under the watchful eye of Tom Belk, could coordinate a complete outfit and get it into production in short order. The buying office was growing, but it had not become so specialized that a committee was required to meet to develop a complete outfit. Often, one or two people got together with Elliott to design a coordinated line, order materials from suppliers, and produce a promotional package for the stores. Located close to textile mills, Belk got good selections and prices on fabric and had no trouble finding manufacturers to cut and sew the clothing.

The increased private-label business was changing the look of Belk stores. At the height of the boys' wear program in about 1960, this department accounted for as much as 8.5 percent of the total store volume, largely on private-label brands produced by the buying office. The national average for boys' departments was about 1 percent. The State Pride label was so successful throughout the region that Byerly was advertising a line of its bath sets called "Pam-Purr" in the Southeastern editions of *Life* magazine in 1962.

The advertising appeared just as the Belk organization was preparing for its seventy-fifth anniversary and ending another period of internal adjustment. After protracted negotiations, the twenty-seven Belk-Lindsey stores in Florida were brought back into the fold in 1960 and restored to full participation in the buying service. The episode was not without another round of lawsuits and family legal fights that resulted in Henry Belk, Jr., being further removed from the business. The settlement did end some confusion for suppliers who for the previous five years had been selling to Belk stores through two separate buying offices.

In 1961, Byerly and Elliott were promoted to vice-presidencies in BSS, strengthening the management of the buying office now firmly under the command of Tom Belk. That same year, John Belk moved Ray Killian from the personnel office at the Charlotte store to BSS, where he became director of personnel and public relations. While some of the larger stores had personnel departments, Killian was the first personnel specialist with responsibilities for the entire Belk organization, which now had more than 20,000 employees.

Killian was from the North Carolina town of Conover. As a teenager, he had clerked in Karl Broome's Hickory store. Broome said he gave him the job because he needed someone from Killian's corner of the county. He believed Killian could attract some business to the store from his hometown. Killian graduated from Lenoir-Rhyne College in Hickory, flew Navy fighters in World War II, and returned home to complete graduate work at Chapel Hill. After a brief stint with the state personnel department in Raleigh, he joined the Charlotte store as personnel manager in 1949.

Killian was John Belk's versatile utility infielder. In addition to his duties as personnel manager of Belk Brothers Company, he organized training sessions for employees from salesclerks to store managers, supervised the publication of the bimonthly company publication *Busy Bees*, and coordinated the biennial managers' conventions. He even performed as Dr. John Belk in a homespun film of the company's history released at the time of the seventieth anniversary in 1958.

Killian's appointment was announced in January 1961. By the time store managers met in May for their annual conference at the Carolina Hotel in Pinehurst, the full implications of Killian's new responsibilities were just coming clear. Killian's department would operate as a placement service for transfers and promotions between stores, regardless of organizational boundaries. No longer would the organization lose a bright young manager who had reached the top in one partner group when another needed experienced help. Killian also announced the beginning of a series of management training seminars, with the first class due in Charlotte in August. Separate programs for other specialized personnel also were being planned. And, Killian told the managers, his office would be looking for ways to improve the public image of the stores in their communities. The underlying message of Killian's announcement was John and Tom Belk's theme for the future—greater cooperation and exchange among all the stores which now numbered nearly four hundred.

When the Belks invited manufacturers, newspaper editors, bankers, and others to their seventy-fifth birthday celebration events in 1962 and 1963, both the company and the region were at critical junctures. For the first time, Belk stores were presented as a united front rather than a string of independent operations. Instead of focusing simply on the past, and the lore of the early days, the anniversary's theme —played out in movies, booklets, speeches, and formal presentations—was the future. Promotional materials included references to fashion, the growing importance of the youth market, contemporary store interiors and design, and, for the first time, national brand name merchandise. The brands were the moderately priced labels from Levi Strauss, Van Heusen, and Hushpuppy, but they reflected Tom Belk's interest in upgrading the bargain image of Belk stores.

By the time of this celebration, the Belks had a twenty-year history of honoring suppliers and manufacturers. In the 1940s, William Henry Belk had periodically hosted suppliers and mill owners at dinners in Charlotte's finest hotels. Bus tours of the stores and the buying office in Charlotte were arranged in subsequent years as Tom and John Belk continued the courtship. The seventy-fifth celebration, however, was a much more elaborate affair. For many of the manufacturers and vendors invited to Charlotte, the event was as much an introduction to the South as to Belk stores. Many saw the South as poor and unsophisticated, its industry old, the social pace slow and conservative. A combination of razzle-dazzle and solid statistical evidence of economic growth helped disabuse a stranger of this stereotype.

The promise made at the company's seventy-fifth anniversary was of a bigger, bolder, and stronger Belk organization. The Belks had backed up the promise with a joint announcement with the J. B. Ivey Company in Charlotte that the two retailers had purchased 500 acres of land south of Charlotte for construction of a major regional shopping center. What they left unsaid, however, was just what kind of Belk store would be there.

The two challenges facing the company were succession and image. Since their father's death, the Belks had relied heavily on the senior partners for direction and leadership in the stores. Along the way, the Belks had made course corrections, but the general operation of the business had changed little, if at all. Now the men the young Belks had depended on in their early years were nearing retirement age, and not all had children who were either sufficiently able or interested in taking their place.

As the cities and towns where Belk operated became more crowded with competing stores, the company leaders also needed to determine what kind of stores Belk would operate in the future. Some in the industry had already announced the death of the department stores. Key men in the Belk organization also had their doubts. Some believed the future lay in the discount business, others favored the traditional middle-of-the-road, moderate-priced market, and some, like Tom Belk, wanted to improve the image and upgrade to appeal to a more affluent shopper. He and brother John believed the future was in the regional malls they had seen in other sections of the nation that were successfully drawing business from miles around.

None felt the pressure of change more keenly than John Belk. Gut instinct and the growth in the Southern economy had guided the expansion and development of Belk stores for generations. "Everybody was just going along doing their own things," John Belk recalls. He knew from his studies and work with the American Management Association that a business the size and complexity of Belk would require careful planning by trained professionals to guide it successfully through the years ahead.

A major task would be the development of a sufficient supply of trained managers who could replace men now retiring after years of service. He dispatched Killian to attend some of the same AMA sessions, and they invited AMA speakers to meet with select groups of store executives and partners. Killian set about creating uniform management language, position descriptions, standards of performance, and other generally accepted management techniques that had been ignored in this large organization. The idea of formal personnel procedures and organization charts was greeted skeptically by many of the old-timers. They said such things would never work in their stores. With Belk's support, Killian expanded the company's training program to accommodate a larger and more concentrated management training component. Hundreds of Belk people, starting from top management down, attended AMA briefings. If they could not change old minds, they would shape young ones. Gradually, with pushing from Charlotte, stores began putting together the first job descriptions and organizational charts in the company's history.

While Killian worked on management structure, Belk looked to Leroy Robinson, an attorney in the BSS legal department, for help in streamlining the grouping of store corporations. Robinson, a quiet, thorough lawyer, had worked closely with John Belk and had helped him and the family navigate through the shoals of internal legal problems, including the 1960 settlement with Henry. And in October 1964, John and Tom Belk added Joe Robinson to the team.

Joe Robinson had been permitted as close a look at the inside of the Belk businesses as any outsider. The Belk connections to the Wachovia Bank and Trust Company were old and strong. So were Robinson's family connections with the

Belks. His father had been president of the Wadesboro bank that had loaned the Leggett brothers the money to open their first store in Virginia. And Robinson's mother had worked closely with Mrs. Henry Belk in joint projects for the Daughters of the American Revolution and Colonial Dames.

Robinson was planning to take a top position with a South Carolina bank when John and Tom Belk asked him to come to work at Belk Stores Services. "You don't have enough to keep me busy," Robinson told Belk. From the outside, Robinson saw a large organization that appeared to have its affairs in order. He was aware of the family feuds, but the stores had capable senior leadership in Arthur Tyler, George Dowdy, and others. Robinson and Belk had talked often about implementing in the retail business the kind of planning Belk had seen as a bank director. Belk persisted in his request and told Robinson, "I guarantee you that if you come with us, you'll have more than you'll ever be able to handle."

Robinson was named vice-president and director of store planning at the same time Belk created four other vice-presidencies. Three went to company lawyers David McConnell, John L. Green, Jr., and Leroy Robinson. The fourth went to I. N. Howard, company controller. Officially, Joe Robinson replaced Gibson Smith, assuming responsibility for the real estate office and architectural and fixtures departments, but his title was sufficiently broad to cover a number of areas.

Early on, Robinson became involved in helping Irwin Belk, whose interest in politics was taking more and more of his time from the business, manage the company's complicated loan portfolio. Tall, friendly, and gregarious like his older brother John, Irwin was serving his third term in the N.C. Senate and had ambitions for higher office when Robinson came aboard. Many of the Belks' bankers already knew Robinson, and the connections helped the Belks and their partners consolidate loans and try new methods of financing. Due to Irwin's outside interests, Robinson assumed more and more of his banking duties.

Robinson also immersed himself in the merchandising

side. He accompanied John and Tom Belk on their trips to stores, listening and looking and getting to know more about retailing. Traveling with Tom Belk was always an experience. On one swing, the two left Laurinburg, N.C., late one day for an overnight drive to Alabama. The trip took longer than usual. Tom had called ahead to the Belk towns en route and arranged for store managers to open up long enough for Tom to make a quick inspection. The two did not stay long. Belk's keen merchant's sense and his eye for detail enabled him to collect more information during his characteristic fast-paced walk through a store than pages of reports. Belk sized up the local operation, and the two climbed back into the car and headed for the next town.

The more Robinson saw once he got inside the business, the more it appalled him. The company was run much as it had been in Henry Belk's day. Decision making "was just as casual as it could be," he recalls. "They'd ride around a town and look at things and make the decision on guts. Just ride around and look, particularly if they had excess money, and most of them did at that time. They'd use no facts, no figures, not even an estimate of cost or financial statements." In addition, company meetings were cluttered with discussion of details most corporate boards left to management. The ragged process, with horseback opinions determining how as much as $22 million might be spent during a single year, disturbed the orderly sense of business that Robinson had cultivated at Wachovia. After several such sessions, Robinson began investigating proposed new locations prior to meetings so he would have important details available.

As Robinson gathered information for these meetings, two things became clear. The potential Belk stores' market was growing larger and larger at the same time it was becoming more affluent. In just five years, the number of households in Charlotte with incomes of $10,000 or more had jumped from one in five to one in four. The trend was the same across the region. "We had a change in the whole makeup of the Southeast going on," Robinson recalls. He investigated further. Contacts in the banking industry and others close to the consumer market told him the South was on the verge of another major economic revitalization.

When Robinson and Nat Howard compared that to the growth of Belk stores, the contrast was striking. Belk companies were making more money from one year to the next, but the size of these increases was getting smaller and smaller. Meanwhile, competitors, most of them public companies that disclosed sales figures, were showing large increases each year. Belk's share of the market was growing smaller and smaller. The trend indicated that Belk stores would be squeezed out of the market, battered by competition from the new wave of discount stores (which now accounted for more retail sales than department stores nationwide) and traditional competitors like Sears and Penney, if no changes were made. Robinson's assessment was that the company needed to make major changes or face serious problems.

Robinson blended the numbers and statistics into a report for John and Tom Belk. The numbers challenged much of the way the company had been doing business for more than seventy-five years. Americans were moving to credit; 87 percent of Belk's sales were still for cash. The move away from downtown was accelerating; 94 percent of Belk's stores were still there. The market was young, stylish, and contemporary, fashion and fashion-label conscious. Belk brands were strong, but could not match the advertising and marketing of national brands. To accommodate the changes taking place in the communities where Belk was now doing nearly $350 million in sales each year would require a major overhaul of the company. Researchers from Lippincott and Margulies were arriving at the same conclusions as they prepared the recommendations for a new image for the stores.

In the fall of 1966, John and Tom Belk, Joe and Leroy Robinson, John Green, Killian, and others wrestled with how best to convince the elders in the business that a major redirection of the business was necessary. It would not be easy. The changes required would cost money, lots of money, and demand the adoption of modern management techniques.

Mindful of the delicate balance needed to keep the massive Belk ship on a steady course, John Belk preferred to work without direct confrontation, developing a consensus among the leaders who would respond. Once again, he called on his old friend Arthur Tyler, who appointed the first long-range planning committee for the Belk stores.

In the months before the committee's first meeting, Killian and Robinson carefully prepared the agenda and briefed key committee members on their findings. On July 12, 1967, the committee members and BSS staff members gathered in John Belk's living room overlooking the golf course at the Dunes Club in Myrtle Beach, S.C. The group included the men who would carry the business into the next decade. Tyler had appointed key senior partners, including William Beery III of Wilmington, Karl Hudson, Jr., of Raleigh, and John W. Hensdale of Fayetteville. Representing Dr. John Belk's side of the family were John Belk Stevens (Frank Stevens's son) from Winston-Salem, and John C. Daughtridge, Jr., from Charleston. Sarah Belk Gambrell did not attend, but all her brothers, except Henry, were present. Robinson, his assistant Joe Lowrance, and controller Nat Howard readied their charts and detailed statistical analysis of Belk markets. Killian distributed the agenda and outlined the schedule of the meeting. Beery opened the meeting.

For the rest of the day and on into the next, the group conducted a free-wheeling discussion of where the future for Belk stores lay. Altogether, the group represented large stores and small, merchants who favored bargain operations and those who were upgrading merchandise to reach a growing, affluent market in the cities. Some had been close associates of the founders, Henry and John Belk. Others knew only the legend. They discussed statistics and trends and digested numbers so large as to be almost unbelievable for a business that had begun with a savings nest egg of $750.

They discussed moving into the discount business and cutting costs by offering more self-service shopping. Henderson Belk favored that, along with adding tires, batteries, and automotive services to the inventory. After all, Tyler's stores operated gas pumps under the name Belko. Henderson suggested that five partners try the discount business as an experiment.

Irwin Belk suggested consolidating corporations to build more financial strength. A single-store corporation was not sufficiently strong to open a store in a large city such as Atlanta. Others said Atlanta was not a place for a Belk store, and they should stay with the markets they knew, the medium- to moderate-sized cities.

Separate merchandising plans for small stores were suggested. Tom Belk said perhaps the smaller stores should have a division of their own and concentrate on lower-priced goods. Hensdale suggested closing all the small stores and concentrating the company's resources on larger regional stores.

Beery, who would open the first Belk store in a regional center just two years hence, asked what the ideal store would be in 1980. Joe Robinson said J. C. Penney was then thinking the average store would be 220,000 square feet, nearly five times larger than the average Belk store. What should the stores' sales goal be in that year? Inflation alone, Robinson said, would generate at least $1 billion by 1980.

John Belk talked about the problem of overlapping territories where partners from separate groups were selling in the same growing retail markets. In North Carolina's largest trading area, the combined Greensboro, Winston-Salem, and High Point market, three separate partners operated stores. The arrangement confused customers, complicated management, and was inefficient. They talked about computers, about larger and finer quarters for Belk Stores Services, about all the things that John Belk and his chief aides had wanted fully aired in this first meeting.

The meeting ended with the taking of only one formal vote. The committee asked for a study of the physical requirements for a new BSS building in Charlotte, because the old building was growing ever more crowded as the business grew. Beyond that, John Belk collected his consensus in a low-key fashion, saying at the appropriate time, "Now, don't y'all think this is a good idea?" His audience nodded consent. On so much as that was the new direction for Belk stores set, to move away from downtowns, into large shopping malls, with a style and flair for action and fashion.

"What that meeting was about," John Belk recalls, "was what did we want to be and what is our goal and what kind of store did we want. Did we want to be a department store, did we want to be a specialty shop, did we want to be a country store? Did we want to be a discount? Rose's was going to discount. Did we want to be a specialty store? Ivey's was going to specialty store. That's when we stated what volume we should do, and then we went about it in each market."

The numbers were bigger, the plans grander than most of the senior partners had ever seen. "I came out of there with a timetable," Robinson recalls. "We'd expand 500,000 square feet a year, and for this company that was unheard of. And we'd remodel another 500,000 square feet a year. That was a big decision. We exceeded that in the first year." Some partners bought into the plan on blind faith. Others balked, and John Belk would be working on changes in their towns for years to come. A key figure, once again, was Arthur Tyler. John and Tom Belk made sure some of the early projects were scheduled for Tyler's towns in eastern North Carolina, first in Elizabeth City and then in Kinston. When the new stores were a success, they referred doubters to the respected Arthur Tyler for a testimonial.

During the next six months, artists from Lippincott and Margulies completed the design for the "Big B" and "Big L." They had proposed several graphic arrangements, and the committee supervising the project had rejected them all. Finally, the artists found an acceptable design and alternative colors, blue or white. The new letters were bold, stylish, with a hint of tradition. The bss board adopted the recommendations, but not without some dissent.

"It's Belk's, not Belk," George Dowdy, the respected old lion of the Charlotte store, bellowed during one meeting. He pointed to Macy's, Ivey's, and a number of other stores that accepted colloquial titles of their stores as their formal name. Dowdy lost the round. His store was the first to receive the 12-foot Belk sign in the new script.

In May 1971, more than 950 Belk managers and partners and their wives gathered at the Daytona Plaza Hotel in Daytona Beach, Fla., for the stores' biennial managers' meeting. These gatherings followed the tradition
of Henry Belk, who once could call all his managers together
around a large table in his office. The founder had used the
sessions with his partners to talk over common problems,
discuss market trends, and highlight successes in one store
in hopes others would duplicate the efforts. Over the years,
as the number of stores and managing partners increased,
the meetings had moved to larger and larger quarters, first to
Charlotte's hotels and then to resorts in Myrtle Beach, S.C.,
and Pinehurst, N.C. Managers relaxed with golf, surf fishing, and good food, but the basic purpose of the conferences
remained the same, to build business and improve the operation through cooperative ventures.

The Daytona Beach session had the usual convention atmosphere with lots of backslapping and good times as Belk
and Leggett managers from across the Southeast renewed
contacts. There also was plenty of work to do. Organizer Ray
Killian, vice-president for human resources for Belk Stores
Services, had lined up his usual impressive list of speakers,
including the president of the country's largest brokerage
house, Merrill Lynch, Pierce, Fenner & Smith, who reported
on the state of the economy and the business outlook for
the 1970s. Experts in insurance, fashion, and organizational
management followed him to the podium during the three-
day conference. Store tours and merchandise shows had
been arranged. But the most important messages of the gathering came from John Belk.

Belk first reported on the impressive growth of the business since the last convention in 1969. Fourteen stores had
been opened in 1969, he said, and sixteen more had been
opened in 1970, including new piece goods specialty stores

called FabricFairs. More than 1.5 million square feet of new sales space had been added to the Belk inventory and stores were getting larger, Belk said. Prior to 1969, the average store size was 28,000 square feet. Now the average was 59,000 square feet. "The average volume per store is 45 percent greater than in 1965, 94 percent greater that in 1960 and 165 percent greater than in 1950 and 555 percent greater than in 1940," Belk said. "In 1980, we expect it to be 100 percent greater than it was in 1970."

In addition, Belk said, modern management techniques had been introduced. More than half of the stores had computers managing their payrolls, three-fourths had a staff organization plan in writing, and nine out of ten had someone in the store responsible for personnel and hiring.

Then, turning to the point of his morning address, Belk said, "Let me emphasize, as strongly as possible, the following facts: Stores in the 1970s will not be managed and operated the same way they were in the 1960s. A new type of leadership will be required: One that is alert, knowledgeable, responsive, one that can manage people and one that can operate in a quantitative or measurement management environment. Simply stated, the management direction of the 1970s involves specific advance planning and management that is capable of successfully implementing the plan developed."

A few hours later, John Belk met separately with the supervising partners and outlined their responsibilities in the coming years. "Frankly, in the past, we have not been fair with you," he told them with candor. "In far too many instances, we have not indicated to you exactly what you were expected to do, what you were being held accountable for, what you were authorized to do and spend and the matters in which you needed to seek board approval. Too often we have applied one set of rules to one partner and a different set of rules to other partners. I am certain, from time to time, we have given you conflicting information and instructions. You have been equally guilty in not clarifying your role as it relates to the store managers and the stores."

Belk then outlined in specific detail the partners' planning, merchandising, and management responsibilities, including maintaining good relations with Belk Stores Services and implementing company-wide objectives, policies, plans, and programs. "We hope in the near future," Belk said, "to develop an overall 'management plan' which will provide a strong, forward thrust to the full potential of the entire organization."

The Belk men have never been polished speakers. After trying to record the often-garbled comments of John Belk at Charlotte City Council meetings, where he presided after his election as mayor in 1969, a *Charlotte Observer* reporter had filled an entire notebook with his honor's malapropisms. This morning, however, the managers and partners responsible for the more than four hundred stores understood John Belk. With unmistakable confidence and clarity, he delivered the message that the Belk leadership knew where it wanted to take the large, growing company and what would be required to get there.

In the five years since the planning meeting at John Belk's Myrtle Beach home, the company had begun to take a new direction not only in merchandising but in management as well. The new, larger stores the company's leaders wanted for the future could not be run out of the manager's hip pocket. The old style of operation where a manager hired and fired at will, planned no further ahead than next month, and considered himself a success if he beat last year's sales might work with stores in the rural hamlets across the South. But these stores were earmarked for oblivion. In the next decade, John Belk would preside over the closing of twice as many stores as he opened.

If there was an extra-solid ring of confidence in Belk's voice, it was because the large organization finally had a plan for the future, and Belk had a consensus among partners, family, and key BSS staff members about how to carry it out.

The reshaping of the company for the future had begun. Most stores now carried the new Lippincott and Margulies signage. During 1969 and 1970, nearly 360 of the new signs

—more than $800,000 worth—were put up on storefronts across the region, giving Belk stores a common identity. The new stores that had been opened, and those about to open, were located in the new shopping malls and were large and contemporary, further emphasizing the new Belk style of fashion and action. Inside, customers found more new lines of brand name merchandise than ever before, and they paid for it with Belk and Leggett credit cards now accepted in any store. In the works were more changes, including reorganization of partner groups around specific market areas, experiments in specialty stores, the introduction of computers to the sales floor, and more new lines of brand name merchandise than many of the old-timers who privately scoffed at these plans had ever dreamed of.

The expansion into regional malls, and the closing of smaller, obsolete downtown stores, was a matter of bricks and mortar and money. A more significant change in the Belk organization was not as apparent, even to some within the business. After many years of family discord that produced conflicting messages to top BSS executives, as well as to the family's partners in the stores, John and Tom Belk had settled the question of family management, at least for their generation.

In mid-1969, John had written to his brothers and sister and asked them to outline their interests and plans for participation in the business, and he had sent along a questionnaire that the American Management Association had helped prepare. The questionnaire also was sent to key BSS executives who, along with the family, were asked to spend a week in close examination of how the business should be run in the future. The questions were pointed and precise, covering everything from image to organization. With the AMA's help, John Belk was putting together a management summit of sorts. Belk wanted to be sure that he had the management team in place to run these stores of the future. It was also an opportunity to settle nagging family problems. "The whole purpose of the thing," John Belk recalls, "was to get the family working together."

Belk received no reply from his older brother, Henry, who now was more removed from the business than ever. Tom would continue to concentrate on merchandise. Irwin was still interested in finance. The responses from Henderson and Sarah were less clearly defined. Belk compiled the results from his family and the others and in the second week of December set off for the Grove at Hamilton, N.Y., an upstate conference center where the AMA staff met with the Belk family and eight top BSS executives.

During the week, the group talked about the changing retail market, the resources of Belk stores, the duties of top BSS executives and family members, personnel, public relations, and long-range planning. It reviewed organizational charts within BSS and the individual partner groups. The discussions were often heated; sparks flew as tensions between family members broke into the open. Henderson insisted that his son be allowed to sit in. John refused, saying this meeting was for his generation and not the next. The next day, both were absent. Old habits of store operation were challenged, and the legend of William Henry Belk hung heavy over the meeting. As retail business declined in small towns, the family would be faced with closing stores. Sarah reminded her brothers that their father had *never* closed a store. More direction and control by BSS conflicted with the tradition of independence at the store level.

The survey of BSS executives pointed up other nagging problems. Merchandise managers in the buying office felt constrained by second-guessing from the family and the partners, by a lack of consistent company objectives, and by the multiplicity of bosses. There were no clear lines of authority and responsibility; decision-making was awkward and ineffective. The ad hoc arrangements of the last decade had strained relations among key staff members. And, again, the question of a new building arose. The BSS offices had expanded beyond the capacity of the East Fifth Street quarters, where partitions and corridors now created a warren of offices and cramped working spaces. Communication within and between departments was difficult at best.

There was also consensus. The group agreed that the business needed more aggressive marketing, modern money management, formal financial procedures, up-to-date personnel and operations management. The business needed new direction and professionals who could specialize in particular areas of the business. BSS needed to be more assertive, exerting more leadership in the stores and thus accelerating the rate of change from budget to fashion merchandise. Planning, rather than reacting, should be part of the standard operating procedure.

The week-long session did not resolve all the problems. It did focus attention on the areas in the organization that needed work, and it established an agenda. Assignments were given to be completed before a return session six months later. John and Tom Belk left the meeting with a confirmation of the plans for development in the 1970s and with certain family problems resolved. They were ready to move ahead.

Belk leaders hoped that they were not too late. While the company prepared for the future, the market was changing rapidly. The South was no longer the nation's economic and social stepchild. Major companies were relocating offices to cities like Charlotte. Suburbanites were moving into new homes and spending money in the new shopping centers and malls opening on the rims of the growing cities.

Nothing had changed the face of retailing in the 1960s more than the explosive expansion of the discount stores that offered brand name merchandise at prices below what customers could find at Belk or other department stores. Ironically, the discount stores threatened to be the price competitors for contemporary Belk stores just as Henry Belk and his early partners had challenged local merchants when they advertised low prices on distressed goods, closeouts, and other odd lots from the markets.

Although discount stores represented the latest wave in retailing, they had been around since just after the turn of the century. In 1909, Filene's Department Store, one of Boston's finest department stores, had added a new dimension to its merchandising, offering discount prices on brand name merchandise. Filene's moved any merchandise that did not sell on its main floors to the Automatic Bargain Basement, where prices were automatically reduced on a given day if the goods were not sold. After thirty days, unsold merchandise was given to charity. Filene's Bargain Basement cost the business money in the early years, but literally saved the company during the depression, when profits from the basement discount sales met the payroll for the entire store.

In later years, other merchants in the Northeast tried discount sales of brand name goods. By the 1950s, several large discount stores had opened. The oldest was Marty's Clothing Mart in South Providence, R.I., which was later joined by Zayre and Bradlees in Massachusetts. These two were specialty shops that had expanded into the discount business. Early discounters used vacant factories and buildings deserted by the apparel industry, which was moving south. Most discount companies grew and survived by trimming their gross margins on sales to half of what was expected in full-price department stores.

In 1960, there were 1,329 discount outlets nationwide. By 1965, discount stores had become a key factor in general merchandise retailing. Kmart, which opened its first store in a Detroit suburb in 1962, had 162 such stores by the mid-1960s. By 1977, nearly 8,000 discount stores would be open. Kmart opened an average of 100 stores in each year between 1967 and 1977.

The South was an inviting location for these new stores. North Carolina, the focal point of the Belk organization, was leading the South in the development of a new urban society fed by a changing industrial mix and the continued migration from the farm to the city. During the decade before John Belk's speech in Daytona, the state had been rewarded with $5.4 billion in new and expanded industry, more than in any other Southern state. In addition, North Carolina's cities were growing. Charlotte's population had increased nearly 20 percent in the previous decade, as had those of Greensboro and Winston-Salem. Raleigh's population had jumped nearly 30 percent. The lights of homes and businesses in

Piedmont towns and cities now created a glowing nighttime arc that began southeast of Charlotte at Greenville, S.C., and extended more than 300 miles northeast to Raleigh.

The changes in the region and the coming of age of the baby boom were creating new Belk customers. Smart merchants whose sales were growing rapidly each year had discovered the youth market. Teenage girls now bought one-fourth of the cosmetics on store shelves, half of all phonograph records, and one-fourth of all greeting cards. Young males were buying more and more cosmetics than ever before. In addition, the active youth population was influencing a trend from spectator to participation sports, making sportswear an essential part of a store's inventory.

The typical Belk customer in 1969, described in Belk's *Busy Bees*, was "a young woman who works, at least part time, and is the chief dispenser of a higher family unit income, has a better and higher education, has developed deeper cultural interests and increased her ability to communicate in a much more mobile society where more activities are shared among family members, fostering greater participation in active sports with a resultant longer life expectancy."

What some called the "peacock era" for men also had begun. Perhaps influenced by young styles and by color television, men now joined women in changing styles from one season to the next. No longer could a menswear buyer be satisfied that he had his stock complete with a limited line of conservative suits, white shirts, and a selection of ties. He had to shop the markets and renew his offerings each year to remain competitive. Shoes were changing shape, with blunted toes and high heels. New fabrics were replacing the traditional wools for suits.

The successful store manager in the 1970s would need more than a sharp eye for styles and merchandise. Killian's management training programs, begun in the mid-1960s, had introduced techniques to store managers accustomed to a more relaxed style of operation, but more was needed. To take care of normal retirements and changes in store management meant finding two hundred new managers virtually overnight. And a new manager would have to supervise hundreds of people, prepare a complicated budget, oversee construction, arrange advertising, and stock his store to meet the demands of a rapidly changing market.

By 1970, Killian had stepped up the BSS training programs at all levels, particularly for middle-management executives, the pool from which the stores would draw the managers of the future. Regular training sessions for hundreds of Belk executives were organized. The programs included training in professional sales supervision, buying techniques, and leadership development. Speaking at these sessions, John and Tom Belk stressed opportunities within the entire Belk organization, not just a single partner group.

The stores these new managers would supervise were part of Belk's most ambitious expansion program. The number of new stores opened each year was the largest since the flurry of openings during the depression and following World War II. Between January 1972 and December 1975, more than fifty stores were opened, adding 4.3 million square feet of new floor space to the business. During the same period, another 1 million square feet of space was remodeled. Altogether, in the decade preceding 1975, the total sales space in Belk stores grew by 66 percent.

The expansion in the late 1960s and early 1970s was a good deal more complicated than anything attempted before. When Henry Belk was opening stores, the procedure was simple, straightforward. Belk or his partner found a vacant building, rounded up the owner, and signed a lease. Suppliers were contacted and shipments of goods were laid out on simple, inexpensive fixtures. A new store could be opened for an initial cash investment of $20,000 or less.

The stores of the 1970s would require much more. They were more expensive; capital requirements were staggering when compared to previous expansion. The new stores opened in malls required a new kind of cooperation with other merchants that other stores never encountered. The new buildings also required more planning. Architects and designers were necessary to produce the most pleasing interiors, and landscaping was now a consideration. Government regulations and zoning laws consumed hours of the companies' lawyers' time.

Although large shopping centers had proliferated as Southern suburbs expanded into the countryside of cities like Charlotte, the Belks could not find developers to take on their early projects. As a result, the first mall stores were in centers that Belk organized or that were handled by a developer whom the Belks recruited.

The job of finding new store designs and coordinating the architectural work for the expansion fell to Jean Surratt, the BSS architect, who had started with the company in 1955. Most of his early assignments were remodeling old stores, adding new storefronts, and generally making the best of the hundreds of old buildings that housed the stores. He also designed the new stores added in the 1950s and 1960s, which were little more than empty boxes with customer traffic patterns arranged in a familiar grid of straight aisles and intersections.

Designing a mall store was something quite different. The store featured a fairly simple exterior. It was a windowless box; only the entrance received special attention. In the early stores, including the first small mall stores for Arthur Tyler in Elizabeth City and Kinston, N.C., architects incorporated the arching columns of the Savannah store, or a variation of them into the store design. The interiors demanded much more attention. Designers matched colors, wall and floor coverings, and layouts to produce a shopping environment, not just sales space. Surratt added designers who created counters and dynamic store fixtures to fit new circular traffic arrangements that encouraged a shopper to linger and shop, not cross quickly from one entrance to another.

Surratt's largest project was SouthPark, the regional center planned for Charlotte. The first thing he had to do was move it. The original SouthPark site, the 600 acres purchased by George Dowdy and George Ivey in 1962, was well south of the city's most ambitious developments. Charlotte had grown and the south side was the hottest area of the county, but John and Tom Belk believed the site was too remote, and they personally arranged to purchase 104 acres of the large Cameron Morrison estate. The land would put SouthPark on the edge of development but comfortably close to the affluent neighborhoods of southeast Charlotte.

Belk and Ivey were equal partners in the development and shared the belief that working together they could create a mall that would discourage any national competitor from capturing their market. They also agreed that Ivey's and Belk together would attract the number of shoppers necessary to make such a large project successful.

The leaders of these two established mercantile operations had different ideas about the mall business, however. John and Tom Belk were committed to building a full-size department store that had plenty of space for the wide range of merchandise customers had come to expect from Belk stores. The Charlotte store had not expanded to other centers in Charlotte because the Belks did not believe a small branch store was the proper investment. George Ivey, meanwhile, had opened stores in other Charlotte shopping centers and wanted to build another small store, of about 40,000 square feet, specializing in ladies' wear. John Belk objected, saying that was too small, and suggested that perhaps Ivey should not be included at all. Ivey increased the size to 150,000 square feet.

The two partners also wanted another major tenant, and on this point the Belks and Ivey parted again. Ivey, whose store would anchor one end of the main wing, wanted to have a J. C. Penney store in the mall. Belk, whose store would be directly opposite Ivey's at the other end of the top of the T-shaped mall wanted to have a Sears store as the major national retailer. Belk liked Sears's operation and was already involved in development of the Savannah mall, which would include a Sears store. In addition, Belk believed Sears's "hard lines," automotive products, appliances, and tools, would complement the project more. Ivey finally agreed, but the standoff delayed construction. One other snag also postponed work. Belk wanted to use a white, glazed brick on the exterior, Ivey's first choice was something darker. The white brick was the final choice.

The large malls in Savannah and Charlotte, and the smaller suburban stores opened in the early period of expansion, were not easy projects. Few, if any, of the nation's large mall developers were doing business in the South during this time, and experienced local developers were not available. This required the Belks to put the complicated and expensive projects together and make concessions in an effort to recruit developers.

By the fall of 1972, Belk had plans on the boards for one hundred new stores and had opened another superstore, the 236,410-square-foot Hudson-Belk store in Crabtree Valley Mall in Raleigh. It was another showcase, like SouthPark, and fit the plan perfectly. But it almost never happened.

Raleigh was North Carolina's fastest growing major city in the 1960s. New industry was attracted to the area to take some of the prime spots in the Research Triangle Park, a unique industrial and corporate research development located strategically between the campuses of the University of North Carolina at Chapel Hill, N.C. State University in Raleigh, and Duke University in Durham. Large state government payrolls boosted the average income of the financial and retail center for eastern North Carolina. Confident of the city's future, Karl Hudson, Jr., had remodeled the downtown Raleigh store in 1964, doubling its size and spending more than $2 million in the process. The new front on Fayetteville Street featured white glazed brick and Georgia marble. Surratt and his staff had dressed Hudson's largest store in their finest designs.

Three years after the remodeled downtown store opened, the city's first major shopping mall, North Hills, opened without a Belk store. Karl Hudson, Jr., was, like most partners at this time, confident in the results of the past and satisfied with the business he had. "Some of us thought we were mighty important in our market," Hudson recalls.

After the mall opened, Hudson-Belk sales began to level off and the store began to lose market share. Now, anxious

about the future, Hudson mustered enough votes to autho-
rize a shopping center store in Raleigh as part of a project
smaller than North Hills, one that would be anchored by a
large, new Kmart store. The location would not be as expensive as a big mall and would permit Hudson-Belk to maintain
its merchandise mix aimed at the moderate- to low-income
shoppers that had been the company's base for two generations.

John and Tom Belk had opposed the location. It was in the
wrong place, they argued, and the brothers did not want a
discounter for a neighbor. The store Hudson had planned
also was too small for what they believed could work in the
expanding Raleigh market. The Belks did not give up the
fight. They hired a consultant to study the market and presented the results to Hudson. The results confirmed the
Belks' assessment. Finally, Hudson agreed that the Kmart
location was the wrong place for his new store and signed on
as soon as the Crabtree Valley location came open. It was
profitable from the start.

During the planning stages for Crabtree Valley Mall, Hudson joined the caravan of Belk executives who had begun a
series of tours of new malls and new stores around the country. These were not casual sightseeing excursions, but serious scouting expeditions. The group followed a busy itiner-
ary that included tours guided by mall developers and store
owners, as well as unannounced and unescorted visits to
new malls, old malls, large and small stores. Tom Belk and
Joe Robinson made arrangements for the trips that took executives to California, where they studied the new stores
being opened by the Nordstrum Company, to New England
for a look at the new Jordan Marsh stores and to the Dayton-
Hudson stores in the Midwest. During the day, the group
split up, with one or two men checking out specific locations. In the evenings, the men convened in a hotel room
and reported on the day's findings. They picked up tips on
new merchandise, point-of-sale displays, fixtures, lighting,
and traffic flow inside and out. They took down the names
of interior designers, mall developers, and store managers

whose work they liked. They saw the best that America's retailers had to offer.

The results of these trips began to show up in North Carolina. Frank Matthews II used a designer whose work he had seen in Dallas, Texas, to lay out the interior of his large new mall store in Gastonia. Von Autry, Jr., the supervising partner who had succeeded John Hensdale in Fayetteville, hired Robert Wildrick away from a fashionable department store in Dallas to become merchandise manager for his group of about a dozen stores from Fayetteville to Winston-Salem. Contacts with mall developers across the country increased builders' interest in the growing Southern market.

The partners who joined the Belks and top BSS staff members on these trips were the men who had emerged as the new generation of leaders for the Belk organization. Most, like Hudson, Matthews, William B. Beery III, and the Leggetts' cousins, had followed their fathers into the business. Hudson had assumed management of the Belk-Hudson organization upon his father's death in 1951. Beery's father had replaced "Mac" Williams's son in Wilmington in the 1940s and the name of the business had been changed to Belk-Beery by the time the large new store was opened there in the early 1950s. Beery now supervised the management of stores from Jacksonville, N.C., south to Savannah, Ga. Matthews was the youngest of Houston Matthews's children, all of whom worked in the business. He had assumed the leadership of the Matthews group after his brother's death in 1971.

Autry had married into the business, taking Frances Hensdale as his wife. A native of Fayetteville, Autry was an Army Air Force pilot in World War II who dreamed of being an engineer. He received his degree in mechanical engineering from N.C. State University with honors in 1949, but by 1951 was assistant manager of the Belk-Hensdale store in downtown Fayetteville. In 1972, upon Hensdale's retirement, Autry became executive vice-president and supervising partner of the Belk-Hensdale group.

Autry was an early follower of the merchandising philosophy preached by John and Tom Belk. Within four years after he became supervising partner, the Belk-Hensdale group had opened two large stores—one each in Fayetteville and Winston-Salem—with a total size of more than 335,000 square feet. In addition, the group opened the network's first regional service center, a 44,000-square-foot facility in Greensboro. The center coordinated sales activities and distribution of merchandise to the large stores concentrated in the Greensboro and Winston-Salem markets.

The service center in Greensboro was followed by another in Fayetteville. In designing the centers, Autry drew on his training and inclinations as an engineer to streamline the receiving, marking, and distribution of merchandise. "The ideal of retailing," Autry said once, "is to have the item handed to the customer straight off the truck." That was not practical, but engineer Autry tried to eliminate as many of the merchandise way stations as he could to cut down the cost of inventory. For example, he designed a system of overhead rails and carriers that cut in half the time needed to load and unload trucks. In time, Autry's system would be exported to other Belk groups. The center broke another tradition, but Autry found the need inescapable. Eighty-five percent of the merchandise in his fourteen stores was the same. It was easier to have it shipped to one central point, checked, tagged, and prepared for the racks than it was to ship to each individual store and have these tasks performed separately.

By the fall of 1975, the Belks and their partners had opened 128 new stores in the previous ten years. Eight thousand more people worked for Belk and Leggett stores in 1975 than were on the payroll in 1965, bringing total employment to 25,000 people. In the past five years, the business had expanded at the rate of 1 million square feet per year. The average new store was now 120,000 square feet, nearly five times what it had been a decade earlier.

The success of each new store helped John and Tom Belk present their case for the next location. Partners reluctant to move into a new store and change from budget or moderate-priced goods to more expensive fashion merchandise could talk with Autry, Karl Hudson, Jr., or Frank Matthews, whose large Eastridge Mall store in Gastonia opened in August, 1976, or Bill Beery in Wilmington and learn whether the new Belk really was going to work.

Some senior partners remained unconvinced, however, and were reluctant to leave the familiar downtown locations. Belk's stores on the Main Streets of Southern towns were an institution. They usually were the largest stores in town, the anchor for the local retail business. The store buildings were paid for, and most stores were making a profit. Relocation would be expensive. In addition, most local managers were part of the established leadership of their communities which, in most towns and cities, were concerned about the vacant storefronts and empty spaces downtown and were struggling unsuccessfully to turn the tide now carrying shoppers to the suburbs and regional malls.

The future of these old downtown stores was sealed. The Belks were closing them with some frequency. The Rutherfordton, N.C., store closed in February 1972, shortly after a regional store was opened in Forest City. Later that year, the Belks closed small stores in the textile villages and farm towns of China Grove, N.C., Union City, Tenn., Galax, Va., and Paris, Tenn. The Belks' first shopping center store in St. Petersburg, Fla., was relocated the following year, and small downtown locations were replaced with mall stores in Washington, N.C., Johnson City, Tenn., and Asheville, N.C. In 1975, Belk left its 80,000 square-foot downtown Greensboro, N.C., store, which was replaced by a store more than twice as large at Four Seasons Mall. The Belk building, one of architect Charles Hartmann's contemporary designs of the 1930s, remained an empty monument to the death of downtown retail business for nearly ten years before it was sold and converted to other uses.

The unique ownership arrangements delayed some decisions to close stores. In some cases, the Belk leadership waited for retirements and death to avoid confrontation with partners reluctant to join the program to upgrade the stores.

In other situations, John and Tom Belk merely persisted until they won out. Neither arrangement was easy and decisions and changes that should have been made years earlier often were postponed.

John and Tom Belk tried to convince their Durham partners, the Leggetts and local manager Wyche Horton, to go into Durham's first mall, Northgate, when it was being built in the late 1960s. They got nowhere. Horton would not budge and remained downtown in what Tom Belk called "a budget store." Durham's downtown continued its decline. Finally, on the next opportunity for a mall location, this time south of the city toward Chapel Hill, the Belks prevailed and the store moved to South Square Mall. In subsequent years, however, with the construction of a new store in Chapel Hill, the Belks ended up with two stores just a few miles apart on the south side of Durham and none on the north side of the city.

Some partners refused to move even when the Belks lost patience and acted on their own. John Belk agreed to put a store in a mall near Hickory over the objections of his father's old partner, Karl Broome. The store was built and ready to be staffed and stocked for opening, but Broome still would not have anything to do with it. Belk finally asked Bill Beery to take the store; Beery sent a manager to Hickory who kept his office in the trunk of his car until Belk finally settled the matter with Broome.

The new stores incorporated new technology as well as new designs and merchandise. Smart cash registers linked to small computers off the sales floor recorded the sale as well as the kind of item sold, which department it came from, and which salesperson made the sale. At the end of each day, the store would have a report on business, and buyers could see which merchandise was moving. Each innovation presented its own challenges to the Belk traditions.

Henry Belk's business had been built on cash sales. His early partners had paid cash for the goods they bought and Belk had little patience for managers who ran large credit balances. When he learned of such, he would call a manager to Charlotte for a stern lecture and specific instructions on paying down the debt. He expected the same kind of honor for cash sales from his customers.

As a result, Belk stores were slow to shed their founder's simple philosophy of cash sales. While some stores, primarily in the larger cities, had introduced charge accounts before Henry Belk died in 1952, the practice was not widespread. In smaller towns, some managers carried certain influential local customers on the books. After Belk's death, credit became more accepted throughout the business and in the 1950s, stores in the larger cities introduced their own credit cards.

The first Belk charge plates in Charlotte were metal and were shared with the other major downtown department stores. Notches in the card allowed a customer to charge sales at Belk as well as the nearby Efird and Ivey stores. It was not until 1967, after the Lippincott and Margulies study, that BSS controller I. N. Howard announced the introduction of a single Belk credit card which would be good in the company's four hundred stores in eighteen states and Puerto Rico. A year later, the BSS board authorized Howard to develop a computer center that would consolidate credit operations for those stores wishing to cooperate in the joint venture.

At the managers' convention in 1969, Tom Belk told the managers to encourage the use of Belk credit cards and increase their percentage of credit sales. In May 1970, Howard's computer center issued its one millionth credit card to one of Frank Matthews's customers in Gastonia. But, two years later, when the managers gathered again, Tom Belk was not satisfied with the progress.

"Now, we are a community of four hundred stores in eighteen states," Belk said, "but we have all said we have one corporate image, one credit card and that we're each part of one organization dedicated to customer service." That was not happening, particularly with credit cards. The goal set in 1969 for the larger stores was 50 percent credit sales. They had averaged 31 percent. The goal for smaller leading stores was 40 percent. They had averaged only 26 percent.

"If we don't get moving in the credit business, the bank cards are going to take over our credit customers and force them to shop at our competitors," Belk admonished the managers. "The Belk family recommends the use of only our own credit cards and not bank cards." In 1976, however, in the face of a blizzard of promotion for bank credit cards, the family policy changed and stores began accepting other credit cards.

The Belk Credit Center had opened in 1970 to handle accounts in Charlotte and Concord stores. In the next few years, other stores and store groups were added. A major change in 1973 increased the demand for central data processing. That year, forty stores installed credit pads and one store installed electronic cash registers that permitted the individual stores to connect with the central credit systems. New stores added newer and more sophisticated equipment and in time, the Belk Datacenter incorporated not only credit management, but merchandising and accounting information into the ever-growing electronic data processing system that linked the center to stores and the New York buying office twenty-four hours a day. Within ten years the system would be serving 2 million Belk and Leggett credit customers a year.

Changes in shopping habits and competition from other retailers changed another Belk family policy: opposition to Sunday openings. Henry Belk had taken seriously the Bible's admonitions about respecting the Sabbath. Belk buyers were not permitted to set off on their New York trips on a Sunday, and all other business was set aside on this day. Sunday store openings were out of the question to Belk's partners and his children, who resisted the early pressure from competitors to open for Sunday business as one local community after another debated the legality of blue laws.

Bradenton, Fla., was one of the early tests of the Belk resolve. "Never on Sunday," said the headline of a large ad store manager M. C. Quattlebaum placed in the Bradenton newspapers during the debate in 1966. "Our folks work hard and deserve this day. We will not take Sunday away from them. Aside from the religious aspect, Sunday opening, save essential services, just doesn't make sense. Isn't seventy-two hours of business activity enough for one week? We feel that six days of twelve hours each is enough."

Not long afterward, the issue of Sunday sales was raised in South Carolina, where a store owner defied law and convention and opened for business on Sunday. Local authorities obtained an injunction to stop the Sunday sales, and the question ended up with the state's legislature. Belk's chief counsel, David McConnell, worked with a legislative committee to draft a new law that was based on the state's right to regulate business and not founded on religious beliefs. It was upheld on appeal to the U.S. Supreme Court.

Despite opposition, prohibitions against Sunday sales fell regularly across the South during the 1970s, though most Belk stores remained closed. By the late 1970s, stores began to yield to pressure from competitors who were open and from mall managements, which were caught between their largest tenant's opposition to Sunday openings and their smaller merchants' desire to increase their business. In some cities, the other large tenants were ordered by their headquarters located outside of the region to open on Sunday. When that happened, as it did in Winston-Salem's Hanes Mall store, the Belk store opened as well. Finally, most stores eased into the change, opening first on Sundays during the Christmas holiday sales season, then continuing the practice after the holidays.

By the end of the 1970s, the Belk organization looked more like the organization that the men who had met in John Belk's Myrtle Beach home had discussed more than a dozen years earlier. Nearly one hundred downtown stores had been closed, some never to be replaced. This included the remaining few Efird's stores, the last of which closed in 1979 in Smithfield. About fifty new stores had been opened, almost all in shopping malls. These new stores put the total number of stores at about the same as when Belk Stores Services was incorporated in 1955, but the amount of selling space had increased by 50 percent.

The new stores also were full-sized department stores; they were not smaller specialty stores that emphasized ladies' fashions or a single department which other department store organizations were opening at the time. Always, the new stores reflected the Lippincott and Margulies image of fashion and action. They had a common identity and common services. A customer from Charlottesville, Va., could use a Leggett credit card in the Belk-Lindsey store while vacationing in Port Richey, Fla. Stores in cities and towns around major media markets like Charlotte had begun to coordinate sales and promotions, combining their advertising to reach the broader audience.

The plans prepared in the late 1960s were reality, including the reorganization of the partnership groups to more clearly reflect the market, not circumstance and history. As the Belks closed stores in the 1970s, and as their father's partners retired without any successors to carry on the work, John and Tom Belk began to change the organization of the Belk network. Whenever possible, they looked for opportunities to reshuffle the deck, as they had in Hickory, N.C., putting stores under the management of strong, able partners, men who had proven management ability and who subscribed to the program of expansion.

In time, Von Autry had assumed responsibility for a dozen stores, most of them in southeastern North Carolina. Bill Beery had assumed responsibility for stores located primarily along the Atlantic Coast, from Jacksonville, N.C., to Savannah, Ga. Leroy Robinson, who had succeeded George Dowdy in Charlotte, had taken on stores in the Charlotte area, from Salisbury, N.C., to York, S.C. Frank Matthews had picked up stores in the Gastonia area and had added his uncle's Georgia stores to his group. The only territories that remained untouched were Tennessee, where the Parkses were the managing partners, and Virginia, home of the Leggetts.

In ten years, the Belk business had emerged more organized and determined than ever before. Belk was setting the pace for retail development, fielding numerous requests from developers to open in new malls just as Henry Belk had received solicitations from local ministers and civic groups eager to get one of his stores in the 1930s. Once virtually ignored as a collection of country stores, Belk was known within the industry as marketwise and strong. At one point, a top executive for Kmart told John Belk, "I just want to find out where you are going. You pick the best places. I'm going to open up right across the street."

Karl Hudson was planning the opening of his large, new Hudson-Belk store at Raleigh's Crabtree Valley shopping center while young Nancy Alderman was finishing her senior year at Wake Forest University in 1972. Alderman had plans to be a teacher. She had studied English and education and felt fully prepared to move to the front of a high school class when she graduated. After receiving her diploma, however, she learned that North Carolina had more than enough graduates to fill the empty spots in its teaching ranks. Karl Hudson, on the other hand, was not quite so fortunate as he surveyed his employment needs for the store he had planned for the regional mall opening soon on Raleigh's busy beltway. He urgently needed people to help him run his grand, new emporium designed to serve the growing suburbs of North Carolina's capitol city.

Alderman had worked for Hudson-Belk the summer before her graduation, selling stationery in Hudson's downtown store. A Raleigh native, she heard about a new training program at Hudson-Belk and applied for admission. She and two dozen other young college graduates found there was some urgency to their program. In two months, Alderman and the others in her class were given a crash course in retailing. Part was classroom work, but Hudson's trainers also put these management candidates into every corner of the business, from the stockroom to the sales floor.

The training exercises played out at Hudson's Raleigh stores would be repeated over and over as the Belks pushed the expansion of the companies' retail business into larger and more sophisticated stores. In addition to better goods to stock the shelves with, the Belks and their partners also realized they would need a better-trained and more-sophisticated crew of managers. The expansion created some anxiety among those responsible for opening these new stores, but the dilemma offered unlimited possibilities for bright young people like Nancy Alderman.

She started as a department manager in lingerie. In a couple of months, she won the job of assistant buyer and despite a serious automobile accident that kept her out of the stores for six months, she was a division manager in the Belk-Hudson organization by the time she was twenty-five. Alderman was not only the youngest person selected to make major buying decisions for the Hudson group, she also was the first woman. Three years later, the group expanded her duties, and in 1981, Alderman moved to the Belk Stores Services in New York as assistant general merchandise manager.

From her corner office five floors above New York's Sixth Avenue, Alderman now, as vice president, supervises the selection and purchasing of millions and millions of dollars in merchandise for hundreds of Belk and Leggett stores across the Southeast. She is tall, attractive, and perfectly manicured. She frequently pushes her dark brown hair away from her green eyes, which remain steady and intent. Her office is clear of work except for what may be the one remaining unsold Belkie Bear; the snow-white stuffed animal with a red and white toboggan atop its head sits on a sofa beside her desk. The bear was one of Alderman's private-label projects which had turned into a sales bonanza during the recent Christmas season. Against the rattle of traffic noise that rises from rush hour traffic below, Alderman talks easily and confidently about the business. She knows it well, from branded lines of better dresses to the bss international market, which she now manages along with juniors' and girls' wear. Clerks are just tallying the final figures from another successful Belk buyers' show completed only the week before and she is preparing for one of her thrice-yearly visits overseas. Alderman's youth belies the fact that during her fifteen-year career with Belk stores she has experienced a retailing revolution that is still underway.

It is a heady experience for a woman from Raleigh, N.C., who had almost become an English teacher. The show that the New York office had just closed in Charlotte had included more than two hundred fashion vendors who were showing their lines exclusively for Belk buyers. Indeed, Belk is a top account with many design houses, cosmetics companies, and top-of-the-line fashion resources. Belk is one of Estée Lauder's largest customers. Levi Strauss makes special television commercials just for airing in Belk market areas. Belk picked up Swatch watches when they were a novelty and within a year had sold more than every other department store chain but one in the United States. Important fashion names like Gucci, Ralph Lauren, Fendi, Alexander Julian, Giorgio, and Liz Claiborne count Belk among their top accounts, as do national brand companies like Haggar, Leslie Fay, Chaus, Izod, Ocean Pacific, Arrow, and many others.

In his Charlotte office jammed with merchandising reports, assorted samples, and buying office paperwork, Tom Belk keeps a thick computer list of the approximately 2,000 principal resources that supply the 350 Belk and Leggett stores. He pinches a few pages together to indicate the stores' most important suppliers of clothing, cosmetics, and brand name merchandise. Most are lines he personally recruited to help fulfill the ambition of the Belks and their partners to transform the Southeast's largest department-store network into the home for fashion in the region's growing metropolitan areas.

The book listing Belk resources is considerably smaller than it was in the mid-1960s. Then, Belk stores bought from just about everybody. Everybody, that is, except the fashion leaders. In 1969, when the Belks opened their first large department store in a mall in Savannah, Ga., the merchandise inside did not match the stylish exterior. A Belk store's best line of beauty products was often popularly priced Revlon. The largest order Belk stores placed with a national brand name clothing company was with Levi Strauss, whose jeans were sold along with work clothes and overalls in the basement departments. Belk and Leggett stores were little known among the nation's major leading retailers and the fashion industry. The company's name seldom appeared in the trade press, and the tradition of local autonomy of store managers restricted any efforts to consolidate buying power to get the attention of the nation's apparel industry. Regional suppliers and manufacturers who produced Belk's extensive line of private-label merchandise courted the Belk business, but the company was virtually unknown outside of the South.

The private-label program was the backbone of the business when the Belk's first regional mall store opened in 1969. Belk's own brands accounted for about half of the average store's total sales. The percentage was even higher in some departments. Belk labels like Ruff 'n Tuff jeans and Andhurst shirts helped push the private-label business to a full three-fourths of the sales in boys' departments. Almost 90 percent of the shoes sold in some Belk stores were manufactured under Belk labels.

The private-label program had served the stores well for years. It kept high-quality and competitively priced goods in the stores' inventories. Belk managers could beat local competitors with less expensive private-label goods and meet prices from large chains, like J. C. Penney and Sears, that had their own private labels. With a small, creative merchandising staff, BSS usually could reproduce contemporary styles in plenty of time to catch the wave of fashion that regularly broke late in the Southeast.

The system was a self-contained world of merchandising. BSS buyers worked out designs for new clothing, arranged for fabric deliveries from Southern manufacturers, and contracted with apparel makers to turn out the lines. Store managers placed their orders at seasonal shows in the BSS building on East Fifth Street in Charlotte, where as many as three-dozen merchandise lines were available in the late 1960s. Belk private labels were not prestige lines, but the merchandise was well made. They were not high fashion, though, on occasion, Belk labels had helped start a fashion trend.

In the early 1960s, when button-down collars and penny loafers were on every high school and college man in the South, private-label manager Paul Godfrey and Sam Elliott, then BSS merchandise manager, created what they called their "Southeastern uniform." The two introduced a complementary line of oxford cloth shirts in dark blue, maroon, and what Godfrey called "Coke bottle green" as part of a promotion that also featured white Bermuda shorts and a belt covered in oxford cloth in colors to match the shirts. They got the outfits in the stores ahead of the annual student migration to the Carolina beaches, where the prep style received an enthusiastic welcome. By summer, the popularity of the casual Carolina look had been spotted by fashion scouts from national manufacturers, who duplicated the sets for their customers elsewhere in the nation.

The success of creations like Godfrey and Elliott's "uniform," as well as popular styles of children's wear and extensive hosiery lines, had helped raise the stature of the BSS buying office to something more than a source of less-expensive goods. In fact, the private-label program laid the foundation for the expansion into national brand name merchandise in the 1970s.

Tom Belk's challenge was to organize the tremendous buying power of the Belk network. He could not do that as long as individual store managers and partner groups operated so independently that individual vendors might not know just how large a customer Belk was. While the system might have frustrated Belk's desire to coordinate purchases, he respected the tradition established by his father and defended the local management as an important difference in the Belk organization.

The system confused many trying to establish Belk as a customer. A salesman for a major lingerie line visited Tom Belk in the late 1950s and the two were reviewing a list of Belk stores that carried his goods. At one point, Belk asked why the line was not in the Belk store in Rock Hill, S.C. The salesman replied that the manager there had told him he was not adding any more lingerie to his inventory. "Go back and call on him again," Belk told the man. When the two saw one another at a subsequent meeting, Belk asked again about Rock Hill. The salesman said he had followed Belk's orders and had called again in Rock Hill. The manager there had been so incensed at the salesman's persistence that he had all but thrown him out of the store. Belk just laughed, and said, "I'll have to do something about that." But the salesman later recalled it was some time before the line was offered to Belk customers in the small South Carolina town.

In the late 1950s, as the complexities of the private-label business required more and better coordination of orders, Tom Belk took the first step toward any central administration of buying for Belk stores. Belk announced that instead of waiting for the stores to place orders for private-label merchandise, the buying office would prepare the stores' initial orders for them. The prepared order forms were sent to the stores in advance of the BSS merchandise shows, where managers would actually see the season's new styles. After looking over the merchandise, managers could adjust the prepared order, adding or deleting items and sizes, but the revised orders had to be in the BSS offices within two weeks of the close of the show or the original planned purchase printed on the blue forms would be placed on their behalf. The procedures left the final purchasing decision with the managers, but for the first time in the company's history, someone besides the store manager was helping decide what went in his store.

This system honored the traditions of founder Henry Belk, and it increased the buying power of Belk Stores Services, which could get better prices, better delivery dates, and better goods into the stores in time for the fashion seasons of the year. The change also improved store profits at locations where complacent or unorganized managers had delayed getting their orders in on schedule or had not ordered in sufficient quantities for the season.

Yet, as strong as the Belk private-label program was for men, boys, and infants, BSS buyers could not copy fashions from the world's fashion markets quickly enough. Belk and Leggett store managers could find Belk label shoes, hosiery, and lingerie at the BSS shows, but they had to shop elsewhere for better lines of dresses, sportswear, and coats.

This independent arrangement perpetuated the inconsistency in the range of styles that shoppers could find in Belk stores. There was an almost endless array of labels. Altogether, at one time Belk suppliers numbered nearly 20,000. And prices varied considerably from one store to the next. "We had stores selling $25 and $29 hats," recalls R. D. McCraw of the BSS New York office, "and we had some stores we couldn't get to go above $5 hats."

As fashion had become more and more important in the South, McCraw had encouraged stores to trade up, gradually adding dresses and sportswear just a little more expensive than the moderate- to low-priced apparel that was the foundation of the Belk business. McCraw argued that if the stores had some fashions priced a little higher than the store's basic lines, then they encouraged customers to buy the best of the store's basic line even if they could not afford the most expensive items in the store. The Charlotte store under George Dowdy picked up better lines, as did larger stores in cities like Gastonia, Greensboro, and Wilmington, N.C., and in Columbia or Charleston, S.C. Most of the small stores resisted pricier items, though years later McCraw fondly remembered one manager who took his advice despite his location in a small southside Virginia hamlet. "That little store in Suffolk, Va., sold more $25 hats than any other."

When the Belks launched the expansion program in the 1970s, Tom Belk looked to his cosmetics counters on which to build the fashion statement that was becoming an important part of the Belk strategy. When the new mall stores began opening, cosmetics accounted for about 3 percent of Belk stores' sales. Belk knew that women were loyal to their favorite fragrances and would return time and again for supplies. A better cosmetics line would not only increase business in that department, but bring in shoppers who might also purchase a new dress, hosiery, or a pair of shoes. Despite repeated attempts, however, Belk buyers could not get the attention of the leading beauty companies. These companies were as image conscious as the season's top fashion models, and were not interested in trading existing outlets in specialty shops that catered to a wealthy clientele or in department stores like Ivey's. But Tom Belk was persistent. He set his sights on Estée Lauder, one of the top names in the beauty products business.

Belk knew Lauder was a well-managed company and produced some of the world's best-selling fragrances. He and others had made unsuccessful attempts to interest the company in adding Belk stores to its distribution. Finally, after several rebuffs by telephone, Tom Belk and partners Bill Beery and Frank Matthews called unannounced on the main offices of Estée Lauder in New York City. Belk was counting on Lauder's reputation for seeing any customer within five minutes to get an audience with a senior sales executive. Within the five-minute limit, the three were ushered into the office of the sales manager for specialty stores, who asked his secretary to bring in the Belk file.

"The secretary knew there wasn't anything in the Belk file," Tom Belk recalls. "*Everybody* in the room knew there wasn't anything in the Belk file. So, she was real smart. She said, 'We don't want to bother Mr. Beery. It's right behind him.' So, he just said, 'oh, forget about it.'"

After more persuasion in subsequent meetings, the Lauder sales manager, Richard Hardigan, agreed to visit Beery's new store just being opened at Myrtle Beach. Belk chartered a plane and flew the Lauder sales manager to South Carolina, gave him a personal tour of the new store, and convinced him that Belk was no longer a low-budget operation. Lauder's line already was promised to a specialty store in the Myrtle Beach area, but Hardigan agreed to give Belk a chance in Myrtle Beach and seven other towns where Lauder products were not then available, all smaller markets, including Salisbury, N.C., Statesboro, Ga., Camden, S.C., and Staunton, Va. Sales skyrocketed. In the last four months of 1975, these eight small stores sold $224,000 in Lauder products. Lauder approved adding eighteen more stores in 1976 and twelve more in 1977, when Belk sold more than $1 million in Lauder products. Two years later, Lauder's Clinique line was added, generating more sales in the first year than the entire Lauder line had produced in its first year at Belk. Aramis, Lauder's fragrance for men, was approved in 1976 and was added in thirty-five stores.

The Lauder coup gave Belk a top name for its cosmetics counters, which were placed right at the entrance in the new stores. Tom Belk now had the leverage he needed to attract other lines, who were shown how well Belk stores treated their suppliers of beauty products.

One by one, the Belk stores picked up some better lines. Jones of New York, one of the leading names for women's and girls' sportswear, finally added a few smaller Belk stores to its list, before committing to larger ones like Hudson-Belk in Raleigh. The slow remaking of the Belk image frustrated buyers like Nancy Alderman, who had pleaded for months with the Jones representative to permit her to buy for the Crabtree store, which had surpassed even Charlotte's South-Park store in sales volume.

William Van Brug watched the change in Belk from his office at Ivey's, directly across Tryon Street from the Belk store. Van Brug had joined Ivey's in 1972, not long after Belk and Ivey's had opened their SouthPark stores. Within a few years, resources that had sold exclusively to Ivey's were telling Ivey's and other stores that they were going to begin giving some business to Belk. At first, new lines—except for Lauder, which protected Ivey's exclusive distribution in Charlotte for several years—appeared in Belk's upgraded cosmetics department. Then women's fashion lines followed in ready-to-wear and sportswear departments. Van Brug recalls that he had observed shortly after coming to Charlotte that Belk was a sleeping giant. He and others now realized it had begun to wake up.

The same year Belk captured Lauder, the Belk Stores Services board made changes in the two top merchandising positions at BSS. The changes reflected Tom Belk's aggressive marketing strategy to recruit new fashion labels for the stores. The Belks replaced Ferd Lawson, who had succeeded R. D. McCraw in 1973, with Robert Wildrick. Wildrick was in his mid-thirties when he took over the office, but he already had run one of the top department stores in Dallas, Texas, and had helped open several new stores for the Belk-Hensdale group. At about the same time, Tom Nipper was named merchandise manager of the Charlotte buying office, taking over Sam Elliott's responsibilities.

Neither Wildrick nor Nipper had been raised in the Belk tradition, and they were among the first outsiders hired to take top merchandising positions. Nipper came from Davison's, the major fashion department store chain based in Atlanta. Nipper knew Belk stores and some of the Belk executives. They had arrived on the floor of his Davison's store in Columbia, S.C., shortly after he had opened it in 1970 next door to Belk. Nipper had deftly aimed the Davison's store at the growing market of affluent shoppers looking for style and fashion, the very market the Belks wanted to capture. John and Tom Belk liked what Nipper had done and talked to him about doing the same kind of merchandising at their stores. Nipper declined, and subsequently he was promoted to run the chain's biggest store, in Atlanta. In 1975, Tom Belk finally recruited him to take a merchandising position in the Charlotte store, where he spent most of his time helping Tom Belk court brand name resources.

Nipper and Belk prepared lists of top lines in men's merchandise. The two laid out their plans for new stores and used the impressive sales figures in Belk's strong men's departments to promote their plans with vendors. "They thought they were happy with their business in this area," Nipper recalls, "but when they saw the business that we started doing, word began to spread that the Belk organization is solid and big and they could sell a lot of merchandise for you."

When Nipper joined the company, Wildrick had been in Fayetteville at the Belk-Hensdale group headquarters for just more than two years. He had not heard of Belk until one of Tom Belk's traveling caravans of partners and BSS executives came to look over the Sanger-Harris store he managed in Dallas in 1972. A few months later, Von Autry, Jr., hired

Wildrick, who had managed the kind of store the Belks wanted and had had experience with the top department store chains in the country. Wildrick was to be Autry's fashion pathfinder.

Schooled in modern business methods, Wildrick found a different management style in the Belk-Hensdale organization. Autry's stores were managed by men who had learned the trade from Frank Stevens, Hensdale's own mentor, and some had worked personally with Henry Belk, who had taken a keen interest in the stores in the small towns of southeastern North Carolina. Most of the stores had changed little over the years. They gave Wildrick a clear picture of the old Belk while at the same time he was helping Autry realize the vision of the new Belk. Perhaps his toughest assignment was in Winston-Salem.

The Winston-Salem store was part of the Belk-Hensdale group, but Frank Stevens's son, John Belk Stevens, still took a proprietary interest in his father's first store in the city's downtown. It had not changed much from his father's day. Home to the first pair of Red Camel overalls, the store still had a large piece goods department, and the old-fashioned counters were stacked high with work clothes for farmers and factory workers. The new, stylish Hanes Mall store was designed to reach the growing affluent suburban market.

Stevens at first was skeptical about John Belk's plans and had resisted moving from the familiar downtown location to Hanes Mall on the western edge of the city, but he eventually approved the plan and Belk signed the papers to include his store in the deal. With John Belk's unqualified support, Autry gave Wildrick a free rein, and Stevens went along. Stevens was shocked, however, when a tractor-trailer rig pulled up to the dock of the new store and the driver asked where the Mr. Coffee coffee makers were to be stacked. When a small space was pointed out, the driver informed the store manager he had a full truckload, not a few crates.

"John Belk Stevens had never bought more than twelve of anything in his life, and I had ordered two truckloads of coffee makers," recalls Wildrick, who had simply applied what he had been doing for years in his previous assignment. "We sold out the first truckload the first day and the second on the second day. From that day on, he thought I was a merchandising genius."

Wildrick and Stevens became good friends, and the Hanes Mall store prospered. So did the large, new Fayetteville store Autry opened in 1975. With Wildrick's help, Autry also opened the first central distribution center for a Belk group.

In 1976, when the Belks were looking for a new head of the New York office, John Belk Stevens backed Wildrick as the man for the job much the same as his father had done when Henry Belk hired McCraw in that position forty years earlier.

When Wildrick arrived in New York, the buyers worked much the same as they had forty years earlier. They were fashion advisors more than buyers with any real money to spend in the nation's fashion houses. While Belk remained set in the past, fashion was ripping into the future. Wildrick knew that Belk stores would never get the better goods—merchandise to match the architecture and cash invested in stores—unless the buying power of the stores could somehow be harnessed.

One of Wildrick's first challenges was to convince managers they should combine their buying power. He found his opportunity with a hot California line called Bronson. The merchandise was so popular that the company usually sold out its entire line within two weeks of opening. That was not enough time for buyers from individual Belk stores to get together, arrange their travel, and arrive on the West Coast to place their orders. If they could not all go, Wildrick argued, then if the buyers would give him their dollars, he would make the purchases for them. He convinced five stores, including the Raleigh stores, to go along with his plan. That season, those who had followed his lead had another major line with which to attract a more affluent customer into their stores.

The new look and merchandise mix built upon the strong Belk base of customers seeking moderately priced clothing and simply added another layer of more affluent shoppers who no longer had to shop out of town to get what they needed. Even stores in smaller towns upgraded, and gradually began layering in new national brands that the New York office courted, on top of Belk's own private-label merchandise.

Yet the focus of the Belk buying operation remained the seasonal merchandise shows that had begun in Sam Scott's sample room with store managers dropping by whenever the word went out that he had special deals. By the 1950s, Tom Belk had organized the shows as the main sales event for Belk's growing private-label merchandise. By the 1970s, the shows were still the principal showcase for private-label lines, but national brand companies also were represented. Hundreds of store buyers were attracted to the seasonal shows for men's and boys' wear, for children's wear, and for shoes at shows in Charlotte's Merchandise Mart. Fewer would arrive for smaller shows for cosmetics, housewares, or accessories. But the volume of business was increasing each year as more stores began participating in sales promotions and cooperative buying programs.

The Belk shows provided a store manager with just about everything he needed to stock his stores, except fashion. For years the New York office had merely coordinated its seasonal fashion reviews with Belk store buyers to coincide with the regular shows of the Carolinas-Virginia Fashion Exhibitors, organized by the regional salesmen for apparel manufacturers. Buyers from the New York office would bring their samples to Charlotte and meet with store buyers a day or two before the Carolinas-Virginia exhibition opened. After the New York office reviewed the new fashions and styles, store buyers would shop the new lines and independently place orders at the Carolinas-Virginia Fashion Exhibitors' show. In many cases, buyers from the larger Belk stores had more clout with manufacturers than the organization as a whole. This was particularly true of buyers from stores in North Carolina's major cities and large stores in other states, such as the store in Columbia, S.C.

In 1982, Wildrick asked Tom Belk to let the New York office produce its own show. It would help consolidate the buying power of Belk shows, he argued, and clearly demonstrate to any doubting fashion resources just how much business was available from the region's largest retail organization. A Belk-produced show would also permit the buying office to manage the growing number of resources better and to help Belk concentrate its dollars on fewer companies. The proposal of the first show was greeted skeptically by Belk, who had had his own anxious moments when he had introduced his first housewares show and had used door prizes and gimmicks to build a crowd. The stores had long-standing relationships with their salesmen. Wildrick was told that resources accustomed to having buyers shop in their showrooms in New York would not bring their goods to Charlotte. Wildrick argued they should give it a try and if it did not work, they could return to the present system.

Wildrick assigned the task of organizing the show to Van Brug. Van Brug arranged with resources already supplying Belk stores to have a sales representative on hand, and he prepared another invitation list to include vendors that Tom Belk, Wildrick, and others wanted to recruit for Belk stores.

The first show in 1983 was small, but it was a success. Wildrick and BSS's New York buyers clearly demonstrated the strength of the Belk stores' buying power to leading fashion houses that did not know Belk well. In turn, sales representatives from more than a hundred lines were able to pick up orders in one location without traveling across the Southeast. Four years later, on the eve of the company's one hundredth anniversary, the show had grown to the point that Van Brug could not accommodate all the companies that wanted to attend. Representatives from the top fashion lines in the nation competed for the best locations in the maze of sales booths and displays at the Belk shows. And the volume of orders handled by the New York office had increased fourfold.

In Charlotte and New York, the people scouting the markets for new lines and preparing the merchandise lineups for

Belk stores had also changed. In New York, where the staff had grown to about 120 by 1987, most of the buyers who had learned by doing under McCraw had retired or left the company to be replaced with men and women who were college-educated and market-tested professionals. A half-dozen held master's degrees in business and most had had retail training at major national department stores before they joined Belk. One of those McCraw brought into the office was Nancy Alderman.

Alderman's staff includes aggressive young buyers like Denise Wendt, who knows the old Belk stores only by what she has heard. A cold, stiff winter wind billows Wendt's coat as she strides purposefully out of the BSS New York office on 40th Street and turns toward Broadway. She is on the lookout for fashionable collections for females fourteen to forty, and is alert to trendy items for teens and sophisticated fashions for career women.

This day, Wendt is between seasons. The summer orders are in; Belk stores have already received shipments of orders placed at the merchandise show several weeks earlier. While she was in Charlotte, she briefed store buyers on what they would see from leading vendors whose booths jammed the rest of the lower level of the Charlotte Merchandise Mart. She also collected orders for planned purchases of national brand merchandise, which had become an extension of the old blue copy program. She and other buyers also counseled managers from the smaller Belk stores, whose contact with the national fashion world is limited. Wendt helped them find less-expensive popular styles that might sell well among the more conservative, small-town customers.

Now the show is behind her, but Wendt still has time to find some special purchases for stores and to track the progress of the season's sales. She is also scouting new lines. About two blocks from the BSS office, Wendt turns into an old office building on Broadway and heads for the tenth-floor showroom of a small firm representing various clothing lines. Laurie, Wendt's contact, has a new sportswear line from England called Pamplemousse. Wendt is not in a buying mood, but the company wants to do business with Belk. The showroom is small, samples hang from racks under dropped spotlights. Wendt and her assistant sit down, pushing their coats back over their chairs. The popular tunes from an FM radio compete with traffic noise from the street. Wendt and Laurie trade comments about their pregnancies—Wendt is due in three months—and then they get down to business.

Wendt is going to be a tough sell. The line is new, but the designs are not. The tops and bottoms in lively colors are much like what Wendt has seen already and will see more of during the day. She asks where the line is selling now and how it is doing. Is there advertising and promotion money available? A new name is hard to sell in the competitive fashion world. The answers are not encouraging. With a new line that has no big reputation and no money for promotion and advertising, Wendt does not give Laurie much hope. "It's going to be hard," she says when asked about orders. Wendt thanks her for her time and heads to her next stop about two blocks away.

Wendt does not bother to remove her coat after she sticks her head in the next cramped showroom which is not much larger than her own small space in the crowded and unpretentious BSS New York offices. "We are very anxious to do business with you," the sales rep says while she pulls selected items from a rack. "I hear that a lot," Wendt says later. "Usually, from vendors we aren't interested in." As the sales rep hangs the tops and bottoms out for Wendt's review, she is talking discounts and concessions as well as highlighting the new line. She has tops featuring sailboats and nautical designs. It's the America's Cup year and designers are cashing in. She has tie-dyed knits, a khaki-and-brown line called Safari—the Banana Republic influence is everywhere—and T-shirt tops with Russian lettering across the front. Wendt is polite, but unimpressed.

Twenty minutes later, Wendt is back on the street and walking toward the St. Michel showroom in a building at 1407 Broadway that is the New York enclave of the women's sportswear market. St. Michel's national sales manager,

Marty Freeman, greets Wendt as soon as she enters. The showroom is stylish, comfortable, and full of the aroma of the popcorn popping in a carnival cart in the corner. The ceiling spotlights reflect off white tabletops. Wendt and her assistant settle into black designer chairs, and the talk is about how good the 1987 line looks. Wendt sees some items she might be able to get in the stores in time to do some good. St. Michel is a popular line in Belk stores.

Within an hour and a half of leaving, she is headed back to her office. Wendt now must determine whether she has enough time to line up the money from buyers in Belk stores to place a late order. If there is some spare money about, she calculates whether orders can be placed in time for the merchandise to reach the stores before late-season markdowns cut into profits. And she must have support from the stores. Despite the changes produced by Wildrick's consolidation of buying, there is not a single buying decision that cannot be reversed by the stores. It is a unique buying system, which links the immediacy of the market with the Belk tradition of local buying.

A hundred years earlier, Henry Belk ran the same questions through his mind as he roamed the streets of New York's garment district. The market has changed, his stores have changed, and buyers like Denise Wendt are just learning about the small country towns that built Henry Belk's business. But like Belk, they mix their own knowledge of the market, the popularity of the styles they have seen, and a history of how they have sold in stores hundreds of miles away. Denise then adds about "20 percent hunch." Then she says with something of the spirit of Henry Belk: "I've made some big mistakes. But, if you aren't making mistakes, you aren't buying."

The lights of Charlotte are far brighter today than they were in the spring of 1970. The city has expanded to fill the woodlands, pastures, and valleys that once separated it and the University of North Carolina at Charlotte campus. New, sleek industrial research facilities and "corporate campuses" are now the university's companions in what once was rural Mecklenburg County. But even with the new development, the floodlights bathing the Belk Tower in the center of the UNCC campus provide a beacon for an air traveler on a clear Carolina night.

The tower stands 147 feet tall, as high as a twelve-story building. From inside the scalloped cylinder sheathed in white quartz come the songs of a 183-bell carillon that can fill the surrounding countryside. The tower was made possible by a $100,000 gift to the university from the family and associates of William Henry Belk, dedicating it in his name to "soar in sight and sound as his achievements soared through his faith in God and man."

During his lifetime, Henry Belk devoted himself to two institutions—his church and his business. With equal enthusiasm, he spread the Gospel according to the Presbyterian Church and direct, honest merchandising according to Belk. He had a commitment to both that began at an early age, long before he was one of the South's wealthiest men. In the early years, Belk and his brother had helped establish as many rural Presbyterian churches as they had bargain stores in the hamlets and communities of Piedmont North Carolina. Later, when his empire spread across more than a dozen states, his business associates say it was often difficult to determine where Belk's interest in expanding the church ended and his interest in building his mercantile enterprise began.

His endowments to the region did not stop with the church. He was a benefactor to colleges and universities, hospitals and clinics, and an untold number of plain folk who just needed help. When Henry Belk, Jr., was settling his father's estate, he wrote numerous letters to retired ministers, nephews, and former store workers inquiring about loans of $200, $500, and $1,000 that had remained unpaid for years on his father's personal accounts.

In the years since his death in 1952, Belk's legacy of giving has been continued by his family and the families and successors of the men he called his partners, who learned a philosophy of giving at the same time they learned how to put the best price on "double L" sheeting. The Belk Foundation remains a source of support for churches, hospitals, and schools throughout the vast trading area of Belk stores.

When he was alive, Belk was perhaps best known for his support of the Presbyterian Church, which he did not join until he was twenty-one years old, despite the devotion to Calvinist tenets that he had learned at home. "I just didn't think I was good enough to join the church," Belk later recalled. "I felt that a fellow, to be a member of the church, ought to be a mighty good person, and I just didn't think I was good enough."

Belk had attended services with his mother, who along with her second husband, John Simpson, had helped organize the first Presbyterian church in Monroe, N.C., not long after they moved there in 1873. When he was twenty-one, Belk went to a revival at the Monroe church and heard the Reverend A. W. Miller of Charlotte's First Presbyterian Church preach to the very point that nagged him so. "You say you are not good enough," Miller told the congregation. "The truth is you are not good enough to stay out. Only the perfect man is good enough. All others need the cleansing of the blood of Christ to fit them for church membership." That was enough for Henry. "I went up to the preacher that night, confessed my sins and accepted the Lord as my savior, and joined the church. And I have never regretted that step I took."

Presbyterians had settled in the Carolinas before the American Revolution. Some church cemeteries hold the remains of soldiers who stood off the British at Guilford Courthouse and Kings Mountain. These early churches were strong, vital parts of the rural communities of the Piedmont. Gradually, as North Carolina towns like Greensboro, Concord, and Charlotte grew, the church grew with them. The Mecklenburg County churches were centers of Presbyterian activity and the closest neighbors to Davidson and Queens colleges, two proud Presbyterian institutions.

The denomination had strong, active, and fervent missionaries elsewhere in the Carolinas, but most parts of North Carolina had little knowledge of the Presbyterian faith. Baptists and Methodists easily outnumbered the Presbyterians, particularly in the rural areas east of the small farms and woodlands of the North Carolina Piedmont. To grow, the church relied on the support of local congregations and the devotion of its members. None were more supportive than the Belk brothers.

Henry Belk was still helping his mother pay off the mortgage on the family farm in South Carolina when he and his brother turned over a portion of the income from their first small store in Monroe to help pay the salary and expenses of the Reverend Jonas Barclay. As superintendent of Sunday schools, Barclay carried the work of the church's Home Missions program to the ends of the dirt roads and the backwoods of the Carolina countryside. His primary circuit was the counties of Union and Anson in North Carolina. Probably at the urging of their mother, whose faith Henry Belk felt he could never measure up to, the brothers increased their tithe to support Barclay's work.

Henry Belk had moved to Charlotte before Barclay retired, but his contributions had continued. In fact, they had grown as Belk and Barclay's replacement, the Reverend William Black, continued to ride Barclay's circuit and extend the circle even further.

Black had been an attorney with a lively practice of law in Greensboro when he became a preacher and was ordained as a Presbyterian minister in 1893. He was a hard-driving churchman whose sermons were straight and direct, complete with a well-organized explanation of the Gospel. Black also was a congenial companion and a frequent visitor to Henry Belk's store in Charlotte. On occasion, Belk even included Black in his entourage of buyers when he made his buying trips to New York.

Black's fervent delivery, his zeal for reaching far into the backwoods of the counties under his care, suited the Belk brothers just fine. Henry Belk believed that any church, no matter how small, continued the Lord's work and helped to fill the larger churches in the cities. People were moving from the farms, and Belk believed that if they did not have religion, preferably of the kind taught by Presbyterians, then the city churches would not grow as fast as they should.

The Belks provided constant encouragement and support for evangelists to develop this theological farm team, and Black was perhaps the most tireless worker of them all. By 1907, Black had held more than 4,000 services and met with congregations in about twenty counties each year. Black's work filled the Presbyterian supply lines with folk who knew the Catechism well before they moved to town. Many city churches reported to the presbytery that their strongest leaders and most generous contributors were those who had pledged their faith in a country church.

By this time, Belk was one of the Home Mission Board's most active members. And he was soon tapped for other duties. Though he continued his membership in the Monroe church, Charlotte Presbyterians, led by the Reverend J. R. Howerton of Charlotte's First Presbyterian Church, did not overlook Belk in 1907 when they organized support to form the Mountain Retreat Association and purchased a failing religious assembly grounds near Black Mountain, N.C., about twenty miles east of Asheville. Belk made a generous contribution and was asked to join the board of what later came to be called Montreat when it was turned over to the Presbyterian Church about ten years later.

In the spring of 1928, Karl Hudson had come to Monroe to talk to John Belk about both the retail business and the religion business. He wanted advice on how to raise money to support the building of more churches, to support the work of more missionaries. The two talked into the evening. When Hudson left, he carried with him Belk's suggestion that he ask the ten largest Belk stores to contribute $100 a year to a fund that would underwrite this work. Hudson liked the idea and was confident the $1,000 a year would go far to extend the Gospel.

Before he could contact the other partners, John Belk had died. Two weeks after the services, Belk managers were called to Charlotte to a meeting. The night before, Hudson was thinking of ways to get money for a specific church project when he decided to ask the managers to create a fund for church buildings in the memory of John Belk. The next day he proposed the idea to his colleagues, and he asked that each store contribute Belk's suggested $100 a year. Hudson would supervise the fund, he said, and each contributing store would be eligible to submit requests for financial help for churches in their communities.

Within the year, the J. M. Belk Memorial Fund was in business. Instead of the $1,000 that Hudson had hoped for, he had a bank account that amounted to $4,000. In addition to the store money, the fund received a portion of the 15 percent of the annual income of John Belk's estate that he had designated for charitable causes and institutions.

For the next thirty years, Hudson was a reliable steward of the J. M. Belk Fund. By the time of his own death in 1952, the fund had helped build more than 150 churches and homes for ministers for congregations of different denominations throughout the Carolinas, Virginia, Tennessee, Georgia, Alabama, and Mississippi. Hudson Memorial Presbyterian Church in Raleigh stands today as a testament to Hudson's steady work.

The same year that John Belk died, Henry Belk lost his trusted companion, fellow churchman William Black. Black and Belk had been an inspiration to Presbyterian evangelists, who during the first quarter of this century had helped boost Presbyterian membership by 40 percent, a far larger increase than the entrenched Baptists or Methodists enjoyed. In a typical year, Black alone reported bringing nearly five hundred members into the fold.

The two men had been a formidable combination. Black's evangelical fire and boundless energy and Belk's financial resources had invigorated mission projects at home and abroad. Belk's money had even kept alive the conservative church newspaper, the *Presbyterian Standard*, whose outspoken editor, the Reverend A. J. McKelway, provoked the wrath of daily papers like the *Charlotte Observer* with his vigorous campaigns for social reform, particularly of child labor laws, and his advocacy of prohibition.

Black's influence on Belk is perhaps most visibly demonstrated in the events shortly before Black's death. In 1926, the nation, particularly the South, was embroiled in vigorous debate over the teaching of theories of evolution. The Scopes trial in nearby Tennessee, in a town much like those where Henry Belk operated his stores, focused attention on an issue that conservative churchmen like Black and Belk considered a threat to the foundation of their faith. At an organizational meeting in Charlotte of the Committee of One Hundred, a group dedicated to electing antievolution members to the 1927 N.C. General Assembly, Black called the theories of evolution the "blackest lie ever blasted out of Hell."

Except for service on the Charlotte school board, Belk had avoided politics and most especially controversy. A quiet, shy man not given to entering disputes, he had left the school board not long after it became divided over the location of a new high school for the city. Belk had proposed a site on high ground, while the majority had chosen an empty lake bed that regularly flooded. In any case, his schedule at the store was full and any spare time was given to his various church committees and boards. When the Committee of One Hundred met, however, Belk was a charter member and one of the most active.

The campaign turned mean that year. The issue stirred men to such feelings and expressions of intolerance, bigotry, and fanaticism that eventually many Presbyterian leaders and laymen withdrew. The effort met with only limited success, but the lukewarm reception at the polls did not deter Black and Belk. Belk remained with the hard-core group, reorganized as the North Carolina Bible League, which proclaimed through its executive secretary that "we are going to keep the fight until we get control of the state and the nation."

Belk's mixture of politics and religion did not last long. He attended the 1928 Democratic Party's nominating convention, where he and other conservative party members forecast disaster upon the nomination of presidential candidate Al Smith. But after the election, Belk withdrew from his public role and returned to his more private support of the church.

In the early 1930s, Belk was on his customary late-winter trip to Florida when he came upon a church-building idea that later came to characterize his own work. He was in a restaurant with Yates Laney, one of his young merchants, when the two men were approached by ladies raising money for a new church building. As they had with other diners, the ladies asked Belk and Yates Laney if they would contribute a dollar to buy a brick for their new church. Belk was intrigued, and impressed. Would the ladies show him where the church would be built? They said yes, and took the two strangers to the site. Before Belk left town, he had contributed the balance of the money needed to buy the brick for the new church.

The Florida encounter was the answer he needed for the ministers and delegates of country congregations who called on him regularly for his support. These visitations had become a virtual Monday morning ritual. Sarah Pharr, Belk's secretary, recalls that Belk's visitors often opened their meetings saying, "Brother Belk, the Lord sent me here this morning." One day, after ushering in the last of the petitioners, she said, "Mr. Belk, it's the strangest thing that the Lord sends them in to you and never sends them to Mr. Ivey." Belk responded that his old friend J. B. Ivey had as many Methodists asking for his help as Belk had Presbyterians.

Belk's response to these requests soon followed from his Florida experience. If the congregation would raise the money for the land, he told the ministers, and contribute labor to build the church, then he would supply the brick. To Belk, the brick meant permanence, a strong foundation for the solid Presbyterian faith. It would last well beyond the present fold and would be there for their children. In time, Belk donated so much brick that Christians across the region believed that, in addition to his dry-goods stores, Henry Belk owned a brickyard.

On occasion, Belk picked out a site and bought the land for a new church without even asking if one was needed. Riding through the streets of Charlotte and other towns, he would spot a likely location for a new church and recommend it to the Home Missions Board. "The Presbyterians ought to have a church here," he would say. "If the committee will buy the lots, I will pay for them."

Often, churchmen, ministers, and local laymen would accompany Belk on his scouting trips that took him deep into the countryside to find sites for the country churches that he called "outposts." He questioned these stewards of the faith about the interest of the local membership and what plans they had to meet their needs. In later years, he wanted to know who was preparing for the care of the new residents in the cities' growing middle-class suburbs and the poorer black communities.

Once a congregation had a building, Belk also was keen on seeing that children received proper instruction in the tenets of the faith. Belk had been raised during a time when not being able to recite the Shorter Catechism, a lengthy statement of Presbyterian basics, was considered a mark of vulgarity. Belk did not impose the Shorter version on youngsters, but he paid $1 to any child who would recite the Child's Catechism. These came to be known as "Belk Bucks," and churches applied every year to the church offices for reimbursement of the dollar payments from a fund Belk kept supplied with money. After his death, churches continued to receive money from the Belk Foundation. Nearly twenty years after the fact, the foundation paid $2 to Gov. Bob Scott of North Carolina, who had been raised as a Presbyterian in the old Hawfields Church in Alamance County, where he had performed the recitation as a young man eager to satisfy his own father, Gov. Kerr Scott.

Belk's interest in Presbyterian institutions extended beyond the church. Atop a hill at the end of Elizabeth Avenue in Charlotte is Presbyterian Hospital, one of the finest and best-equipped hospitals in the impressive Charlotte medical complex. Henry Belk helped bring the hospital to life when Charlotte had but a few trained physicians.

One of the leading Presbyterian families in Charlotte at the turn of the century was the Irwin family, whose forebears had helped settle the territory. Dr. John Irwin was a surgeon and active churchman, and his early offices were located in a building on Charlotte's square, almost midway between Henry Belk's store and the lush lawns and stately trees of First Presbyterian Church. Irwin was the first Charlotte surgeon to specialize in gynecology and abdominal surgery and among the first in the city to have any formal medical training. In 1897, he assisted in the first operation in the state in which an X-ray machine was used. With a unit developed at Davidson College, Irwin and other doctors dislodged a thimble stuck in a six-year-old girl's throat.

Irwin helped organize the Charlotte Medical and Surgical Institute, later renamed Charlotte Private Hospital, which was given to the Presbyterian churches of the city in 1902. Belk was one of the first contributors, donating $5,000 to the hospital after the churches assumed responsibility for its operation.

In 1917, Belk and other community leaders were trying to raise $100,000 for a new home for the hospital. It was a controversial campaign with organizers divided over the location of a new facility. The campaign was short of its goal, and dissent had about stalled all hope of success. Finally, in June, the campaign directors decided on the purchase of part of the property vacated by Elizabeth College, a small girls' school that had relocated to Salem, Va. The spacious school buildings and large grounds were well suited.

It appeared to be a perfect arrangement, but the purchase

Thomas M. Belk, left, and John M. Belk, president and chairman,
respectively, of Belk Stores Services, Inc., Charlotte, and of most of the
Belk stores, pose with a bust of their father, company founder William
Henry Belk, in 1987.

almost fell through. At 4:00 P.M., as the deal was about to
close, the hospital board realized it was $35,000 short. Ten
men, including Belk, agreed to underwrite a loan for $20,000
and further agreed to endorse another note of the same size
if additional money was needed.

Presbyterian Hospital's home was assured, though its fi-
nances were still shaky. In 1924, the hospital was threatened
again with foreclosure. Belk and four other men arranged for
additional money from a life insurance company that sus-

Creative visual merchandising techniques are used in modern Belk stores to display merchandise and create an exciting shopping environment. This display of women's sportswear features the company's Red Camel label, which was originally used on denim work clothes and work shoes when introduced in 1931.

The first Big B was hoisted to the east wall of the downtown Charlotte store in 1968. A New York marketing and design company created a complete Belk alphabet, including the distinctive curlicue capital B, for use in company signing and advertising. Originally designed with a dark center to the letters, the final version had a white interior.

World-renowned fashion designer Oscar de la Renta, fourth from left, was the star of a preview gala for the grand reopening of Charlotte's Belk SouthPark store on September 21, 1986. With him in this photo are, from left, Leroy Robinson, executive vice-president, Belk Brothers Company, John M. Belk, Deborah Harris, de la Renta, Jocelyn Dienst, and Thomas M. Belk. Mrs. Harris and Mrs. Dienst were president-elect and president, respectively, of the Junior League of Charlotte. The black tie event raised $25,000 to benefit Junior League charities.

This three-by-five-foot assemblage containing historical artifacts and company memorabilia was created by Hallmark Cards, Inc. as a gift to the Belk organization upon its 100th anniversary in 1988. Hallmark Chairman Don Hall presented the work to Belk family members in Charlotte on May 11, 1988.

pended its rules against lending money to charitable institutions. The five men endorsed the note, and Belk personally guaranteed another $60,000 in loans from local banks.

While Henry was busy with Presbyterian Hospital in Charlotte, brother John was working on a similar project in Monroe. In 1916, John Belk's neighbor, Ellen Fitzgerald, died and left her large home to the city of Monroe to be used as a hospital. The bequest caught the City Council by surprise. The council hastily organized a board of directors that included Belk and set them about outfitting the town's hospital. The world was at war, however, and America's entry into the conflict postponed any real work. The first patients were not admitted until October 1921. By the time John Belk died in 1928, the Ellen Fitzgerald Hospital had a qualified medical staff and a school of nursing.

The latest in architectural design is reflected in this rendering of the new
Belk Stores Services office complex and showroom, located in southwest
Charlotte, near the airport and major interstate highways. The 562,000-
square-foot facility unites the support organization's approximately 1,100
employees, who were previously in five different office locations in
Charlotte.

From left, North Carolina Governor Jim Martin with Katherine Belk, her
husband, Tom Belk, and their daughter, Katie Belk Morris, of Southern
Pines, N.C., during the dedication of the Katherine and Tom Belk
Gymnasium at the University of North Carolina at Charlotte on
September 25, 1987.

*John Belk at the podium during a dinner in his honor at his alma mater,
Davidson College, in May 1981. President Gerald Ford was one of the
guests for the dinner. (Photograph by Bill Giduz, Davidson College)*

The William Henry Belk College Center at St. Andrew's Presbyterian
College in Laurinburg, N.C. Dozens of churches and school buildings
throughout the South bear the Belk name as a result of the family's
philanthropy.

Nearly 400 Belk and Leggett store managers and other top executives form
a giant 100 on the top of a hotel parking garage in downtown Charlotte
during a 100th anniversary preview celebration on May 26, 1987.

Sophisticated Belk circulars, along with many other forms of print and broadcast advertising, reach millions of people daily in the company's extensive market area in the Southeast and neighboring regions.

In 1921, the Belk brothers combined their efforts to build another hospital, this one in China. The story of the hard work of Dr. R. B. Price at a small Presbyterian mission in China was related to the Belks' mother by friends who had visited the clinic. It was housed in native huts in the northern province of Kiangsu, in the town of T'ai-chou. She arranged a meeting between her sons and the doctor when he returned for a brief visit in 1920. The next year, Price had money to build the first outpatient clinic to serve the small village and the surrounding area.

The clinic helped, but Price needed more help. On the strengths of his reports, the brothers obliged. Five years later, they had paid for the installation of a power generator to supply electricity, and they had arranged for a deep well to be dug. The water was so plentiful that it generously sup-

An example of newspaper advertising used during the company's 100th anniversary in 1988. The ads proclaimed Belk and Leggett's celebration of a century of providing fashion, value, quality, and service to its customers.

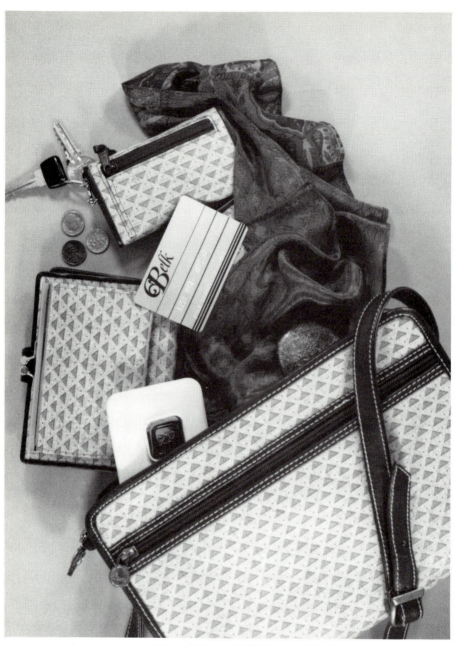

Far from the days of William Henry Belk's "no credit" policy days, Belk and Leggett stores now have millions of company credit card customers.

Mrs. George McClellan, whose husband served as manager of the Belk store in Monroe, N.C., from 1928 to 1952, cuts a cake commemorating the Monroe store's 90th birthday in 1978. Looking on, from left, are Tom Belk, Irwin Belk, Charles Hunley, former Monroe store manager, John Belk, and Henderson Belk.

Ted Venis of Surratt, Smith, Abernathy/Williams Associates, the company's in-house architectural firm in Charlotte, puts the finishing touches on a model of the North Myrtle Beach, S.C., Belk store.

Buyers from the New York and Charlotte offices of Belk Stores Services brainstorm ideas for the company's upcoming 100th anniversary during a workshop in Charlotte in February 1987.

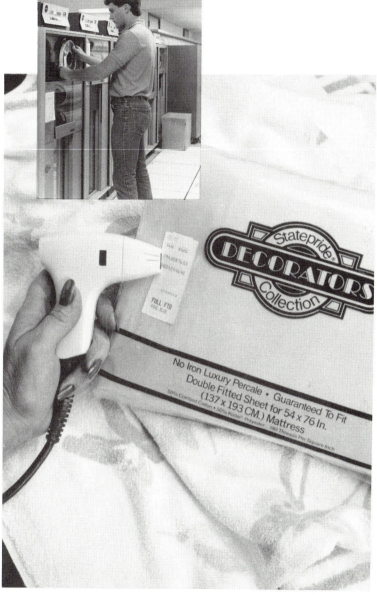

A computer wanding device is used to "capture" pricing and inventory
information from a merchandise tag. The company uses the latest
technology, coordinated through major computer data centers in Charlotte
and in Orlando, Fla., to help it manage its complex financial and
merchandising information systems.

John and Laura Pomerantz, center, executives of the Leslie Fay Companies, Inc., in New York receive an Eagle award from John and Tom Belk during a Belk 100th anniversary preview meeting with the company's top merchandise resource companies on September 28, 1987, in Charlotte. Leslie Fay, one of Belk's top resources, was one of nearly 150 companies to receive special Eagle and Falcon awards for its sales volume and service record with Belk.

Tom Belk, right, at commencement exercises at the University of North Carolina at Charlotte in 1982, with Chancellor E. K. Fretwell, Jr., left, and commencement speaker U.S. Senator Paul Simon of Illinois, who ran for the Democratic nomination for the presidency of the United States in 1988. Tom Belk served as chairman of the university's board of trustees from 1982 to 1984.

On October 27, 1985, Presbyterian Hospital's Belk Heart Center in Charlotte, a regional heart center equipped with the latest surgical technology and equipment, was dedicated to the Belk family "for their enormous support to Presbyterian Hospital since its founding in 1903."

The Belk Residence Hall at Davidson College.

The Belk store at SouthPark Mall, Charlotte, opened in 1970 with 220,000 square feet of space. A major remodeling in 1986 added a new shopping level and 70,000 square feet of space, and established the store as the company's flagship store. (Photograph by Gordon Schenck)

The 177,000-square-foot Belk-Beery store at Independence Mall in Wilmington, N.C., features large mosaic tile murals of Wilmington area scenes located at each of its three exterior entrances. The store opened in August 1979. (Photograph by Gordon Schenck)

Belk of Pinecrest Plaza, Southern Pines, N.C., opened in October 1987, with 64,000 square feet of space. (Photograph by Rick Alexander)

Belk entered the Chattanooga, Tenn., market in August 1987 with this 136,000-square-foot store at Hamilton Place.

Belk joined the island resort community of Hilton Head, S.C., with the opening of this 57,000-square-foot store at the mall at Shelter Cove in April 1988. (Photograph by Gordon Schenck)

A sleek modern design was used for this 106,000-square-foot Belk-Lindsey store, which opened in October 1982 at the Melborne Square Mall in Melborne, Fla. (Photograph by Gordon Schenck)

Leggett of Staunton Plaza, Staunton, Va., opened in February 1987, with nearly 65,000 square feet of space. (Photograph by Gordon Schenck)

A traditional architectural design was used for the Belk-Leggett store in Piedmont Mall in Danville, Va., when it opened in 1984, with nearly 127,000 square feet of space. (Photograph by Gordon Schenck)

Cosmetics counter at Belk SouthPark, Charlotte.

Women's fashion apparel area at Belk SouthPark.

China, crystal, silver, and gifts area in the lower level at Belk SouthPark, Charlotte. (Photograph by Gordon Schenck)

Cosmetics area at Belk of Hamilton Place, Chattanooga, Tenn. (Photograph by Gordon Schenck)

Center court at Belk of Hamilton Place, Chattanooga, Tenn. (Photograph by Gordon Schenck)

Center court of Belk-Leggett store at Piedmont Mall in Danville, Va. (Photograph by Gordon Schenck)

Checker-board aisles lead customers to the fashion apparel areas at the Belk of Pinecrest Plaza, Southern Pines, N.C. (Photograph by Rick Alexander)

plied both the hospital and the town. In 1928, a permanent hospital building was added to the facility that now was called the Sarah Walkup Hospital, in honor of the Belk brothers' mother. None of the reports about the work of the hospital, periodically detailed in the *Charlotte Observer* by Belk's friend, the Reverend J. G. Garth, make clear why the brothers chose their mother's maiden name.

Altogether, the brothers donated more than $60,000 to the hospital, which was confiscated and used by the Japanese

Belk sales associate assisting customer at Belk SouthPark, Charlotte.

A computerized gift registry system assists customers with their gift-giving at Belk SouthPark, Charlotte.

army when it invaded China. Belk got a firsthand report on the hospital in 1942 when Dr. Price and other missionaries returned to the United States after the outbreak of World War II. Price visited Belk in Charlotte and told him that during the two decades of operation, about 30,000 people a year had been treated at the hospital. Price told Belk that the Japanese army commander who took over the hospital said it would be returned at the end of the war.

The hospital survived World War II and continued operation briefly under the Nationalist regime. In 1948, a young Chinese doctor studying medicine in the United States visited Belk in Charlotte and personally reported on the hospital's contribution to the region. Within the year, the hospital was lost from sight when the Bamboo Curtain closed on the country.

Belk had attracted to his business young men who cared about their church and their communities. Some, like Arthur Tyler of Rocky Mount and John Hensdale of Fayetteville, helped public and private colleges and universities extend education to rural areas of the state. Tyler was a driving force behind the growth of East Carolina University in Greenville. Others, like Karl Hudson, worked in the church. Hudson also was an active and generous supporter of the 4-H programs in the counties where the Hudson brothers operated stores.

Belk stores were in and of their communities. Local store managers often would pass along small contributions at Henry Belk's direction and they were expected to use a portion of their profits for community projects.

During the 1930s, Henry Belk and his chief buyer, Sam Scott were traveling through the rural counties of the Carolinas and talking about the condition of the Southern farm economy. They were distressed that the future of the farm families in the region depended so heavily on the area's two money crops, tobacco and cotton. Prices fluctuated wildly, driven by conditions well beyond the control of the farmers and unrelated to the quality of their crop. These changes also were reflected on the balance sheets of the local Belk stores.

If farmers had a bad year, they would be spending less money as they struggled to make ends meet. Farmers needed to wean themselves from such dependence, and the two men decided to do something about it.

In 1940, Scott gathered managers of twenty-four stores in twenty-two counties to enlist their support for building dairying as another source of income for North Carolina farmers. Scott and J. Horton Doughton, Belk's partner in Statesville, asked the managers to help sponsor a calf-raising competition among the children from area farms. While older farmers might be set in their ways and reluctant to change old habits, the two believed that their children might be encouraged to learn something new. The managers agreed. With the help of the state agriculture specialists, they announced that $5,000 in prize money would be awarded each year to young farmers who showed the best animals.

The next year, in Statesville, 201 animals from farms in twelve counties were shown. The program was a hit. Children as young as eight and nine years old participated. Three years later, a similar program was started by stores in the eastern part of the state. By the 1950s, a third North Carolina contest was organized, and a program was begun in South Carolina. Both states experienced dramatic growth in their dairy industries during the decade.

Less than two years before his death, Davidson College honored Henry Belk for his many contributions to his church and his community. Belk had passed up a college education to make way for his brother, but on Commencement Day in 1950, Belk pulled on the robes of a doctor of laws and walked across the shaded lawn with the procession to receive his honorary degree. He was one of five men honored that year. Another was Davidson graduate Dean Rusk, who later would become President Lyndon Johnson's secretary of state.

The Davidson honors carried special meaning for Belk, whose family had been part of the small Presbyterian institution for generations. Davidson was not even ten years old when the first Belk attended classes there in 1847. Before the Civil War, four of Belk's uncles had been graduated. One of the four, James Thomas Kitchin Belk, represented the Synod of the Presbyterian Church from South Carolina on the college's board of trustees from 1866 to 1874. In addition, Belk's father-in-law, Dr. John Irwin, and many in Irwin's family were Davidson graduates.

There is no indication that Belk was ever eager to follow his uncles to Davidson. Belk seemed more intent on furthering his business career when he was a young man of college age. When he arrived in Charlotte in 1895 to find a location for his new store, his connections with the college and its founders were renewed. His first store building, the small brick structure on East Trade Street, was leased at very reasonable and convenient terms from the Davidson family, which had donated the property to the college sixty years earlier. Belk's lease continued without ever being reduced to writing for more than fifty years.

Davidson College was Charlotte's foremost institution, although it was located well into the country in a village about twenty miles north. The early *Charlotte Observer* carried regular reports of college activities, including a rundown of the ages and backgrounds of incoming classes. Belk supported the college through the church for years, but he became more involved in Presbyterian institutions away from his home base.

In 1916, Belk was named to the first board of trustees of Montreat College, later called Montreat-Anderson, which was located at Montreat Assembly and was organized to train teachers for schools in the North Carolina mountains. About ten years later, at the urging of the Reverend William Black, Belk also helped organize Presbyterian Junior College in Maxton, N.C. He was the first board member elected, and he signed the application for the college's charter in October 1928.

Presbyterian Junior College, which later merged with other church colleges to become St. Andrew's College in Laurinburg, N.C., had a very shaky beginning. Belk and R. L. McLeod of Maxton personally carried a large part of the debt required to underwrite operations of the school during its formative years. Finally, in 1939, the two made a contribution of $20,000 to the school to repay the loan. Belk continued with periodic contributions, making his last, a $50,000 challenge gift, just a few months before his death.

Henry Belk's own sons attended Davidson, as did the sons of partners Karl Hudson and Houston Matthews. Of the five Belk sons, however, only John finished his college career on that campus. The others had their education interrupted by World War II; when they returned, they earned degrees at other North Carolina universities: Duke and the University of North Carolina at Chapel Hill. That did not suit their father, who considered John to be the only one to have earned a real diploma!

The same year that Davidson College honored Belk, the Belk Chapel was dedicated on the campus of Queens College in Charlotte, his wife's alma mater. The chapel, built on modified lines of early Greek temples, with Doric columns across the front, was the gift of the families and business associates of Henry and John Belk. A year earlier, Henry Belk's partner Erskine Gallant, whose uncle had been one of the missionaries the Belk brothers had supported years before, presented Henry Belk to the congregation of the William Henry Belk Presbyterian Church in Anderson, S.C. The church was named in his honor and was paid for by the congregation with the help of money raised by Gallant and his associates in the Gallant-Belk stores.

Shortly after Henry Belk's death, the *Mecklenburg Presbyterian* said of his remarkable life: "Mild-mannered, soft-spoken, courage of a lion, but gentle as a lady, devotion to family and friends, the zeal of Paul, a double portion of the foundation grace of humility, much of the compassion of our Lord, God's good man—William Henry Belk—will be speaking for generations to come."

Indeed, Belk's good works survive. Henry Belk did not apportion his estate as did his brother, John, stipulating that a certain share of its income go to continue what he had begun. But he encouraged his heirs to continue and to remind themselves regularly of their Christian duty to advance God's work. In time, the J. M. Belk Foundation was combined with part of Henry Belk's estate to form the Belk Foundation, which has presented major gifts to colleges, churches, and other institutions.

A large $300,000 residence hall at Davidson College, the money for which was pledged before his death, was opened in his name in 1953. The next year, Mary Irwin Belk stood with others in her Queens College class of 1901 and dedicated a new residence hall there. Over the years, contributions have gone to state campuses at Appalachian State University, the University of North Carolina campuses at Asheville and Charlotte, and East Carolina University. Smaller colleges such as Coker College, Chowan College, Converse College, Elon College, Erskine College, Meredith College, Mars Hill College, and Methodist College have received gifts from the foundation. Members of the Belk family also have been instrumental in raising money for St. Andrew's College, Union Theological Seminary in Richmond, Va., and Johnson C. Smith University in Charlotte.

Community involvement and support of local institutions have been part of the fabric of the Belk organization beyond Charlotte. Belk managers in the southeastern part of North Carolina helped raise money to build St. Andrew's College. When the Presbyterians picked Laurinburg as the site for St. Andrew's, Belk partner John Hensdale helped organize supporters to bring Methodist College to Fayetteville. The Hensdale Chapel on the Methodist College campus honors Hensdale's contributions. His personal gifts also extended to Fayetteville State University and Campbell College in nearby Buies Creek.

In time, Belk's children have extended the reach of the foundation and their own giving to include hospitals, parks, the YMCA and YWCA, and the Boy Scouts of America. John Belk and other Belk executives like John Hensdale and Robert Wildrick have received the highest scouting awards for their work. John Belk, an avid Scout as a teenager, continued his scouting work when he was helping resettle families during the Korean War, by organizing Scout troops and even submitting a weather project he had completed as an adult for an unfinished merit badge from his youth.

Three Belk men, Tom, Irwin, and John, have served on the board of trustees of the University of North Carolina at Charlotte, a campus Irwin helped create as a state senator when he introduced the bill authorizing the state to convert Charlotte College to a campus of the university system. Tom made the first of several donations of land, giving ninety acres for the campus. All three have been active with the school's foundation and have helped raise millions of dollars for the school, making their own large personal contributions.

No institution has had as long an association with the Belk family as Presbyterian Hospital in Charlotte, literally the Belks' next-door neighbor. The hospital remains on the site chosen by Henry Belk and others, despite attempts through the years to merge with other medical facilities. The core building was constructed after the last merger attempt in 1939 and has been added to through the years. Henry Belk died in the hospital in 1952. When Mary Belk died in 1968, she left 3.2 acres of land, including the large Belk home, to the hospital, which purchased additional land from the Belk family. A few years later, with John Belk leading the campaign, the hospital raised $5 million, $2 million over its goal, to expand services, so that now it serves more than 100,000 patients a year.

In 1985, the hospital's board of trustees, of which Tom Belk is a member, dedicated the Belk Heart Center to Dr. John Robinson Irwin, William Henry Belk, Sr., Mary Irwin Belk, and their children, whom Board Chairman William H. Barnhardt called "North Carolina's finest assets."

Henry Belk's mercantile business, a quarter-century old, was one of the most successful enterprises in the Carolinas when, in 1913, E. W. Grove opened his magnificent Grove Park Inn overlooking the French Broad River valley at Asheville, N.C. Grove's mountain workmen built one of the South's most unusual hotels out of the huge boulders they hauled up the side of Sunset Mountain. The building rose floor by floor from the mountainside as they fashioned each bold hunk of granite into a comfortable fit with its neighbor.

In the summer of 1986, Henry Belk's successors gathered at the Grove Park Inn to lay plans for their future. Their stores, once as random and different as the boulders in the walls of the magnificent Grove Park, now were united in a unique mercantile network that had not only prospered for nearly one hundred years, but had remained a family business in an age of mergers and acquisitions and corporate control.

As they approached their second century, the Belk and Leggett organizations dominated the retail market in more than 80 percent of the more than 325 cities in which they did business. Often, the toughest competitor for a Belk store was another Belk store in a nearby city. And the Belks and Leggetts were on the move again after a decade of regrouping and relocating from downtown to regional shopping malls in communities where they had done business for years. Large, suburban department stores were opening or were planned for new markets in Florida, Virginia, Kentucky, Texas, Tennessee, and Delaware. Altogether, Belk stores would be in a composite trading area serving more than 80 million people.

The new generation of stores was as elaborate and stylish as any in the nation. The $455 million that Belk stores had spent on remodeling old stores and building new ones during the previous ten years had established the business as the retail fashion leader in its markets and had helped win the stores national awards for outstanding architectural design. While the partners met in Asheville, workmen were putting the finishing touches on the $13 million remodeling of the Belk SouthPark store in Charlotte. The interior displays that Belk Stores Services' interior designers would create for Gucci shops installed in Belk and Leggett stores in the Southeast would be replicated for Gucci shops at other department-store chains throughout the United States.

In the booming metropolitan areas of the South, Belk stores had successfully met the demand for fashion that in the 1970s had replaced the conservative tradition of shopping for value and durability. Belk customers, many of them transplanted from major cities in the Northeast and Midwest, now expected the latest in fashion and popular design labels in much the same way as Henry Belk's early customers had looked to him for bargains and inexpensive work clothes.

The Belk-Leggett private labels were being revived. The old, faithful Red Camel label, first used on men's denim overalls, now was sewn to the collars of trendy women's and girls' sportswear. (Ironically, Belk designers had picked it for its character, not its tradition. Those who knew its connection with work clothes had at first rejected it.) The stores' faith in the organization's ability to generate successful merchandise would soon be shown in the introduction of a line of fashionable lingerie. The first order to manufacturers would be worth $10 million.

During this period of dramatic change, Belk had not replaced the large group of loyal customers who shopped for moderate-priced merchandise with a smaller, though more affluent, group of customers seeking more expensive fashion items and trendy styles. Not every city was a Charlotte, and not every store was a local version of the Belk "store of the future" at SouthPark. Instead, throughout the system, Belk had successfully added a new layer of buying opportunity for customers looking for fashion. As they had from the very early days under Henry Belk, store managers still tailored the merchandise mix to suit their stores in towns and small cities where payrolls and pocketbooks were more modest than those in the wealthier suburbs of metropolitan areas. After nearly one hundred years, there still was no *one* Belk store. In fact, many of the 350 Belk and Leggett stores were still located in smaller towns and cities across sixteen states from Delaware to Texas.

The blanket coverage of Belk in the Carolinas had given the organization stability and ready outlets for large quantities of inexpensive durable merchandise designed, produced, and manufactured under the careful attention of Belk Stores Services. During the previous twenty years, however, one small store after another had been closed as the inefficiencies of these small outlets became inescapable. Those that remained now participated in more group purchasing, centralized merchandising, and consolidated services.

The Belk tradition of local autonomy, the varied personalities of the communities in which Belk stores did business, and the marked changes in the South had now produced three categories of stores in the Belk and Leggett organizations. There were the large fashion stores like SouthPark, Raleigh's Crabtree Valley (which would complete a $7 to $8 million face-lift in the centennial year), the Leggett store in Roanoke, Va., and Greensboro's large Four Seasons store. These stores were comparable in style and design to the best any department-store chain in the nation had to offer. At the next level were medium-sized stores in smaller towns. These locations featured national brands and private-label fashions, but the stock was moderately priced and designed to compete with Belk's traditional rivals such as J. C. Penney or Sears. Finally, the network included a few bargain and budget stores, some of them called BudgetFair, that carried popular-priced merchandise for the workingman and his family. These stores more closely resembled the Belk stores as they were at the height of Henry Belk's day in the 1920s and 1930s.

This collection of stores, consolidated now under about 225 separate corporations in twenty-nine partner groups, was the result of the planning that had begun more than twenty years earlier at John Belk's home on the Myrtle Beach golf course. Through the years, subsequent planning sessions had focused on specific segments of the business. Modern management techniques, fashion, financing, sales promotions and joint advertising, and succession planning each had been carefully considered at separate planning retreats. Altogether, these meetings had helped the Belks and Leggetts not only reach but double the volume of sales they had set in 1966 as their goal for the business.

The business clearly reflected the style of John Belk, the tall, affable chief executive of most of the store corporations and chairman of the board of Belk Stores Services. Belk supervised the vast network of stores from his crowded office in downtown Charlotte. The head of the country's largest family- and management-owned business worked with his door open, only lightly guarded from visitors by Carol Cannon, his secretary for more than thirty years.

The office reflected his passions—the business, his family, and sports, particularly basketball and big game hunting. Belk's desk was forever a foot deep in paperwork. Only a few spots of polished wood could be seen on any of the bookcases, which were covered with an assortment of memorabilia including national Boy Scout awards and the brass footing and a cash carrier from the days of the Lamson pneumatic tube system. An oversized map of the United States, printed before interstate highways were laid across the country, covered the wall to his left, the trophy from an African safari hung high on another, and an award from the National Retail Merchants Association, of which he had served as president, was on another. A small television with a broken antenna was in a corner. The office, like Belk, offered no pretensions.

From the beginning, Belk had used encouragement and suggestion rather than direct intervention to shape the business. Change had come more slowly, but Belk's measured pace capitalized on the strength of his partners and local managers whose investment in their stores was personal as much as financial. Contemporary economists and students of business management had recently discovered this system, which for the Belks was rooted in nearly one hundred years of business. The combination of corporate structure with local ownership that tapped the entrepreneurial spirit was now called Japanese Management.

That summer of 1986, during a very private two-day meeting at the Grove Park Inn, John and Tom Belk had met with the forty-five men and women most responsible for the future of the company. Together, they had listened to outside analysts and management specialists report on what they saw ahead for the company and the retail business in the Southeast. They had studied the future markets for the stores and the strengths and weaknesses of the Belk organization and had reviewed the results of earlier planning meetings. These sessions were similar in style to previous management retreats, but they differed in one major respect. For the first time, the Belk and Leggett leaders were putting together a unified plan that would deliver the business into the hands of the next generation of professionals and a third generation of family leaders.

A few months later, one of the analysts assigned to the project reported on the highlights of the meeting, sharing in democratic fashion with men and women from stores large and small much of the same information the Belks and their partners had considered in Asheville. The future of the stores rests with the people who are hired, trained, developed, and promoted through the ranks, Peat Marwick's Michael Turillo told the group of company personnel and operations managers. The company must remain market driven, he said, responding to customers' requests, with Belk sales associates giving special attention to the same quality of service that "Mr. Henry" and "Dr. John" Belk had preached to their early partners. The business would need the best systems for rapidly moving the merchandise from the manufacturers' shipping docks to the customers' hands. And the company should build on the strengths of the unique Belk management formula. "You have something others are envi-

ous of," Turillo said, "the balance of entrepreneurial ownership and the bigness of corporate structure. That's what
they're trying to replicate. Let's operate as if we are locally
owned and managed stores. Whatever you do, don't lose
that."

A few months later, on the eve of the company's one hundredth anniversary year, the stockholders of the 350 stores
were reminded of the same spirit by members of the Belk
and Leggett families who greeted them for a special one-
hundredth anniversary preview meeting. Gathered together
in a meeting room of the Radisson Hotel in Charlotte were
the heirs of Henry and John Belk and their early partners
Karl Hudson, Houston Matthews, Erskine Gallant, J. G.
Parks, and others. "It's fitting that we begin our one hundredth anniversary celebration kickoff with you, our Belk
and Leggett stockholders," John Belk told the group meeting
on this special occasion. "You're the reason our company
has grown from a small bargain store in Monroe in 1888 to
the country's largest family- and management-owned department store organization."

Seated throughout the room were many of the next generation from the Belk and Leggett families. When he took his
turn at the podium, crew-cut T. C. Leggett of South Boston,
Va., president of Leggett stores, confidently displayed a picture of five young Leggett sons who already had assumed
various jobs within the Leggett stores. "These young men
started at the freight chute, cleaning up the store, delivering
packages, being an assistant division manager, division manager, and now two of them are managers of stores," Leggett
said.

A like number of the young men and women of the next
generation of Belks and their partners also had followed their
fathers into the stores. Tom Belk's three sons, Tim, McKay,
and John, were working in stores in Charlotte and Gastonia.
His daughter, Katie, previously had worked in Karl Hudson's group. Irwin Belk's son, Bill, was in a management position in the Columbia, S.C., store and another son, Carl,

was working in Asheville, N.C. Henderson Belk's son, Paul, and Belk Daughtridge, grandson of Dr. John Belk, held management positions in the Belk-Hensdale group offices.

A third generation from the Belk partners' families was involved. In Gastonia, Gene Matthews, son of Houston Matthews's youngest son, Frank, was preparing for a retail career. In Raleigh, Karl Hudson's grandsons, Richard and Karl III, were already in the business. Erskine Parks's son, George, was manager of the Bristol, Va., store.

The forebears of many of those meeting in the hotel in downtown Charlotte had learned the merchant's trade in the Belk store located just across Trade Street. The original three-story brick building, where Henry Belk and his young protégés had worked from early morning to past supper and then retired to rooms above, was long gone. A small pocket park was in its place. The impressive south front of the building that Henry and John Belk had introduced as their grand emporium in 1928 remained. It was partially obscured by an enclosed overstreet walkway that connected the store to the bustle of a downtown mall and towering office building that stood where Henry Belk had taken his meals at the Central Hotel.

In December of 1986, a portion of the land upon which the downtown Belk store is located was sold to a joint venture of NCNB National Bank, Charter Properties, and Lincoln Property Company, which planned to develop an office/retail building complex in conjunction with a proposed performing arts center for the city. Another portion of the land, valued at $3,150,000, was donated by Belk to the Foundation for the Carolinas to support the development of the City of Charlotte's new performing arts center.

As with other birthday celebrations, Belk kicked off its one hundredth anniversary by inviting first 350 suppliers, including the heads of some of the nation's largest and most popular fashion houses, and then later two hundred newspaper and media executives who benefited from the stores' annual $70 million advertising budgets in the 16-state area to elaborate luncheons and dinners to unveil plans for the anniversary. The company also rolled out the red carpet for about 200 leading bankers and business leaders. Guests heard John Belk announce company news, including the opening of eleven stores in the company's centennial year. The new stores would add 725,000 square feet to the organization's total of 20 million square feet of selling space.

During the suppliers' visit, thirty-five parent apparel and textile companies were recognized by Belk as top-volume leaders, and during a midafternoon awards presentation on the Queens College campus, chief executives dressed in formal wear picked up the Belk's Eagle Club Award, made by Steuben. Another 101 vendors were presented Falcon Club Awards made by Baccarat.

"If you're going to be important and try to dominate this area," one leading sportswear manufacturer told a reporter for a national industry publication, "one's relationship with Belk is essential."

Speakers for the celebration also included Senator Sam Nunn of Georgia, former U.S. secretary of transportation Elizabeth Dole, former astronaut William Anders, former CIA director Admiral Stansfield Turner, industrialist Ross Perot, and former chairman of the Federal Reserve System Paul Volcker. The governor of North Carolina, James Martin, whose father-in-law was an executive in the Columbia, S.C., Belk store, was an invited speaker along with chief executives of Estée Lauder, Liz Claiborne, Levi Strauss, the Leslie Fay Companies, and Milliken and Co., all major Belk resources. These presentations, and others, included reminders that the Belk organization still relied on such human elements of the business as integrity, compassion, imagination, courage, and resourcefulness, all embodied by founder Henry Belk.

Perot, who had met John Belk more than twenty-five years earlier in an AMA seminar, summed up the Belk contribution to business and the region with its unique organization saying, "the Belk family has been a great steward for one hundred years in providing very fine, stable jobs and opportunities. I'd give anything if they would teach in the business schools that if you really want to bring out the best in your talented young people, then give them a chance to own a part of the business."

The Belks' concentration on human values had built a company that was ranked among the largest privately owned businesses in the country. In recent years, these basic tenets had been supplemented by sophisticated computer systems that permitted a customer to order a particular shoe from a manufacturer right from the shoe department, allowed a salesperson to track a special-order bridal gown, or let a store manager know exactly when important popular merchandise would arrive at the dock. The nexus of the business remained in the heart of Charlotte, a city as certain of its destiny as it was the day Henry Belk stepped off the train to find himself a new store.

Charlotte now was home to more than 350,000 people; 5 million more potential Belk customers lived within 100 miles of the city. Cranes and construction crews were changing the face of Charlotte daily, building new homes and offices for corporations listed among the nation's largest. Again, Belk was part of the growth. As John Belk spoke to the guests in high-rise hotels in downtown Charlotte, workmen and heavy equipment were clearing a building site, in an office park located south of the city, for a new home for Belk Stores Services.

Three times during the past twenty years, Belk architects had designed a new building to replace the East Fifth Street quarters that had been too small almost by the time the building opened in 1949. Each time, the plans had been put back on the shelf in favor of more important options. Throughout the 1970s, the Belks and their partners were more intent on putting their money into new stores. Moreover, the shape and size of the BSS functions and staff also had been in a constant state of change. John Belk found it hard to recommend a building for a future home when it was not clear what functions would be housed there. This time, however, the building was on. Construction had begun on a 32-acre site near Charlotte's new 25,000-seat coliseum just off the Billy Graham Parkway near the airport. The offices were due to open in the summer of 1988.

The new offices would be five and a half times larger than the old building, combining under one roof the buying and operations sections, as well as the executive offices for BSS. Cramped quarters and overstuffed offices would no longer be a way of life for the 1,100 BSS employees, who worked at eight locations throughout the city, from East Fifth Street and offices on the upper floors of the downtown store to space in Charlotte's Merchandise Mart and a warehouse located just off Interstate 85. The discomforts were shared equally. For years, after moving from the open work area of the buying office, Tom Belk's office had been a converted law library. It was so jammed with paperwork, merchandise samples, and reports from the stores that there was room for no more than one visitor at a time. In his proportionately small outer office, two secretaries worked in space too small for one. One worked in what once had been a storage closet.

Jean Surratt's architects and their consultants had designed a building as functional as Henry Belk's rolltop desk and as elegant as the new SouthPark store. Three large, multistoried wings, each designed for specific tasks, extended from a central, skylighted mall. The 560,000-square-foot building also included a 100,000-square-foot merchandise showroom, enough space to operate the average Belk department store. The main entrance to this impressive building, set back from a reflecting pond, was to be a grand, four-story, glass-enclosed atrium framed by tall columns supporting a graceful arch.

The new home would be more than simple relief for overcrowded quarters. It was designed to coordinate the work and future of the more than 35,000 Belk employees and hundreds of millions of dollars in purchases from resources around the world. Since 1971, just after the first scouting trip by Belk merchandise specialists to Hong Kong, BSS had operated Belk International, which shopped throughout the world for goods for Belk stores. The international business grew rapidly during the next decade, becoming strong and profitable, but Belk remained loyal to American manufacturers, many of which had plants and facilities near Belk stores in the Southeast. About 95 percent of Belk private-label goods were made domestically. The international buying power of BSS, the computer networks and the planning and distribution, personnel, legal resources, sales promotion, and administration services put even the smallest Belk store in a unique competitive position.

After nearly forty years, John and Tom Belk finally had the suburban location they had wanted for the buying office when it had outgrown the upper floors of the Charlotte store. John Belk had argued to his father that if the buying service was to succeed and to serve the increasing number of stores properly, it would have to be separate from the Charlotte store to shed its image as a corporate stepchild. His father had been set on the downtown location. Henry Belk had only reluctantly moved from the store to his new, large, paneled office down the street prepared for him by his children. That was far enough from his beloved sales floor. At least he could still hear the Southern Railway trains he once rode north rumble into town delivering goods for his stores.

After more than a decade of corporate reorganization and building for the future, BSS had come of age. As much as anything, the building represented the fulfillment of John and Tom Belk's goal to unite the collection of Belk stores into a well-organized merchandising business unsurpassed in the South. Meeting with the Belk and Leggett resources, John Belk said proudly, "It's exciting to be 99 going on 100. We've come a long way and (borrowing from a promotional slogan) we want everyone to 'take a look at Belk today.' We have lots to be proud of, and we're doing everything we can to keep the momentum going. We look forward to the future," Belk said. "1988, our centennial year, marks the dawn, the bright sunrise, of a promising new century for us."

Index

Illustrations are indicated in italics.

Advertising, for the Belk stores: in the late 1800s, 20, 37, 38, 42, 44; in the early 1900s, 30, 58; slogans, 39, 75, 116, 164, 180; for the Charlotte store (1938), 171; circulars, 264; example of print advertising (1988), 265
Albemarle, N.C., Belk store in, 65
Alderman, Nancy, 231, 239, 245
Allied Stores Corporation, 155, 157, 173
American Management Association (AMA), 192, 201, 212, 213–14
American Tobacco Company, 46
Anderson, E. A., 108, 109, 136, 146
Anderson, S.C., Belk store in, 69, 98, 125, 128, 133
Anthony, Ruth, 41
Arkins, Harry, 153
Arkins, Sidney, 153
Athens, Ga., Belk store in, 133
Austin, Ed, 19
Austin, John, 13, 21
Autry, Von, Jr., 222–23, 224, 229, 240–41

Barclay, Jonas, 250
Barnhardt, William H., 287
Barringer, Osmond, 47
Baruch, Herman, 35
Beck, Vance, 133
Bee Hive store, the, 36, 39–40, 42, 52
Beery, William B., III, 10, 11, 205, 206, 225; management role of, in the 1970s, 229; and the Estée Lauder deal, 238
Belk, Abel Nelson Washington, 13
Belk, Hallie, 75
Belk, Henderson, 4, 29, 72, 145, 187; during World War II, 146, 147; and the Thomasville store, 150; and the Tampa store, 159–60; in a family portrait, 162; with Billy Graham, 170; at the Monroe store's 90th birthday, 267
Belk, Henry, Jr., 4, 9, 29, 113, 135; initial participation in the Belk business, 145–47, 148; design for store fixtures, 151; and the first Belk stores in Florida, 158–59; and the formation of BSS, 160; in a family portrait, 161; and the reacquisition of the Belk-Lindsey stores, 198; and the Belk business, in the late 1960s, 213
Belk, Irwin, 4, 29, 147, 187, 202; in a family portrait, 162; with Billy Graham, 170; at the Monroe store's 90th birthday, 267
Belk, James Thomas Kitchin, 284
Belk, Dr. John, 14, 18, 71; partnership with Henry Belk, 22, 26, 32, 39, 91–93; and the establishment of the cooperative buying network, 40–41; and Henry Belk, comparison of, 46–47, 93; management style of, 53, 135–36; and Karl Hudson, relationship with, 66; and Fred Leggett, relationship with, 76, 78; and the break with the Leggetts, 86–87; support of the Presbyterian Church, 91; death of, 92–93
Belk, John (son of Tom Belk), 293
Belk, John (son of William Henry Belk), 2, 29, 188, 190–92; and the Belk image outside the South, 5; and the hiring of Joe Robinson, 7, 8; and the Savannah store, 10; and his father's death, 143; during World War

II, 147; and the buying services, 152, 153–54; and the Efird purchase, 160, 165–67, 173–76, 191; and BSS, 160, 187; in a family portrait, *161*; and the opening of the Friendly Center store, 189; and the development of the Belk business in the 1960s, 201; at the Daytona Beach manager's convention, 209–10, 215; and the resolution of family management issues, 212–13; with Tom Belk, 257; at the reopening of the SouthPark store, *259*; at the podium, during a dinner at Davidson College, *262*; at the Monroe store's 90th birthday, *267*; community involvement of, 286–87; management style of, 291

Belk, Katherine McKay, 193, *261*

Belk, Mabel, 93

Belk, McKay, 293

Belk, Mary Irwin, 71, 72, 91, 113, 286; in a family portrait, *161*; with Billy Graham, *170*; and the opening the newly expanded Charlotte store (1956), 177; death of, 287

Belk, Nealie, *22*, 76

Belk, Ralph J., 48, 64

Belk, Sarah. *See* Gambrell, Sarah Belk

Belk, Sarah Walkup (mother of William Henry and John Belk), 13–14, 33, 47

Belk, Tom, 1, 2, 3, 4, 145; and the Belk image outside the South, 5; and the hiring of Joe Robinson, 7; in family portraits, *29*, *161*; during World War II, 147; and the buying services, 154, 233, 235; at a piece goods meeting in New York (1953), *167*; with Billy Graham, *170*; and the Efird purchase, 174, 175; role of, in the Belk business in the 1950s, 192–93; and the Belk private-label business, 196–97; and the resolution of family management issues, 212; research trip of, to study new forms of retailing, 221–22; with John Belk (brother), 257; at the reopening of the SouthPark store, *259*; at the dedication of the Katherine and Tom Belk Gymnasium, *261*; at the Monroe store's 90th birthday, *267*; at commencement exercises at the University of North Carolina, *270*; community involvement of, 287

Belk, William Henry, 3, 11–15, 17, 22, 32, 47; as a leading benefactor, 5, 248–85 passim; and the New York Racket, 12–33 passim; apprenticeship to Heath, 13, 14, 21, 45; cash-sales policy of, 15–16, 19, 21, 31, 116, 225–26; advertisements written by, 20, 37, 38, 42; and the original Belk store in Charlotte, 34–55 passim; eye for opportunity, 36–37, 45; keen sense of promotion, 36–39, 44, 68; rapport with customers, 38–39, 40, 45, 47–48; early sales strategy of, 39; establishment of a cooperative buying network, 40–41; and John Belk (brother), comparison of, 46–47, 93; managerial style of, 53, 63–64, 105–7, 124–25, 136–37; recruiting system of, 53–54; marketing strategy of, in the early 1900s, 58; and the Presbyterian Church, 61, 62, 91, 103–4, 143–44, 248–85 passim; and Karl Hudson, relationship with, 66–67, 127; marriage to Mary Irwin, 71; and the New York office, 84–85; and the break with the Leggetts, 86–87; mansion of, near downtown Charlotte, 91–92; and John Belk's death, 92; and the start of the Great Depression, 100–101; merchandising philosophy of, 108, 118;

and Houston Matthews, relationship with, 127; yearly meetings with partners and managers, 141–42; death of, 143–44, 158, 287; will of, 145; on real estate investment, 146; in a family portrait, *161*; and J. C. Penney, *161*, 178; photograph of, at his desk, *162*; with Horton Doughton, *172*; exemplary character of, 285
Belk Credit Center, 227
Belk Foundation, 249, 255, 286
Belk-Lindsey Company, 104, 158, 159, 160; Florida stores of, 197–98
Belk logo, the, 5, 60, 123, 180; illustrations of, *25, 26, 27, 259*; the "Big B" and "Big L," 179, 182, 207–8, 211–12, *259*
Belk stores: reputation of, for value, 4, 5, 8–9; 75th anniversary of, 4, 6–7, 9, 197, 199–200; and the Belk name, 4–5; image of, outside the South, 5; State Pride label of, 6, 194–95; buying power of, 40–41, 48–49; basic business premises of, 41; management style of, in the early 1900s, 62–64; attitude toward customers, 63, 137–38; loss-leader selling style of, 78; merchandising style of, 81, 131, 182, *258*; and the Great Depression, 99, 112, 116, 131–32, 138; insurance coverage for, during the 1930s, 108–9; inception of a group insurance program for, 109; 50th anniversary of the, 120, 124; new concern for ambience and appearance, 132, 134–35; as a "merchant's democracy," 135–36; change from budget to fashion merchandise, 152, 153, *172*, 214; and the Efird purchase, 160, 165–67, 173–76; annual convention of, display at, *169*; and the L&M report, 179–82; need for a new corporate image, 179, 182–83; entry

into the insurance business, 185; and discord in the Belk family, during the 1950s, 185–86; in the suburbs, advent of, 188–90; the private-label program of, 196–97, 234–36, 243, 298; introduction of modern management techniques, 201, 204, 210, 214; changing market of, 203–4, 216; introduction of credit cards, 204, 212, 225–27; introduction of computers to the sales floors, 212; management training programs of, 216–17, 231; total sales space of, in the decade preceding 1975, 217; and the issue of Sunday sales, 227–28; and the Estée Lauder deal, 237–39; 100th anniversary celebration for, *263*, 293, 294–95, 298
—buying services of, 95–99, 101–3, 109, 112, 119; early buying practices, 41, 68; the New York office, 84–85, 118, 120, 139; and Sam Scott, 95–99, 101–3, 112, 151–52, 154–55; during World War II, 139, 140; expansion of, during the 1940s, 151–54; a piece goods meeting in New York (1953), *167*; during the 1950s, 193–94; since the 1970s, 232–33, 235, 236, 242–47; first fashion show coordinated by, 244; staff planning for the 100th anniversary, *268*
—expansion of: style of, 60, 61–62; during the early 1900s, 64–71; after World War I, 70; during the 1930s, 103, 132–34, 141, 151, 217; during the 1940s, 140–41, 150, 217; during the 1950s, 167–68, 188; during the late 1960s, 209–10, 217; into regional malls, 212, 218–21; during the 1970s, 217–24, 228–29. *See also* Advertising, for the Belk stores; Belk logo, the
Belk Stores Association, 83–84, 136

Belk Stores Services, Incorporated
(BSS), 2, 185, 186–87, 211, 261;
formation of, 160; Myrtle Beach
meeting (1967), 205–7, 291; new
building for, 206, 297–98; meet-
ing of, with AMA staff, 213–14;
Grove Park Inn meeting, 288,
292
Bell, Alexander Graham, 36
Belmont, N.C., Belk store in, 126
Bennettsville, S.C., Belk store in,
84
Benton, William A., 19
"Big Belk Country," theme of, 6
Black, William, 22, 250–51, 252–
53, 284
Bloodhound label, 110
Bloomingdale's (company), 2
Broome, Karl W., 65, 70, 98, 198;
as a senior partner, 125, 225
Brown, Henry, 19
Bryan, William Jennings, 20
Burlington, N.C., Belk store in,
77, 133
Busy Bees, 159, 198, 216
Byerly, Guy, Jr., 152, 154, 193; at a
piece goods meeting in New
York (1953), 167; and the State
Pride label, 195, 197; promotion
of, to vice-president, 198

Caldwell, J. P., 46
Camel cigarettes, 74, 110
Cameron Village, 170, 188–89
Cannon, Carol, 291
Cannon, James W., 16, 34
Cannon Mills Company, 6, 16, 34,
40, 64–65; bath towels from, 90,
112
Carolinas-Virginia Fashion Exhibi-
tors, 243
Cash-handling systems, 89. See
also Lamson system, the
Cash-sales policy, 15–16, 19, 21,
31, 116, 225–26
Chapel Hill, N.C., Belk store in,
225
Charleston, S.C., Belk store in, 84
Charlotte, N.C., Belk store in:

original store, 23, 24, 28, 30,
34–55; new five-story building
(1910), 54–55; growth of, in the
early 1900s, 57–98 passim;
opening of the new store
(1927), 88–90; expansion of
(1937), 112, 113, 120–22; fires
at, 114–15; 50th anniversary of
the, 150; photograph of, during
the 1950s, 165; expansion of
(1956), 176–77. See also Park
Road Shopping Center; South-
Park Mall, Belk store in
Charlotte Chamber of Commerce,
61, 150
Charlotte National Bank, 44, 51,
100
Charlotte News, 112, 144, 148–49,
177
Charlotte Observer, 28, 35, 54,
72, 113; "Ivey's Weekly Store
News" in, 58; on the Belk
Chain of Stores, 69, 80; on the
opening of the new Belk store
(1927), 88, 89; on the fire at the
Belk store (1930), 115; on the
opening of the new Belk store
(1937), 121; on the expansion of
the Belk store (1956), 177; on
the Sarah Walkup Hospital,
280; reports on activities at Da-
vidson College, 284
Charlotte Private Hospital, 256
Chattanooga, Tenn., Belk store
in, 273, 277, 278
Chester, S.C., Kluttz Department
Store in, 31, 40, 41, 48, 49
China, Belk support of hospital
in, 264, 280, 282
China Grove, N.C., Belk store in,
150
Civil War, the, 13, 15, 42, 283
Cline, Ray, 119
Clinton, N.C., Belk store in, 84
Coble, Carrie Rudge, 19
Cole Cotton Planter Manufactur-
ing Company, 44
Concord, N.C., Belk Store in, 64,
65

Cone, Ceasar, 34
Cone, Moses, 34
Cone Mills, 34, 49
Consumerism, rise of, in the late
    1800s, 57
Cook, Homer, 186
Cooper, S. T., 36, 39
Country Club Plaza, 156
Crabtree Valley Mall, Belk store
    in, 220, 221, 239, 290
Craddock, Abe, 152
Craddock-Terry Shoe Corpora-
    tion, 6, 40, 110, 128, 194
Credit cards, introduction of, at
    the Belk stores, 204, 212, 225–
    27
Crowell, Walter, 19
Currance, R. D., 167

Daily Advance, 134
Daily News Record, 158
Daily Observer, 36, 37, 42, 43
Dallas, Tex., Sanger-Harris store
    in, 240
Danville, Va., Belk-Leggett store
    in, 4, 78, 85, 114, 126, 166; in
    Piedmont Mall, 275, 279
Daughtridge, John C., 184
Daughtridge, John C., Jr., 205
Davidson, E. L. Baxter, 36
Davidson College, 35, 36, 72, 147,
    256, 271; and Henry Belk, 283–
    84, 286
Davison's (store), 182, 240
Declaration of Independence, the,
    43
de la Renta, Oscar, 1, 2, 259
Depression, the Great, 99–100,
    112–13, 116, 131–32, 138
Depression of 1893, 26, 31–32, 34–
    35
Dienst, Jocelyn, 259
Dillon, S.C., Belk store in, 141
Dixie Lad label, 194, 195
Doughton, Horton, 171, 283
Douglas, Ben, 113
Dowdy, George, 113–14, 116, 118,
    119–20, 147; offer given to, to
    assume management of the

Efird stores, 166; with Billy
    Graham, 170; as a senior part-
    ner, 185; and the new Belk
    logo, 208
Duke, James B., 46, 57
Durham, N.C., Belk store in, 68,
    79–80, 114, 126, 225; remodel-
    ing of, 132

Eagle Stores, 132
Eastridge Mall, Belk store in, 224
Efird, Hugh, 52
Efird, J. B., 61, 64
Efird, Paul, 161, 165–67, 173–76
Efird department stores, 30, 58,
    69, 80, 116; and the merger
    with the Belk stores, 161, 165–
    67, 173–76; closing of the, 228
Elizabeth College, 72, 91, 256
Ellenboro, N.C., Belk's textile mill
    in, 90
Ellen Fitzgerald Hospital, 260
Elliott, Rebecca, 137, 138
Elliott, Sam, 115, 117, 148, 149–50;
    and the Dixie Lad label, 194; as
    merchandise manager, 196–97;
    promotion of, to vice-president,
    198; and the private-label pro-
    gram, 234–35
Ervin, Sam, Jr., 177
Estée Lauder (company), 233,
    238–39

Fain, O. N., 107
Fantl, Alfred, 84, 118
Farmers: political strength of, in
    the 1880s, 15; and Henry Belk's
    system of cash sales, 15–16, 19, 31
Fendi (company), 1, 233
Filene, Edward Albert, 57
Filene's Department Store, 214–15
Fitzgerald, Ellen, 260
Ford, Gerald, 262
Ford Motor Company, 57–58, 79
Four Seasons Mall, Belk store in,
    224
Fretwell, E. K., Jr., 270
Friendly Center, Belk store in,
    188–90

Gallant, W. E., 68–69, 70, 78, 98, 103; as a senior partner, 125, 128–29, 130; and the William Henry Belk Presbyterian Church, 285

Gambrell, Sarah Belk, 4, 29, 152, 187, 205; in a family portrait, 161

Gardner, Charles, 175

Garth, J. G., 280

Gastonia, N.C., Belk store in, 22, 50, 54, 126–28, 190, 224

Gastonia Merchants Association, 130

Gilmer's Department Store, 87, 98, 119

Godfrey, Paul, 234–35

Goldsboro, N.C., Belk store in, 131, 133

Graham, Billy, 170, 178

Green, John L., 175, 202, 204

Greensboro, N.C., Belk store in, 25, 44, 133–34, 224; opening of, 48–49; featured in a Founder's Day display, 168. See also Four Seasons Mall, Belk store in; Friendly Center, Belk store in

Greenville, S.C., Belk store in, 68, 188

Grove, E. W., 288

Gucci (company), 1, 233, 289

Hall, Don, 260

Hallmark Cards, Inc., assemblage by, given to the Belk organization, 260

Hamlet, N.C., Belk store in, 19

Hampton, Archie, 106, 108, 175

Hancock, John, 43

Hanes Mall store, 241

Hardigan, Richard, 238

Harris, Deborah, 259

Harry, Arthur, 50

Harry, D. R., 25, 49

Harry, Reece P., 31–32, 41, 49

Harry, Sam, 49, 50

Harry and Belk Company, 31–32, 40, 41, 49

Hart, Emma, 59

Hartmann, Charles, 133, 134, 168, 224

Heath, B. D., 13, 14, 21, 45, 59

Heath, Jim, 59

Hensdale, John, 106, 125, 128, 139; and the Efird purchase, 174; as a senior partner, 205; at the Myrtle Beach meeting (1967), 206; community involvement of, 286

Hickory, N.C., Belk store in, 65

Hilton Head, S.C., Belk store in, 274

Hocutt, Sam H., 131

Hodges, Luther, 6, 177

Horton, Wyche, 139, 225

Houston, Sarah, 28, 54–55, 84, 89

Howard, I. N. "Nat," 175, 176, 202, 204, 226

Hudson, Grier, 66, 67, 132–33, 167

Hudson, J. L., 57

Hudson, Karl, 66–67, 68, 78–79, 101, 231; and the New York office, 84; work of, in the Presbyterian church, 130, 251–52, 282

Hudson, Karl, Jr., 205, 220–21; and the decision to maintain Hudson-Belk's downtown location, 157

Hudson, Will, 66, 67, 130, 132

Hudson-Belk Company, 4, 66, 67–68, 76–77, 134, 157–58

Hunley, Charles, at the Monroe store's 90th birthday, 267

IBM (company), 192

Irwin, John R., 71, 72, 256, 284, 287

Irwin, Mary. See Belk, Mary Irwin

Ivey, George, 219

Ivey, J. B., 52, 58, 79

Ivey's department stores. See J. B. Ivey and Company

J. A. Jones Construction Company, 112, 120

J. B. Ivey and Company, 5, 30, 58, 116, 121; regional shopping

center of, shared with the Belk business, 200, 219; colloquial title of their stores, 208
J. C. Nichols Company, 156
J. C. Penney stores, 109, 110, 129, 132, 178; expansion of, in the 1940s, 158; and the Belk stores, competition between, 173, 194, 195, 219, 234
J. G. Hood and Company, 40
J. M. Belk Memorial Fund, 252
Jones, J. A., 120
Jordan Marsh stores, 221

Kannapolis, N.C.: Cannon's cotton mills in, 16, 34, 40, 64; Belk store in, 64, 65
Killian, Ray, 6, 198–99, 209; influence on management structure in the Belk business, 201, 205, 216–17
Kimrey, D. S., 167
Kindley, Will, 50, 127
Kindley-Belk Company, 22, 50, 54, 127
Kinston, N.C., Belk store in, 133
Kirkpatrick, John W., 59, 68, 127
Kirkpatrick-Belk Company, 59, 68, 127
Kluttz, Alex, 31
Kluttz, Fred, 48
Kluttz Department Store, 31, 41, 48, 49
Kmart stores, 173, 215, 221, 230
Kress department stores, 173

Lamson system, the, 23, 24, 82, 89, 134
Laney, Yates, 68, 103, 140, 254
Lawson, Ferd, 239
Leader Stores, the, 107–8
Leggett, Fred, 75–76, 86, 114
Leggett, George, 75, 77
Leggett, Hallie, 77
Leggett, Harold, 75, 77–78, 85–86
Leggett, Julia, 77
Leggett, Robert, 75, 77, 85, 86; and the Durham store, 79–80
Leggett, T. C., 293

Leggett, Tom, 188
Leggett, Will, 75, 76, 77–78, 85, 86
Leggett family, the, 85–87, 94, 103, 125–26, 185
Levi Strauss (company), 199, 233, 295
Life Insurance Company of Virginia, 42
Life magazine, 197
Lincolnton, N.C., Belk store in, 126
Lindsey, Colin, 104, 105, 159
Lippincott and Margulies (L&M) study, 179–82, 204, 211, 226, 229
Little, Hallie. See Belk, Hallie
Lord and Taylor (company), 16
Loss-leader selling, style of, 78
Lowrance, Joe, 205

McCain, John, 13, 21
McClellan, George, 116
McClellan, Mrs. George, 267
McClure, Charles G., 143
McConnell, David, 148, 175, 202, 228
McCraw, R. D., 119, 136, 139, 140, 153; at a piece goods meeting in New York (1953), 167; remarks on pricing in Belk stores, 237
McDonald, Herbert, 70, 96
McKay, Katherine. See Belk, Katherine
McKelway, A. J., 253
McLaurin, H. A., 82
Macy's (company), 2, 56, 57, 174, 182; colloquial title of their stores, 208
Mahoney, A. F., 92
Mail-order service, 40, 57, 80, 84
Margulies, Harold, 180. See also Lippincott and Margulies (L&M) study
Marshall Field's (company), 56, 57
Martin, James, 261
Marty's Clothing Mart, 215
Matthews, Elizabeth, 190
Matthews, Eugene, 126

Matthews, Frank, 53–54, 55, 71, 81, 82–83; and the New York office, 84; and the Belk whole-sale business, 87; collaboration with Stevens, in manufacturing the Red Camel, 110; and the fire at the Charlotte store (1930), 115; retailing style of, 117–18; as a senior partner, 126; as organizer of the annual con-ventions, 136–37; as organizer of individual associations for buyers, 137

Matthews, Frank, II, 126, 190, 222, 229

Matthews, Henry, 86, 140

Matthews, Houston, 22, 54, 81, 126, 127–28

Matthews, Houston, Jr., 126, 190

Matthews, W. M. ("Mac"), 53–54, 126

Mecklenburg Declaration of Inde-pendence, 42–44

Mecklenburg Presbyterian, 285

Melborne, Fla., Belk store in, *274*

Mellon's (store), 116, 118, 121

Memphis, Tenn., Belk store in, 188

Merrill Lynch, Pierce, Fenner & Smith (company), 209

Merritt, Thomas, 103

Miller, A. W., 249

Money-back guarantees, 56

Monroe, N.C., Belk store in, *267. See also* New York Racket, the

Monroe Journal, 31

Montgomery Ward, 116, 132

Montreat Association, the, 72

Montreat College, 284

Morgan, J. D., *167*

Morris, Katie Belk, *261, 293*

Morrison, Cameron, 2, 100; road system begun by, 75, 90, 101

National Retail Merchants Asso-ciation, 166, 192

New England Dry Goods Com-pany, 97

News and Observer (Raleigh), 67

Newton, N.C., Belk store in, 65

New York Racket, the, 12–33, *20*, 39, 40; cash-sales policy of, 15–16, 19, 21, 31; advertisements for, 31

Nipper, Tom, 240

Nordstrum Company, 221

Northgate Mall, 225

North Hills Mall, 220, 221

Norwood, Alice, *19*

Ocala, Fla., Belk store in, 104

Oestreicher brothers, the, 36

Oglethorpe Mall, Belk store in, 10, 11

One-cent items, 40

One-price selling system, 16, 56

Overstocking, 83, 95–96

Palestine, Tex., Belk store in, 159

Palmer, Hendrix, 114–15

Paris, Tex., Belk store in, 151, 191

Parker, John J., 75

Park Road Shopping Center, 170–71, 178, 188–89

Parks, C. E., 65

Parks, J. G., 64–65, 66, 70, 83, 87, 125

Parks-Belk Company, 64, 65

Payne, Gene, 188

"Peacock era" for men, 216

Penney, J. C., *162*, 178. *See also* J. C. Penney stores

Perot, Ross, 192, 295–96

Pharr, Sarah, 82–83, 105, 113, 117, 142, 149

Pickens, Stanton, 123

Piedmont Fire Insurance Com-pany, 44, 52

Polk, Leonidas L., 15

Pomerantz, John, *270*

Pomerantz, Laura, *270*

Presbyterian Church: Henry Belk and the, 61, 62, 91, 103–4, 143–44, 248–85; Karl Hudson and the, 130, 251–52, 282

Presbyterian Hospital, 257, 260, *271*, 287

Presbyterian Junior College, 284–85

Presbyterian Standard, 253

Price, R. B., 264, 282
Progressive Farmer, 15
Prohibition, 51
Proximity Mill, 34, 49
Puerto Rico, Belk stores in, 180

Quattlebaum, M. C., 105, 228
Queens College, 72

Radio, advent of, 113
Raleigh, N.C.: Hudson-Belk store
  in, 4, 66–68, 131; the Pilot Mills
  in, 130–31, 220, 221, 239, 240
Red Camel label, 110, 111, 194,
  258
Reichard, Henry, 167
Reynolds, R. J., 74, 77, 110
Rich's (company), 57, 182
Ridenhour, George, 65
Robinson, Ginnie, 104
Robinson, Joe, 7–9, 11, 174, 201–7,
  221
Robinson, Leroy, 175, 201, 202,
  229, 259
Robinson, Virginia Bond, 194
Rockefeller, David, 177
Rock Hill, S.C., Belk store in, 235,
  236
Rocky Mount, N.C., Belk store
  in, 184
Roland Park Shop Center, 156
Rudge, William, 19

St. Andrew's Presbyterian Col-
  lege, 263
St. Louis World's Fair, 56
St. Petersburg, Fla., Belk store in,
  158, 159, 224
Sarah Walkup Hospital, 280
Savannah, Ga., Belk store in, 10–
  11, 188
Scopes trial, the, 253
Scott, Bob, 255–56
Scott, Kerr, 256
Scott, Norman, 129
Scott, Sam, 87–88, 94, 107, 118,
  148; and the buying services,
  95–99, 101–3, 112, 151–52, 154–
  55; at a piece goods meeting in
  New York (1953), 167; with

Horton Doughton and William
  Henry Belk, 172; and the Belk-
  sponsored calf-raising program,
  282–83
Sears, Roebuck and Company, 10,
  116, 132, 219; expansion of, in
  the 1940s, 158; and the Belk
  stores, competition between,
  173, 234
Self-service shopping, 159, 205
Sells Brothers Circus, 37–38
Seneca, S.C., Belk store in, 133
Shea, George Beverly, 170
Simon, Paul, 270
Simpson, Bessie, 116
Simpson, John R., 14, 249
Simpson, Sarah. *See* Belk, Sarah
  Walkup
Simpson, Will, 32
Smith, A. Tuttle, 159
Smith, Gibson, 8, 146, 147, 202
Smith, W. I., 82
Southern Pines, N.C., Belk store
  in, 273, 280
Southern Railway, the, 34
SouthPark Mall, Belk store in, 1,
  2, 10, 218–19, 272, 276, 277; re-
  modeling of, 259, 289; sales
  personnel assisting customers
  at, 281
South Square Mall, Belk store in,
  225
Spartanburg, S.C., Belk store in,
  65, 132
Springs, Elliott, 140
State Pride label, 6, 194–95
Statesville, N.C., Belk store in,
  164
Stern, Eugene J., 54
Stern Brothers (store), 157
Stevens, Frank, 76–77, 86, 87–88,
  125; and the New York office,
  84, 118–19; positive characteris-
  tics of, 93–94; and Scott, relationship with, 96; merchandising style of, 108, 109–11, 118,
  189–90; yearly meetings held
  by, 142; photograph of, 163;
  and the Efird purchase, 174
Stevens, John Belk, 205, 241, 242

Stevenson, Adlai, 43
Surratt, Jean, 218, 297

Tarboro, N.C., Belk store in, 133
Television, impact of, on marketing, 171, 173, 216
Textile mills, 16, 34, 49, 51, 98; after World War I, 74; during the Great Depression, 100, 112–13, 123
Thigpen, D. E., 136
Thomas, Frank, 19
Thomasville, Ga., Belk store in, 150
Thomasville Chair Company, 102
T. L. Alexander and Company, 41
Todd, Baxtor, 43
Truman, Harry, 154
Turillo, Michael, 292
Tyler, Arthur, 10, 125, 128, 131, 133; and the Efird purchase, 174; strong influence of, on the Belk organization, 183–85, 207; as chairman of BSS, 186; community involvement of, 282

Union, S.C., Belk store in, 31–32, 40, 41, 49

Van Brug, William, 239, 244
Van Heusen (company), 199
Vanity Fair (company), 7
VanWie, Mary, 29
Veldown Corporation, 99
Venis, Ted, 267
Virginia Bond label, 194

Wachovia Bank and Trust Company, 7, 100, 174, 201, 203
Walkup, Henry, 19, 44
Wallis, W. L., 88
Wanamaker, John, 16, 56, 57

"Want slips," use of, 83
Washington, N.C., Belk store in, 133
Washington Mills, 196
Waxhaw, N.C., Belk store in, 48, 59, 64, 66–67
Weiss, Emma, 118, 120
Wendt, Denise, 245–47
West Palm Beach, Fla., Belk store in, 159
Wheeler, Oliver D., 54
White, Cyrus, 65, 70, 125
White-Parks-Belk Company, 65
Whitney, Eli, 57
Whitney, Grant, 170
Wildrick, Robert, 222, 239–42, 286
William Henry Belk Presbyterian Church, 285
Williams, Hugh McRae, 59–60, 222
Williams, Jim, 59, 66, 84, 137–38
Wilmington, N.C., Belk store in, 60, 66, 272
Wilson, Grady, 170
Winston-Salem, N.C., Belk store in, 76–77, 86–87, 119; Hanes Mall store, 241–42
Women's Wear Daily, 4, 160
World War I, 57, 65, 70, 74, 129
World War II, 110, 138–40, 146–47, 156–57
W. T. Grant stores, 173
Wyatt, Henry, 43

Yates, Ogburn, 150
Ybor City, Fla., Belk store in, 159–60
York, S.C., Belk store in, 59, 68, 127
Young, Kermit, 151
Young Manufacturing Company, 151